SYLLOGE OF COINS
OF THE BRITISH ISLES

SYLLOGE OF COINS OF THE BRITISH ISLES

Published by the British Academy, except Nos. 8 and 34, published by the Trustees of the British Museum, and Nos. 16, 31, and 33 published by Spink and Son Ltd.

All quarto, cloth bound

SYLLOGE OF COINS
OF THE BRITISH ISLES

35

Scottish Coins
in the
Ashmolean Museum, Oxford
and the
Hunterian Museum, Glasgow

BY

J. D. BATESON
Curator of Coins and Medals,
The University of Glasgow

AND

N. J. MAYHEW
Assistant Keeper in the
Heberden Coin Room, Ashmolean
Museum

PUBLISHED FOR THE BRITISH ACADEMY
by the OXFORD UNIVERSITY PRESS
and SPINK & SON LIMITED
5-7 KING STREET, ST JAMES'S, LONDON S.W.I
1987

Oxford University Press, Walton Street, Oxford OX2 6DP

Oxford New York Toronto
Delhi Bombay Calcutta Madras Karachi
Petaling Jaya Singapore Hong Kong Tokyo
Nairobi Dar es Salaam Cape Town
Melbourne Auckland

and associated companies in
Beirut Berlin Ibadan Nicosia

Oxford is a trade mark of Oxford University Press

British Library Cataloguing in Publication Data
Sylloge of Coins of the British Isles.
Vol. 35: Scottish coins in the Ashmolean
and Hunterian collections.
1. Coins, British—Catalogs
I. Bateson, J. D. II. Mayhew, N. J.
III. British Academy
737.4941′074 CJ 2476
ISBN 0–19–726047–0

Printed in Great Britain
at the University Printing House, Oxford
by David Stanford
Printer to the University

CONTENTS

APPENDIX

INDEX OF MINTS

INDEX OF MONEYERS

INDEX OF FINDS

PREFACE

THE Scottish coins in the Ashmolean Museum, Oxford and Hunterian Museum, Glasgow have been brought together in this joint sylloge volume. The idea arose out of an invitation to one of the authors to be the Robinson Visiting Fellow to the Heberden Coin Room in 1980. While studying the Scottish series housed there both of us lamented the fact that neither the Oxford nor Glasgow Scottish coins had been syllogized. Indeed such a project for separate volumes had been raised earlier by the respective Cabinets but it was felt that while each contained great rarities neither covered the series in enough depth to justify a separate volume. Glasgow's coins were still primarily those of William Hunter who had not counted Scotland among his main areas of interest while Oxford's strength lay in its gold derived from Alderman Hird's collection. It therefore seemed a logical idea to combine the two collections to produce a volume on a series hitherto absent from the Sylloge series. The proposal was put to the Sylloge Committee with the encouragement of the late Dr Colin Kraay, Keeper of the Heberden Coin Room, and was readily accepted.

It had been hoped that the volume might appear to coincide with the celebrations to mark the tercentenary of the foundation of the Ashmolean Museum and the bicentenary of the death of Dr William Hunter. However, the recent cuts in university funding so affected the Hunterian Museum that this has not proved possible. Nevertheless this volume does recall these two events and will now indeed appear at a time which also recalls the 850th anniversary of the start of the Scottish coinage under David I and the centenary of the publication of the still standard work *The Coinage of Scotland* by Edward Burns.

We would like to acknowledge the help and encouragement of Dr Michael Metcalf, Keeper of the Heberden Coin Room and Professor Frank Willett, Director of the Hunterian Museum and Art Gallery. Subsidies towards the cost of publication from the Publications Committee of the University of Glasgow and the Royal Bank of Scotland should be gratefully placed on record. We are also grateful to the Sylloge Committee especially Mr Christopher Blunt, for his help and guidance. Dr Ian Stewart was particularly generous in obtaining specimens to fill outstanding gaps in both collections and has kindly contributed an appendix on the important Alexander III transitional short cross penny of Glasgow. Colonel and Mrs Murray have also made many helpful suggestions, corrections, and comments, and looked through most of the Oxford casts. This was a major undertaking and we are most grateful to them for their help. The casts at Glasgow were started by Mr Hugh Forbes who before being transferred to another department in 1982 had spent over thirty years preparing casts for various

Hunterian catalogues; the work was continued by Mr Roy Dingley until his own departure and was only completed by the kindness of the Heberden Coin Room whose own casts were made by Miss Oonagh Rennie. Finally Mrs Mary Beattie, of Glasgow was responsible for turning a difficult manuscript into an excellent typescript.

The editors also wish to record their thanks to Colonel and Mrs Murray and to Dr Ian Stewart for help and advice in preparing the material for the press.

INTRODUCTION

THERE is a total of 1,838 coins listed of which 1,168 belong to the Ashmolean collections and the remaining 670 to the Hunterian cabinet. The coins from the two groups are integrated in the sylloge but with an indication of their ownership.

Even now Edward Burns' *The Coinage of Scotland* is the standard work on this series and with few exceptions reference is made to his catalogue. However, a comprehensive and up-to-date guide will be found in the second edition of Dr Stewart's *The Scottish Coinage* and extensive use has been made of his arrangements. Stewart's further study of the Scottish mints in the Baldwin *Festschrift* is particularly useful for the medieval period and his publications of the 1963 Renfrew hoard and the Glenluce and Rhoneston billon hoards has done much for our understanding of the Alexander III second coinage and the billon pennies of James II-IV respectively. Much is also owed to the various reviews undertaken by Colonel and Mrs Murray especially on the coinages of James III-IV, those of Mary before and during her marriage to Francis and the precious metal issues of Charles I and II. The new classifications offered in these are all used here. Finally mention may be made of Murray and Stewart's consideration of the copper coinage between 1642 and 1697 as well as Stevenson's work on the earlier Stirling turners of the 1630s. There have therefore been many advances since Burns' time and the large group of Scottish coins listed here has been classified making use of this recent research. Further detail is given at the appropriate place below and a select bibliography of the works used appended.

The basic arrangement in the catalogue is by reign and then by metal in the order gold, silver, billon, and copper. The coins are then listed according to coinage followed by mint, denomination, and class. Each entry has its own sylloge number accompanied by an A or H to denote an Ashmolean or Hunterian source. This is followed by its weight in grains and grammes, the die axis by degree, a note on chipping, piercing etc. if present and after 1539 the date when included. A full reading of the legends is given for all coins up to the introduction of the long cross penny in 1250 and a reverse reading only for the long cross coins up to 1280. Thereafter readings are only given occasionally to clarify the classification. If the lettering is illegible but known from other specimens it is given within the brackets, while uncertain letters are noted by empty brackets. From the second coinage of David II all stops of whatever type (e.g. saltires, roses, etc.) when they occur in the text are indicated by the use of a single mid-line stop. With few exceptions a Burns reference follows and noteworthy variation is noted by 'but . . .' with a brief description of the difference. A Burns reference should not nevertheless be taken always to suggest exact correspondence. However, if the entry is a die duplicate of the Burns specimen this is noted. This is followed by a reference to any more recent classification or publication. When the details of classification and, where applicable die-identity, are identical in adjacent entries, the later entry is annotated 'As . . .' with a reference to the number of the first coin of this exact type. Die-duplication is only implied by an 'As . . .' entry of this type if it is noted in the first common entry. Every entry ends with the provenance and pedigree if known. Donations, including bequests are indicated by the letter D. P indicates purchase, E exchange, and L a loan. These letters are followed by the date of acquisition. To avoid repetition, Bodleian, Ashmolean, and Oxford college coins are entered without explanatory letters and date, as are the splendid Hird and Hunter benefactions. The details of these acquisitions may be gleaned from the notes on the Sources of the collections which follow this introduction.

Further details on the arrangement of the coins of each reign follow.

David I. Burns divides the earliest coinage into four classes of which three are of the most numerous type with the cross fleury reverse. Class I coins are of good workmanship and lettering while class II are poor copies with blundered legends; class IV are of better style but the legends remain unintelligible. Class III consist of those coins of David with English types on the reverse. Stewart at first (1955 edn.) followed Burns but more logically numbered the cross fleury groups I–III and the English reverses group IV. Later (1967, 191–2; Scottish Mints, ch. III) he argued that the types with English reverses were the earliest, and this was soon confirmed by the Prestwich hoard. The English types (group IV) belong to phases (*a*) (1136–early 1140s) and (*b*) (mid-1140s), and the cross fleury groups (I–III) began late in David's reign and probably continued posthumously. During David's reign several types were issued by his son Prince Henry who died in 1152; one struck at Newcastle (in Stephen's name) is included in this volume (5/A), but two others (in Henry's name) are included in *SCBI 12* (nos. 291–2).

Malcolm IV. As was to happen regularly in the Scottish coinage the last types of the earlier reign continued to be struck into the new reign. Thus some of the class II and IV (Burns) coins of David are probably posthumous. However, there are coins in Malcolm's own name (Stewart, 1967, 8) and the least-rare, continuing David's cross fleury type, is represented by a sole example.

William I. The (brief) first coinage follows the cross fleury tradition but is unrepresented. His second coinage better known as the 'crescent and pellet' issue readily falls into two groups distinguished by the shape of the sceptre head: either square headed as on Henry II's 'Tealby' coinage from 1158 or with cross pommée as on the short cross coinage from 1180. Dating the Scottish coinage is complicated by the loss of the castles, and presumably the minting places therein, of Edinburgh, Roxburgh, and Berwick by the Treaty of Falaise in December 1174. However, it may have begun as early as 1170 (Stewart 1977, 67–8) and is generally accepted as having been replaced in 1195. Earlier issues with the square headed sceptre were struck principally at Perth and Roxburgh and also occur without mint names struck by moneyers using colons between the letters of their names and by one named Raul Derling. The later pommée headed coins emanate mainly from Berwick, Edinburgh, Roxburgh, and again without mint name by Raul Derling. The specimens here are listed by mint with a note of the sceptre head much as Burns though in different order but for the best discussion see Stewart ('Scottish Mints', 197–201). The third issue of this reign is the short cross coinage introduced according to the Chronicle of Melrose in 1195. Burns lists it by mints followed by those issues with the names of moneyers only, particularly Hue Walter, the latter group divided in six classes. Apart from the order of the mints this system is followed by us. Stewart (see especially, 'Scottish Mints', 202–5) adopts a chronological system for the short cross series assigning the coins to phase (a) to (e) though the precise dates for each phase are still uncertain (Stewart 1977, 68–9). Those short cross pence with the mint names (Edinburgh, Perth, Roxburgh) belong to the earliest phase (a) from the introduction of the type in 1195 to about 1205/1210. These are then replaced by phase (b) coins with the names of the moneyers only to the end of the reign (1214) and beyond probably terminating towards 1230. Though phase (c) coins with William's name clearly belong to the middle of Alexander II's reign they are listed together with the earlier short cross pennies of his father's reign.

Alexander II. As with Burns only the short cross pennies bearing the name Alexander are listed under Alexander II. However, those included here all possess the bearded portrait of Stewart's phase (d) struck in the last years of Alexander II's kingship.

Alexander III. A single example of the short cross phase (e) is listed of the type bearing this name but now with beardless portrait. This specimen of the transitional issue of 1249/50 is a unique coin of Glasgow about which Dr Stewart has added a separate appendix (Appendix, pp. 244–6 below).

In 1250 the Scotichronicon notes the introduction of the long cross type in Scotland and this forms Alexander III's first coinage, the majority of which had been struck by the early 1250s (Stewart 1977, 69). Burns divides the long cross coinage into five classes and lists the coins by mint and then class (B i. 118–62, esp. 121). However, understanding of this series was greatly advanced by the study and reclassification into eight classes of the large parcel included in the Brussels hoard. This work of A. H. Baldwin was first applied to the Scottish long cross pence in the Lockett sale (Lockett 1957, 10–15) where it is accompanied by a series of useful illustrations. The arrangement was published shortly afterwards (Stewart 1958–9, Brussels) and in turn applied to Burns (Stewart 1970) but has since been discussed further particularly with the added information of the parcel from the 1969 Colchester hoard which has led to several varieties being noted among class VIII

('Scottish Mints', 205–13 esp. table G of mints, moneyers, and classes and Stewart 1974, 48–61). The eighty-four long cross pennies in the present work follow this arrangement being listed first by the classes (I–VIII) and then by mint in alphabetical order.

About 1280 Alexander III followed Edward I in introducing a new single long cross type of penny. Burns (i, 163–83) divides this large second coinage into two groups on the shape of the head and each group into three classes by the lettering; there is also a small late anomalous group. Group II, class III depicts three varieties of head. All group I reverses possess four mullets of six points but the group II reverses display much greater variety with both mullets and stars giving a wider range of total points. Within each group the various classes sometimes interchange their reverses and Burns lists these at the end of the respective groups. Stewart (1967, 20–2) follows Burns in the arrangement of this coinage though substitutes letters for the various classes/groups thus giving the following concordance:

Burns	group I/class I	I,II	I,III	II,I	II,II	II,III	Anomalous
Stewart	B	A	C	D	E	FG	H I ('Baliol')

The 1963 Renfrew hoard presented an opportunity to apply this system to a large group (Woodhead and Stewart, 1966, esp. 139–40) and forty-four pence from this find are among the Hunterian coins. Unfortunately the Scottish coins do not follow their English counterparts in retaining the name of the mint though attempts have been made to identify these from the total number of points displayed by the mullets and stars ('Scottish Mints', 216–18). The bulk of the coinage appears to have been struck between 1280 and 1281 and few were issued after Alexander III's death in 1286 (Stewart 1967, 194).

In this sylloge we follow the basic arrangement giving the Burns group and class and the Stewart letter headings though the interchanges are listed at the end of each class rather than at the end of the two groups. Furthermore with group II this class is subordinated to the reverse mullets and stars combinations.

The 1279 coinage in England witnessed the first regular striking of halfpence and farthings and small numbers of the same denominations were subsequently issued by Alexander III in Scotland. Burns' numbering (i, 183–5) is followed for the few included here.

John Baliol. The division of Baliol's coinage into an earlier 'rough issue' and later 'smooth' issue by Burns (i, 222–8) remains the basic arrangement and is followed here. Halfpennies exist, though are more common in the smooth issue. St Andrews is the only named mint but the coins without mint name are now believed to have been struck at Berwick (Stewart 1967, 194) while the majority of coins appear to have been struck between 1292 and 1296 ('Scottish Mints', 222–3).

Robert Bruce. The pennies, and especially the halfpennies and farthings, of Robert I are not numerous and cause no problems of arrangement (B, i, 228–31). The

Renfrew hoard again provided the evidence for their date of issue shortly before 1321 (Woodhead and Stewart 1966), and the capture of Berwick in 1318 lends weight to the suggestion that minting of this issue commenced shortly afterwards (Stewart 1967, 194 and 'Scottish Mints' 223–4).

David II. The return of David II from captivity in England in 1357 marks the central point of his coinage. Those coins struck prior to this date constitute his first coinage which Burns (i, 232–9) took to form one group apparently struck in the early 1350s though it has since been recognized that two issues are involved (Stewart 1967, 195 and 'Scottish Mints' 223–41, though see also 1977, 70). A small issue of halfpennies and farthings both with mullets of five points seems to have emanated from Berwick between 1329 and 1333 while a much larger issue of pennies and halfpennies was struck after 1351, possibly at Edinburgh since Berwick was then once more in English hands. However, of these various coins only the pennies, albeit with thirty specimens, are represented in the present catalogue.

David's second coinage from 1357 included an attempt to introduce a gold coinage into Scotland but the issue seems to have been small and only four of these nobles have survived, two of which are included here (B, i, 267–9). Other new denominations are the groat and halfgroat struck alongside the penny, principally at Edinburgh but also at Aberdeen. Burns (i, 239–66) organizes the silver by the shape of the head though this is not always clear and his system has been simplified and expanded to deal with the varieties arising from the first use of privy marks by Stewart (1967, 28–31 and 195). This may be summarized as follows:

Burns	Stewart	Varieties
small head	A	A1–A9
first intermediate head	B	B1, 2a–b, 3a–d
second intermediate head		
third intermediate head	C	C1–C3
Robert II head	D	D1–D3

Stewart's arrangement has been adopted for this sylloge and each coin listed has been given a Stewart variety reference.

In 1367 a reduction in weight gave rise to David II's third coinage with the 'Robert II' head and its distinguishing mark of a star on the sceptre handle. Though Burns (i, 256–8) separates this issue from the earlier groats, he lists the halfgroats and pennies with the 'Robert II' head issues (i, 263 and 266). Again we follow Stewart (1967, 31–2) in listing this coinage separately though with Burns' numbers.

Robert II. The coinage of this reign consists of silver only, groats to halfpenny, struck at Edinburgh, Perth, and Dundee. It is a straightforward continuation of the third coinage of David II though with Robert's name now as well as the 'Robert II' head and there has been no noteworthy advance since Burns (i, 269–82).

Robert III was responsible for introducing a regular gold coinage, changing the portrait on the silver from the normal Scottish profile to the usual English facing bust and leading the way towards the later prolific billon coinage by debasing the minor silver denominations. The major coinage, the 'heavy' coins, consisting of lions, demi-lions, groats, halfgroats, pennies, and halfpennies, was issued from the start of the reign in 1390 to about 1403 when a reduction in weight resulted in the striking of 'light' gold coins and groats only. The earlier silver was struck at Edinburgh, Perth, and Aberdeen while for the later 'light' groats Dumbarton replaced Perth. For the gold we follow Burns (i, 340–65) in listing the two coinages together and dealing with all the lions and then the demi-lions. The silver is very numerous and complicated and falls into two major issues, the first possessing three pellets on the cusps of the tressure, the second issue displaying trefoils with a neater bust. The 'light' groats have not survived in large numbers. Again we follow Burns (i, 285–340) except that the 'light' groats are not included with the main issue of groats but are treated as a separate coinage after the halfpennies of the first coinage. A concise and up-to-date statement on the coinage of Robert III will be found in Stewart (1967, 36–40 and 'Scottish Mints', 229–32).

James I and II. James I was in English captivity when he acceded in 1406 and it was 1424 before he was freed to rule in person. Though some coins in his name appear to have been struck prior to this, the bulk of James I's coinage dates from 1424 and similar types continued to be issued after his death in 1437. It was not until 1451 that James II altered the types for his second coinage. The gold coin introduced by James I was the demy, and this continued up to 1451, along with a small number of half-demies struck in James I's reign only. These have therefore been listed together but follow Burns' numbering for the two separate reigns (ii, 30–46 and 89–94). The shape of the quatrefoils on the reverse subdivides the demies into four groups corresponding with the silver and billon (B, ii, 33 and Stewart, 1967, 45).

The distinctive silver coin of the period 1424 to 1451 is the fleur-de-lis groat called after the lis found in two of the angles on the reverse; the bust continues to be facing. The fleur-de-lis groat falls into four main varieties. The first, and largest group, possesses a tall neat bust with lis and saltire stops and was struck at Edinburgh, Linlithgow, and Perth. The second variety, with a larger crown and lis, annulet, and crescent stops has Stirling added to the previous three mints. The crown on the third variety, not struck at Perth, is tall but thin and the stops on this less numerous group are crescents and annulets. The crown on the fourth variety has a tall central lis, clothed bust, and saltire stops. It was struck only at Edinburgh in small numbers. In addition a scarce initial variety of fleur-de-lis groats is now recognized (Stewart, 1967, 43). The usual division of the fleur-de-lis groats was to give the first and second varieties to James I and the third and fourth varieties to

James II (Burns, ii, 3–30 and 62–71) but it seems more likely that the second variety covers the later years of James I and the early years of his successor ('Scottish Mints', 243, note 21).

The fleur-de-lis groats are thus listed together by variety with reference to Burns.

A small number of billon pennies and halfpennies was also issued corresponding with the various varieties of gold and silver (Stewart, 1967, 45). These have been divided into four groups A–D (Stewart, 1967, 44, 46, 139). This system is adopted here with the coins being placed along with the groat varieties with appropriate Burns references (ii, 46–55).

James II second coinage. This was introduced in 1451 and lasted beyond James's death at Roxburgh in 1460. It falls into two issues the first of short duration and now scarce while the second is large with much variety and falls into four groups (Stewart, 1967, 46–50). The gold consists of lions and a few half lions, the latter of the second issue only. The silver groat differs from the previous coinage in having the fleur-de-lis on the reverse replaced by crowns (hence the 'crown' or 'crown and pellet' groats) and also in the disappearance of the sceptre beside the bust. The majority were struck at Edinburgh but for the third group of the second issue the capital was joined by Aberdeen, Perth, Stirling, and Roxburgh. A small number of halfgroats was struck at Edinburgh, Aberdeen, and Perth. Billon pennies occur in both issues. The halfgroat and first issue penny as well as the Roxburgh mint are not represented in the catalogue where the gold is treated as a unit but the groats follow the two issues with the second issue pennies at the end though otherwise treated as Burns (ii, 94–8, 71–94 and 99–104).

James III. Several innovations occurred during the prolific coinages of James III and these are most ably described by Stewart (1967, 57–67 and 198, also 51–6 and 197) though Burns (ii, 104–70) sets the basic pattern. Two new gold coins appeared, the rider and the unicorn. The rider is the earlier with two varieties, depending on which direction the king is riding, and accompanied in the second variety only by a half rider and quarter rider. The unicorn forms part of the major coinage of 1484 but does not appear to be an extensive issue.

The silver is divided by Stewart (see 1967, 142–3) into six groups (I–VI) though group V is now assigned to the following reign (Murray, 1971, 68). Group I possesses a facing bust with mullets of six points in two of the angles and was struck from about 1467 at Edinburgh and Berwick with halfgroats from both mints, some designating the king for the first time with a numeral 3. The introduction of a portrait facing partly right along with thistles on the reverse make the alloyed silver groat struck from approximately 1475 to 1484 doubly noteworthy. Accompanied by rare halfgroats they bear only the Edinburgh mint signature (see also Murray and Stewart, 1970). Group III was introduced in 1475 but Group II groats continued to be struck. Issued at Edinburgh and Berwick they are of similar type to the group I groats. Halfgroats of Berwick and silver pennies of Edinburgh exist but are not represented here.

The third issue of 'light' groats of James III was first struck about 1482. These group IV groats differ from groups I and III in having five-pointed mullets. Edinburgh, the sole mint, also produced halfgroats and silver pennies. These only lasted until the major new coinage of 1484 when a portrait, now facing half left, reappeared on the groat struck at Edinburgh and Aberdeen.

This reign also saw the introduction of a larger billon coin, the plack and its half. The bulk of these were seemingly struck throughout the 1470s and later while a small group with an I in the centre of the reverse belongs to the start of the 1485 coinage (Stewart, 1967, 198). Stewart (1967, 143 and 198) divides the billon pennies into four groups (A–D) and references in the catalogue are to this arrangement.

Yet another innovation of James III was the striking of copper coins which became known as 'black money'. Two issues are known (Burns, ii, 167–70 and Stewart, 1967, 144). Only an example of the first issue is represented. Other copper issues termed 'ecclesiastical' were also struck during this period (Stewart, 1967, 51–6) though there is the suggestion that the *moneta pauperum* farthings may be regal (ibid., 197). The so-called 'Crossraguel' or *crux pellit* pennies were not known to Burns and are here arranged according to Stewart (ibid., 140–1). Their origin is still a matter of uncertainty however ('Scottish Mints', 241–2; Archibald, 1981, 54; Murray and Van Nerom, 1983).

A summary of these numerous issues of James III links them as follows:

date	gold	groat	features	billon	billon pence	copper
1467–75	*rider* first variety king to right	I	6-point mullets +ET; *halfgroat*	*plack*	A	*black farthing* first issue
1470–84		II	portrait facing right; *halfgroat*	*plack*	B	*black farthing* second issue
1475–82	*rider* as above	III	6-point mullets +Z; *halfgroat, penny*	*plack*	C	
1482–4	*rider* second variety king to left	IV	5-point mullets; *halfgroat, penny*	*plack*	C cont.	
1484–8	*unicorn*	VI	portrait facing left; *halfgroat*	*plack* +I	D	

(the *crux pellit* pennies may have been struck throughout much of the reign—the position of the *moneta pauperum* farthings is unclear)

James IV. Edinburgh was the only mint during this reign which was otherwise distinguished by a change-over to Roman lettering late in the reign, and by the fact that James was more often designated as the fourth of that name. Otherwise the various issues do not fall so readily into pattern and the picture is somewhat complicated (Stewart, 1967, 68–74 and 199–200). The unicorns fall into two major divisions having three and five lis respectively on the crown on the neck (Burns, ii, 183–9) and while following this system in the catalogue more recent references are added for the unicorns and their halves (Murray, 1971). Gold crowns were also struck in small numbers (Burns, ii, 189–93).

The first groats of James IV, a continuation of the 'heavy coinage' from the previous reign, have caused problems but have now been more satisfactorily arranged into two groups, B with crowns and pellets and C with one of the crowns replaced with a lis (Murray, 1971, 78; the C group formerly being considered one of the issues of James III i.e. Burns, ii, 131–3 and Stewart V). Murray B and C belong from 1489 until about the mid-1490s. These were superseded by an issue of light groats with pellets and mullets of five points with several varieties based on the form of 'the fourth' (Murray, ibid., 96; Stewart, 1967, 145, group III; Burns, ii, 174–80). Half-groats and pennies (Burns, ii, 180–2) accompanied these but are not represented.

The placks are a very numerous issue constituting much of the late coinage of this reign and are arranged, along with their rare halves, by their Old English/Roman lettering, the numeral and the stops (Burns, ii, 203–16; Stewart, 1967, 72–3 and especially 145–6). The billon pennies, which were seemingly all struck before the introduction of the Roman lettering (Stewart, 1967, 72), fall into two issues. The first issue, associated with the 'heavy' issue groats of the early part of the reign, possess pellets only on the reverse along with the mint name and are here listed according to Stewart and Murray (Murray, 1971, 90). The second and larger issue is easily recognizable from the reverse with crowns and lis in alternate angles. One group (I) has the *salvum fac* legend on the reverse but groups II–IV revert to the mint name (Stewart, 1967, 146; Burns, ii. 219–27).

James V. The coinages of James V's reign are not as numerous as before and as literary evidence becomes more plentiful and dates begin to appear on the coins they can more readily be arranged in fairly straightforward patterns. Three coinages are clearly discernable the first running from the start of the reign in 1513, the second commencing in 1526 and the third in 1538. No silver was produced during the first coinage (1513–26) which is made up of unicorns and placks. The second coinage (1526–38) consists of gold crowns and silver groats but not billon while the third coinage (1538–42) is made up entirely of two new types, the gold ducat and billon bawbee. Edinburgh remains the sole mint though the then separate Holyrood was the site of the mint for the crowns or 'abbey crowns' as they are appropriately known.

Gold was struck in the three coinages noted. The unicorns of the first coinage are listed according to Stewart (1967, 75 and 146–7) whose class I is countermarked on the reverse with a cinquefoil. Coins of Ia use a reverse die of James IV while Ib and II possess the usual mullet found in the centre of the reverse of this group. There is a half unicorn of class II and denominations here otherwise fall into Burns' arrangement (ii, 242–44). The crowns introduced in 1526 as part of the second coinage are classified, like the groats, on the shape of the crown and shield and the stops used (Stewart, 1967, 147, classes I–IV and 202, class V which may be post-1539). The ducats of 1539 and 1540 and their parts of 1540 are the first Scottish coins to bear dates and present no problems of classification (Burns, ii, 250–2).

Silver groats were struck only during the second coinage from 1526 to 1538 and like the contemporary crowns are classified according to the crown, shield, and stops as well as the king's mantle (Stewart, 1967, 147, groups I–IV but see p. 202 where the order of groups III and IV is reversed i.e. the catalogue follows order I, II, III (old IV) and IV (old III) with reference still to Burns (ii, 233–9, though his order has now been superseded). One third groats of (new) group IV also exist.

The billon of the first coinage consists only of placks distinguishable from those of James IV by the absence of the numeral and the substitution of two of the crowns by saltires on the reverse. It is a numerous issue classified by the stops used (Burns, ii, 253–61). Virtually no billon was struck from 1526 until 1538 when the start of the third coinage introduced what was to become one of the best known of Scottish coins. The I and 5 on either side of the crowned thistle on the reverse clearly point to the source of the bawbee. The bawbees are readily arranged according to the absence or use of an annulet on the obverse into classes I–V which are a reversal of the former order (Burns, ii, 267–8; Stewart, 1967, 148, Ia–c and IIa–b). A rare half bawbee is also known.

Mary. The major events of Mary's reign divide it neatly into five periods:

period 1	pre-marriage	1542–58
period 2	marriage to Francis	1558–60
period 3	first widowhood	1560–5
period 4	marriage to Lord Darnley	1565–7
period 5	second widowhood	1567 (abdicated)

The coinage is not dealt with primarily by metal as normal but follows the system adopted by Burns and Stewart (1967) of treating all the issues of each of the above periods as a separate unit.

The relatively long period of Mary's childhood up to her marriage with Francis, dauphin and then king of France, witnessed numerous issues which indeed included the bulk of gold coinage of the reign as a whole. An early issue of Abbey crowns was followed by the appearance of twenty shilling pieces in 1543 and by forty-four and twenty-two shilling pieces ten years later in 1553, all three issues bearing the cinquefoils associated with the regent James, Earl of Arran. A fourth gold issue of ryals or three pound pieces, and halves, with a rather unflattering portrait took place between 1555 and 1558. The essential pattern of the gold is to be found in Burns (ii, 282–91) but recent work has not only added to our background knowledge of these issues but provided more detailed classifications and die identities. There is therefore usually an added Murray reference in many cases referring to the actual specimen listed here (1543 issue—Murray, 1979; 1553 issue—Murray, 1968, 98–102, 104–5, 107–9; 1555 issue—Murray, 1979).

The silver issues of this pre-marriage period consist of the testoon and half-testoon. First issued in 1553 with a portrait this was replaced in the second type of 1555 by a crowned M which in turn was replaced by the arms of Scotland on the third type struck from 1556 to 1558. They are listed in groups I–III (Stewart, 1967, 149) with reference to Burns (ii, 269–82). More recent variety numbers are added (Murray, 1968, 102–4) for the 1553 testoons along with a reference to the list of known specimens (Murray, 1981, 347).

A large number of billon coins survive from this period. There is great variety among the bawbees which are divided into eight classes (I–VIII) by Burns (ii, 296–305). Half bawbees also occur in classes I and II of these Edinburgh bawbees (ibid., 306). There was also a short issue of bawbees only from Stirling, the last striking of coins outside Edinburgh (ibid., 305–6). This issue has been dated to the latter half of 1544 (Murray, 1966, 306).

Billon pennies bearing a portrait at first young, then older, appeared from 1547 and were replaced by another in 1554 when two lis replaced the cinquefoils on the reverse (Burns, ii, 309–10). They thus consist of three types 1–3 (Stewart, 1967, 149–50).

A new and slightly larger billon coin appeared in 1555 and 1556—the lion or hardhead of three halfpence (Burns, ii, 310–12). Non-portrait pence were struck in 1556 (ibid., 312–14). The following year saw a large issue of small placks (ibid., 314–16) and a further issue of lions or hardheads took place in 1558 (ibid., 316–17).

Mary's marriage to the dauphin in April, 1558 ushered in the second period of her coinage. A small issue of rare gold ducats depicting the couple facing each other is not represented in the catalogue (Burns, ii, 324–5). The silver of the second period again consists of testoons and their halves. They fall into two groups before and after the accession of Francis to the French throne and within the second group are divided into two types depending on the ending of the obverse legend (Burns, ii, 318–24; Murray, 1967, 95; Stewart, 1967, 86–7 and 150).

The billon of the second period consists of the new and numerous fine billon nonsunts dated 1558 and 1559 (Burns, ii, 326–8) and base billon lions or hardheads dated 1559 and 1560 (ibid., 330). Both bear the FM monogram and the dolphins associated with Francis. This was the last billon struck during Mary's reign.

No sooner had Francis ascended the French throne than he died leaving Mary to return to Scotland as a young widow. Excepting the unique and probable pattern crowns of 1561 (Burns, ii, 334–6) no gold was struck during the period of her first widowhood. This third period lasted until 1565. A portrait makes a re-appearance on the testoons and half testoons of 1561 and 1562 (ibid., 332–4) and these now rare coins are the only ones struck during this period.

In 1565 Mary married Henry, Lord Darnley. The coinage of this fourth period is made up only of silver ryals along with their fractions, two and one thirds, dated between 1565 and 1567 (Burns, ii, 339–42). The main issue bears the arms of Scotland on the obverse but a very rare type of ryal dated 1565 depicts Henry and Mary facing each other (ibid., 338).

Following Darnley's murder in 1567 there was a short time of second widowhood, period 5, before the queen's marriage to Bothwell and subsequent abdication. The issue of ryals and their fractions continued as before though now with Mary's name alone in the title (Burns, ii, 343–4).

James VI and I. James VI succeeded his mother in 1567 and ruled Scotland alone for thirty-six years before succeeding Elizabeth I as James I of England in 1603 and occupying both thrones for a further twenty-two years until his death in 1625. Consequently there are a very large number of issues belonging to this long reign though they present no real difficulties in classification. The year 1603 marks a crucial point of change in the coinage of Scotland in so far as the post-1603 types more closely follow their English counterparts. The coinage of James VI/I is therefore usually treated in two parts pre-accession to English throne (1567–1603) and post-accession (1603–25).

There is a good account of the reign's coinage readily available though this classifies the issues by the individual coinages (Stewart, 1967, 91–104, 151–5 and 203 and Stewart 1983 (a)) whereas here we follow Burns' arrangement by metals with the various issues readily falling into a chronological pattern (Burns, ii, 349–441). Between 1567 and 1604 there were eight coinages with gold in each except for the first. The earliest gold coins are the magnificent twenty pound pieces of 1575 and there is an interesting variety of issues up to the sword and sceptre pieces first struck in 1601. The gold is well represented in the catalogue with all types present and only an occasional absence of a variety of date.

Silver was struck as part of seven of the eight pre-accession coinages and displays an even greater number of types than the gold (Burns, ii, 348–84). The only outstanding gap in the silver listed is the very rare forty shilling piece of 1582 though the four and two shilling pieces of 1581 are also lacking as well as a small number of dates of otherwise well represented types. In 1578 a re-valuation of several earlier issues took place by the counterstamping of the coins with a crowned thistle. Any coin bearing such a counterstamp has been listed under its original issue but a brief separate list of counterstamped specimens has been inserted at the appropriate place among the silver in the catalogue.

The billon types of this period are not numerous and fall into three issues of 1583, 1588, and 1594 (Burns, ii, 402–11; Murray, 1972). Prior to this in 1575 there had been a countermarking with a heart and star of the genuine billon placks and lions or hardheads of Mary's reign and again there is a separate listing of the small number of these represented at the start of the billon section of the catalogue. The first billon issue of 1583 consists of placks and half placks also called the eightpenny and fourpenny groat. A hardhead or twopenny plack along with a penny plack was issued in August 1588 with a shield on the reverse (type I) but in November of the same year was replaced by one with a more distinguishable lion rampant (type II). A saltire or fourpenny plack struck in 1594 completed the billon issue.

Once again an official copper coinage made its appearance during this period in the form of turners or twopences bearing a close resemblance to the contemporary French double tournois (Burns, ii, 411-14). Very rare pennies also exist of this issue of 1597.

Much of the interesting variety went out of the Scottish coinage after the union of the two crowns in 1603 when the coin types of the two countries were also unified leaving only minor differences to distinguish the two, apart from the twelve to one ratio in terms of value between the Scots pound and the English sterling. The Scottish coins of the post-accession period between 1603 and 1625 fall into two groups, the first (or ninth coinage) struck from 1605 to 1609 and the second (or tenth coinage) from 1609 to 1625. The main difference between these two rather similar issues is the position of the Scottish arms on the shield. The lion rampant occupies only the second quarter of the shield in the former but is found in the first and fourth quarters of the latter. Gold, silver, and again copper but no billon were struck.

The arrangement again deals with the coins by metal and then coinages as Burns (ii, 414-41). There are five denominations of gold none bearing a date or value and all are represented. The silver ranges from the sixty shilling piece to the one shilling piece (five shillings to penny sterling) and of these the six shilling piece bears a date for most years from 1605 to 1622. The major types are again represented with the exception of the one shilling piece though several of the dates among the six shilling pieces are absent. Issues of copper turners again took place in 1614 and 1623. The portrait of the earlier type is, however, replaced by a triple-headed thistle and there is a lion rampant on the reverse. The turners were accompanied by pennies which are very rare and not represented here.

An overall view of the Scottish coinage between 1567 and 1625 is as follows:

coinage	dates	gold	silver	billon	copper
PRE-ACCESSION 1567-1603					
first	1567-71	—	ryal*		
second	1571-80	twenty pound	noble/½ merk 2 merk/thistle dollar*		
third	1580-1	ducat	16 shilling*		
fourth	1582-8	lion noble*	40 shilling*	plack*	
fifth	1588-90	thistle noble	—	hardhead*	

coinage	dates	gold	silver	billon	copper
PRE-ACCESSION 1567–1603 (*cont.*)					
sixth	1591–3	hat piece	balance half merk*		
seventh	1594–1601	rider*	10 shilling*	saltire plack	turner*
eighth	1601–4	sword and sceptre	thistle merk*		
POST-ACCESSION 1603–25					
ninth	1605–9	unit*	60 shilling*		
tenth	1609–25	unit*	60 shilling*		turner*

* indicate fractions also struck.

Charles I. Apart from the work of Burns (ii, 441–92) and Stewart (1967, 105–11, 155–7, and 204–5) the gold and silver coinage of this reign has been recently thoroughly re-considered (Murray, 1970). References are to this latter work though as usual Burns numbers are also given and the arrangement of Burns by metal is adhered to rather than by each coinage as a whole.

The bulk of Charles I's Scottish coins was struck between 1625 and 1642 with only issues of copper after 1642. Within this period the greatest number of issues took place during the third coinage from 1637 to 1641. The first coinage is similar to the last coinage of James VI and lasted until 1634 when it was followed in 1636 by a small coinage of the lower silver denominations only and of which rare milled patterns were also struck by the newly appointed mint master Nicholas Briot. Milling became the norm in the huge third coinage which is divided into five issues (1–5) of which the first is Briot's issue distinguished by the use of the initial B on the range of gold and silver coins. There is a small issue, the intermediate issue, of thirty shilling and twelve shilling pieces only, without an initial, before Briot departed from Scotland leaving the next issue to his son-in-law, Sir John Falconer, whose initial F is found on this—3, Falconer's first issue, and also on 4, Falconer's second issue. The final issue of the third coinage lacks an initial and is known as 5, Falconer's anonymous issue. Early in 1642 a small issue of three shilling and two shilling pieces took place constituting the fourth coinage. The table on page 114 of Murray (1970) neatly summarizes the position.

In addition to the coinages in the precious metals there were three issues of copper, all turners or twopences. The first issue of turners took place in 1629 and follows the last type of James VI—a penny was also struck (Burns, ii, 284–5). The second issue of turners is quite different being smaller and lighter as well as having an obverse design of a crowned C II R with the thistle, now single-headed, moved to the reverse. The profit on this coinage had been granted to the Earl of Stirling and his name is often given to the issue which is also noteworthy in being the first Scottish coins struck on the new mill presses by Briot. These Stirling turners are very common but have been the subject of a detailed study based on the crowns and mintmarks (Stevenson, 1959). References are given to this as well as to the less satisfactory listing in Burns (ii, 486–8).

Burns too had considerable difficulty with the third issue of turners (ibid., 489–92). This type was larger and heavier and similar to the later issue of 1663. The chief difference between the two being the presence or absence of a II behind the CR on the obverse. Burns listed a few varieties of each together though in the wrong basic order and it is felt that no purpose would be served by giving a Burns number here for such pieces. Fortunately recent work on the two series has sorted out the problem and these *without* the II are assigned to Charles I making up the known strikings of 1642, 1644, 1648 and, albeit after the king's death, 1650 (Murray and Stewart, 1972). References are therefore given only to this work.

Charles II. No gold was struck during this reign but the silver is plentiful and falls into two distinct groups. The first coinage with the head to the right and bearing interlinked Cs along with the mark of the value was issued between 1664 and 1675. Four types run from the four merk to half merk piece with a greater variety of dates on the two lower denominations. The head faces left and thistles replace the Cs on the coins of the second coinage minted from 1675 to 1682. Five types from the dollar to a sixteenth dollar no longer bear a mark of value. Again there has been a recent review of this coinage (Murray, 1969) and references are given to its list of main varieties (ibid., 123–5) as well as to Burns (ii, 493–501).

There was an extensive issue of copper turners in 1663 with, as noted above, a II after the CR. This was followed between 1677 and 1679 by the first issue of the common large late-seventeenth century copper bawbee bearing a portrait and a crowned thistle as well as a further issue of turners now with a crowned sword and sceptre crossed and a thistle on the reverse. References are to Murray and Stewart (1972) for all the Charles II copper as well as to Burns (ii, 501–3) for the 1677–9 coinage.

James VII. James struck only two denominations in silver during his reign. These are the forty shilling and ten shilling pieces both issued in 1687 and 1688 (Burns, ii, 506–7).

William and Mary. During this joint reign a series of five silver coins from the sixty shilling down to the five shilling piece was struck bearing the monarchs' conjoined portraits with a mark of the value beneath (Burns, ii, 508–13). Copper bawbees and turners were also struck each year from 1691 to 1694 (ibid., 514–15). The bawbee is of similar type to that of Charles II but the turner carries a crowned WM monogram on the obverse.

William II. The coinage of this reign is noteworthy for the issue of the last Scottish gold coins. A pistole worth twelve pounds Scots and a half pistole were struck bearing the date 1701 (Burns, ii, 519–21). Otherwise the silver follows the pattern of the joint reign but without the largest denomination and with a thistle on the reverse of the five shilling piece (ibid., 518–19). Similarly there were issues of copper bawbees and turners between 1695 and 1697 (ibid., 523–3). References to Murray and Stewart (1972) continue to be given also for the copper issues of these two reigns.

Anne. Only silver was struck during the reign of Queen Anne whose coinage is divided up by the Act of Union in 1707. Anne's pre-union coinage consists of ten and five shilling pieces, similar to those of William II and issued in 1705 and 1706 (Burns, ii. 523–5). After the union the coins struck at Edinburgh were similar to their English counterparts except for the addition of an E beneath the portrait. Crowns, half crowns and particularly shillings and sixpences make up this second coinage which ended with the half crowns and shillings dated 1709 (Burns, ii, 525–35). This ended an independent Scottish coinage.

Forgeries. These are listed at the end of the catalogue and include only the obvious forgeries, the small number of questionable copies being kept with their contemporary official specimens. The forgeries fell into two types either contemporary or 'modern'. The series as a whole is relatively free of copies of both sorts. The former mainly appeared among the billon issues of the second half of the sixteenth century and indeed gave rise to the countermarking of 1575 when the genuine placks and hardheads of Mary were punched with a heart and star to distinguish them from the copies. The copper turners of Charles I and II were also extensively copied though none is included here probably because such were deliberately shunned by the original collectors. The few 'modern' copies include a penny of Robert I and an example of the work of the nineteenth-century Dunfermline forger, Jons.

THE SOURCES

(*a*) The Ashmolean Museum

AMONG the 1,168 Scottish coins in the Ashmolean Museum two sources predominate: the collections of Ian Stewart, and of Horace Hird. In 1953 Alderman Horace Hird gave to the Heberden Coin Room in the Ashmolean his collection of 327 Scottish coins comprising 165 outstandingly beautiful gold coins and 162 silver. Hird, born and bred in Bradford, and the town's Lord Mayor 1951–2, was prominent in business and local government. He was a noted philanthropist, working chiefly for the deaf and dumb, and for the local branch of the Royal National Lifeboat Institution, but he also found time to pursue his antiquarian and numismatic interests. A collector of Scottish coins since the 1920s, his collecting and philanthropic interests combined to move him to present his collection to the Ashmolean. Despite his extensive knowledge of his chosen series, and of the wider field of antiquities (he was elected a Fellow of the Society of Antiquaries of London in 1947), Hird was, above all, a collector. His love of his collection was such that he did not wish it to be dispersed, though his understanding of the interests of other collectors made him shy of publicity for his gift to Oxford. But such was his collecting passion that having formed and given away a most remarkable collection of Scottish gold, he began at once to build another which finally came to auction after his death. Indeed in the week of his death he telephoned Spinks from his hospital bed about a purchase.

It was early intended that this munificent Hird donation should form the basis of a Sylloge of Scottish coins in the Ashmolean, as a public record of and monument to this outstandingly generous collector. It is indeed a source of much sadness that this project should only come to fruition after the death of the benefactor who inspired it. Ironically, the delay arose, at least in part, from the spectacular nature of the Hird donation: the gold was so breathtaking as to unbalance the collection as a whole, presenting a somewhat distorted picture of Scotland's coinage.

However, since the Hird donation, the Ashmolean collection has been considerably rounded out by the acquisition of 158 coins from the collection of Dr Ian Stewart. As is well known, Dr Stewart has actively pursued an interest in Scottish coinage, both as a scholar and collector, since boyhood. Whether by gift, sale, or exchange, Dr Stewart has enabled the Ashmolean to acquire quickly a range of select specimens which it would scarcely have been possible to obtain by ordinary collecting on the open market.

The most perfunctory glance through the catalogue will reveal the importance of the Hird and Stewart sources. Coins formerly in their collections occur on almost every page. The other sources which now make up the Ashmolean collections are noted below, with a reference to the number of the coin or coins concerned. Of course some coins with a long pedigree will occur under the names of several collectors. Apart from the usual Oxford sources (e.g. Browne Willis, Bodleian, Knight), Hird coins were often acquired from a range of both well and little known collectors of Scottish coins from the first half of this century, while some of these pedigrees stretch back into the nineteenth century. In many cases collectors' principal sales are noted; this is intended to place the collector in context, and, because of private sales, does not necessarily mean that the coins in question occurred in that sale, although this is usually the case. Purchases made from dealers in the London market without further provenance are not noted here; nor are single donations or sales by individuals without numismatic connection. Finds now in the Ashmolean are included in the list of sources, but this subject may perhaps be more easily researched by reference to the Index of Finds which covers both the Ashmolean and the Hunterian collections together.

Aberdeen golflinks	1033.
Aberdeen Upperkirkgate Hoard	Discovered in 1886. Lent/given by the city/university of Aberdeen 1975. 276.
Addington	Most of Samuel Addington's collection was sold privately to Montagu in 1883, but there was a portion sold by Sothebys in 1886. 357, 507.
Advocates	Two sales of duplicates of the Faculty of Advocates and Society of Antiquaries of Scotland by Dowell of Edinburgh, 1873 and 1874. 10, 98, 322, 525, 634, 690, 886, 889, 891, 901.
Antiquaries	See Advocates. This distinction between Advocates and Antiquaries duplicates is based solely on Hird's tickets and the Cochran-Patrick 1936 sale catalogue. 24, 45, 715.
Ashmolean	Coins already in the Ashmolean Museum in 1833. 105, 107, 117, 131, 133, 143, 215, 248, 361, 403, 796, 866, 869, 1006, 1088, 1250, 1261, 1309, 1372, 1456, 1463, 1484, 1510, 1527, 1581, 1602, 1638, 1645, 1684, 1709, 1765, 1799, 1811.
Atholl, Duke of	Coins sold privately. 521-2, 529, 671, 734, 818, 832, 836, 838, 882, 1160, 1391.
Baldwin	Gift of A. H. Baldwin & Sons Ltd, 1964. 360, 363, 366.
Barnard	Gift of Dr F. Pierrepont Barnard, Honorary Deputy Curator of Coins, 1917–28. 335, 860, 1464.
Barrett	Coins of Thomas Barrett of Lee near Canterbury, acquired by Knight (q.v.) and bequeathed to the university by him in 1795. 990, 996, 1119.
Bearman	T. Bearman's collection was purchased and re-sold c.1922 by Baldwins. 292, 753, 789, 1169, 1354.

Bodleian	Coins transferred from the Bodleian Library in 1920. 54, 63, 78, 80, 238, 240–1, 247, 253, 271–2, 275, 283, 308, 377, 386, 392, 417, 419, 421–2, 443, 447–8, 450, 475, 490, 502, 600, 609–10, 645, 651, 669, 695–6, 855, 913, 934, 937, 939, 950, 957–8, 969, 974, 1032, 1061, 1065, 1071, 1107, 1114–15, 1202, 1208, 1223, 1225, 1236, 1244, 1247, 1256–7, 1263, 1266, 1273, 1281–2, 1285, 1293, 1298, 1302, 1306, 1308, 1315, 1335, 1352, 1363, 1369–71, 1373, 1375, 1377–9, 1385, 1411, 1422, 1430–1, 1433, 1440, 1449, 1451, 1454–5, 1462, 1469, 1471, 1480, 1482, 1488, 1495, 1497, 1502–4, 1509, 1516, 1522, 1528, 1534, 1537, 1540, 1543, 1545–6, 1548–9, 1553–4, 1556–9, 1562–5, 1570, 1578, 1590, 1594, 1598, 1601, 1603, 1606, 1608, 1612, 1615, 1620, 1632, 1635, 1644, 1647, 1649–51, 1653–5, 1659–61, 1663–5, 1667, 1670–1, 1673, 1680, 1697, 1700, 1702, 1704, 1710, 1714, 1717, 1722, 1724, 1726, 1729, 1736–7, 1753, 1757, 1762, 1770, 1774–5, 1778–9, 1782, 1786–7, 1789, 1791, 1798, 1803, 1813.
Bouchier	The bequest of Edmund S. Bouchier, 1930. 547, 1133, 1679, 1793.
Brand	The collection of V. M. Brand of Chicago was sold privately over some time to a number of dealers, including Seabys in 1935. 357, 507, 637, 691, 733, 899, 985, 988.
British Museum	Duplicates sale. 839.
Browne	Christopher Corbally Browne, Sothebys 1935. 622, 739, 904, 993, 1357, 1359.
Browne Willis	See Willis.
Brushfield	A. N. Brushfield, Glendining 1940. 32, 518.
Brussels	Coins from the Brussels hoard. See Stewart 1958–9 Brussels. 85, 94, 100, 108, 113, 118–21, 124–6, 138, 144, 155, 169.
Burton-Jones	A customer of Baldwins before the last war. 689.
Bute	Marquess of Bute, Sothebys 1951. 344, 692, 738, 828, 884, 892, 999, 1145, 1358.
Campbell	The Reverend I. C. G. Campbell of Weeping Water, Nebraska, made an extensive donation of chiefly oriental and modern coins to the Ashmolean in 1981. 1652.
Carlyon-Britton	The collection of R. Carlyon-Britton was bought by Seabys in 1940, 1949 and 1959. See also Stewart 1981, 235. 30, 34, 841.
Chalgrove	Found at Chalgrove, Oxon, and donated by the finder, 1962. 293.
Christ Church	The Christ Church collection of coins was deposited on loan in the Heberden Coin Room in 1940. 29, 178, 186, 196, 207, 211–12, 217–21, 249, 254–6, 306, 398, 416, 445, 612, 820, 906, 949, 959, 1010, 1054, 1060, 1099, 1104, 1113, 1132, 1152, 1157, 1164, 1176, 1184, 1189, 1197,

	1209, 1246, 1252, 1258, 1264, 1284, 1294, 1344, 1360, 1392, 1399, 1442–3, 1450, 1458, 1460, 1481, 1491, 1493, 1496, 1512, 1576, 1618, 1625, 1639, 1643, 1658, 1686, 1698, 1708, 1750, 1763, 1767, 1788.
Cochran-Patrick	See Stewart 1981, 241. Sothebys 1936. 3, 4, 6, 10, 16, 24, 40, 42, 45, 48, 98, 101, 109, 127, 137, 156, 322, 477, 506, 525, 619, 628, 634, 670, 677, 690, 701, 715, 754, 827, 883, 886, 889, 891, 893, 976, 989, 992, 1141, 1153, 1346, 1405, 1407.
Corpus Christi College	Collection deposited on loan in the Heberden Coin Room, 1933. 324, 1183.
Cozens	Bequest of W. Cozens, 1915. 71, 158, 1305.
Cree	J. E. Cree of North Berwick (d. 1929). 620, 638, 823, 896.
Cuff	J. D. Cuff, 1781–1853. Sothebys 1854. 908.
Cumming	Gordon Cumming named on Hird ticket. 1139.
Dakers	C. H. & H. J. Dakers, Glendining 1946. 3, 21, 79, 88, 132, 135, 315, 322, 618–19, 657, 677, 715, 722, 724–7, 787, 790, 1166, 1232, 1234.
Daniels	N. H. Daniels, Glendining 1936. 331–4, 336, 338–9.
Dick Institute	(Kilmarnock). 1826.
Douce	Francis Douce 1757–1834 bequeathed his coins to the University. 847.
Drabble	G. C. Drabble, Glendining 1939, 1943. 27, 37, 85, 114, 440, 793, 840, 1172, 1194.
Dyke	Dyke Hoard (Metcalf 1977, no. 7). 29.
Eynsham	Found at Fruitlands, Eynsham, Oxon, (1931) and presented by the finder. 74.
Finch	The gift of R. Finch, 1834. 1587, 1690.
Gambier-Parry	Bequest of T. R. Gambier-Parry, 1935. 1814.
Gaunt	Alderman C. F. Gaunt, Glendining 1927, 1929. 908.
Glenluce	Glenluce hoard, (Stewart 1958–9 Glenluce). 723, 794, 797–8, 800, 804, 865, 868.
Grantley	Lord Grantley (Blunt 1976), Glendining 1944. 192, 608.
Great Bedwyn	Coin found at Great Bedwyn, Wilts 1982. 83.
Griffith	Gifts of F. Llewellyn Griffith, 1921. 364, 1286, 1289, 1291, 1520–1, 1529–30, 1591, 1614, 1696, 1796, 1807, 1821.
Haddington, Earl of	Glendining 1938, 1947. 728, 825, 1141.
Hastings, Lord	Sothebys 1880. 357, 908.
Hawkins	E. Hawkins of the British Museum. 357.
Hussey	Gifts of Edward L. Hussey 1893. 92, 1795.
Huth	R. Huth, Sothebys 1927. 994.
Innerwick	Coins from the Innerwick hoard (Caldwell 1982) purchased through the Q and LTR. 709–11, 720, 740–2, 745, 747, 755, 757, 759, 761, 763–4, 769–71.
Jesus College	Jesus College collection, deposited in the Ashmolean on loan in 1933. 7.

Kay	The gift of A. C. Kay 1912. 187, 408.
Keble College	Keble College collection including that of Canon H. P. Liddon, deposited in the Ashmolean on loan in 1934. 188, 252, 1052–3, 1213, 1267, 1300, 1494.
Knight	Thomas Knight bequeathed his collection to the University in 1795. 990, 996, 1093, 1106, 1119, 1129, 1188, 1237, 1397–8, 1413, 1417, 1420, 1438, 1448, 1461, 1466, 1468, 1476, 1524, 1572, 1575, 1609, 1622, 1629, 1641, 1718, 1725, 1747, 1754, 1766, 1773, 1781, 1784, 1792, 1800, 1806, 1818.
Lincoln College	Lincoln College collection deposited on loan in 1940. Many of the Lincoln College coins were given to the college by its fellow, J. Knollis, in 1803. 201, 1579, 1595.
Lindsay-Carnegie	Major Lindsay-Carnegie of Spynie and Boysack who bequeathed his coins to the Royal Scottish Museum in 1911. 685.
Lingford	H. M. Lingford. Glendining 1951. 1144, 1171, 1218, 1230, 1234, 1312–13, 1320–1, 1336–8, 1346, 1835–7.
Lockett	R. C. Lockett, Glendining 1957, 1960. 94, 100, 118–19, 121, 124, 126, 138, 144, 190, 292, 407, 503, 506, 715, 746, 753, 789–90, 793, 795, 799, 854, 857, 863–4, 867, 870–6, 879–81, 945, 1070.
Longstaffe	J. E. D. Longstaffe, Sothebys 1903. 292.
Mackenzie	Sheriff T. Mackenzie, 1831–1916. T. Chapman & Son 1883, Sothebys 1921. 840, 1082.
Mallet	James Mallet, Glendining 1923. 1401.
Mann	Alexander Mann, Sothebys 1917. 503.
Marr	The collection of H. J. Marr was bought by Spink in 1965. 96, 152, 841.
Marshall	W. S. Marshall, Glendining 1946. 4, 32, 87.
Martin	J. W. Martin, Sothebys 1859. 357.
McCallum	An unknown contact of Hird's, apparently from Ayr, c.1935. 395, 479.
McFarlan	D. McFarlan of Stirling, collected in the 1950s. 41, 616, 684.
Merton College	The Merton College collection was deposited on loan in 1951, but contained within it the cabinet of the Reverend Joseph Kilner (1767). Merton: 941, 1271, 1361, 1681, 1735. Merton, Kilner: 1694, 1706, 1742, 1785.
Milne	Gifts of J. G. Milne, Deputy Keeper of Coins in the Heberden Coin Room 1931–51. 426, 457, 463, 1518.
Morrieson	H. W. Morrieson, Sothebys 1933. 1234.
Murdoch	J. G. Murdoch, Sothebys 1903–5. 190, 192, 357, 507, 621, 753, 825, 908, 988, 994, 1357.
Murray	A gift of J. K. R. Murray, 1971. 560.
Napier	D. S. Napier, Glendining 1956. 41, 387.
Newcomer	Waldo Newcomer of Baltimore, active in the 1930s. 509, 730, 817, 835, 898, 987, 1148, 1175, 1733.

Northumberland, Duke of	14.
Oriel College	Oriel College collection deposited on loan in 1932. 1260, 1531.
Oxford	Local finds, viz: Botanic Gardens in 1883. 1838.
	Broad Street in 1938. 1831.
	Clive Road in 1953. 290.
	site of Keble College in 1868. 1187.
	Port Meadow allotments in 1932. 1518.
Parsons	H. A. Parsons, Glendining 1954. 8, 23, 84, 341, 400, 602.
Plummer	L. H. Scott-Plummer, Sothebys 1929. 629.
Pollexfen	J. H. Pollexfen, Sothebys 1900. 355, 440, 508, 789, 987, 1354.
Prestwich	Prestwich hoard 1972 (*Coin Hoards* 1 (1975), 91–2). 5.
Radcliffe	Received from the Radcliffe Trustees in 1861. 70, 206, 425, 580, 780, 1427, 1479.
Rawlinson	Gifts of Richard Rawlinson to the University, 1734, 1756. 1533, 1536, 1539.
Rees	D. P. Rees, Sothebys 1936. 908.
Richardson	A. B. Richardson of National Museum of Antiquities of Scotland. Scottish coins sold privately to J. G. Murdoch about the turn of the century. 192, 357.
Roberts	Barré Charles Roberts, Student of Christ Church, Oxford, died in his twenty-first year. His coins were acquired by the BM in 1810. 839.
Roth	B. Roth, Sothebys 1918. 190 not this sale but for Roth pedigree see Lockett catalogue.
Royal Scottish Museum	685.
St John's College	St John's College collection deposited on loan in 1957. 204, 415, 1394.
Selkirk	Found on a new housing site, Selkirk 1946. 737.
Selkirk-Hunter	Not traced. 1826.
Shand	F. J. Shand, Glendining 1949. 305, 1171.
Shortt	H. de S. Shortt of Salisbury Museum bequeathed his collection in 1976. 200, 202, 246, 1544.
Somerville College	The Somerville College collection deposited on loan in 1954. 591, 713, 1004, 1059, 1083, 1220.
Spufford	Peter Spufford, Cambridge. 342.
Stobart	J. M. Stobart, Christies 1903. 1169.
Stuart-Menteth	F. M. Stuart-Menteth. 359, 483, 648.
Tennant	James Tennant, Sothebys 1946. 631, 635.
Thellusson	A. Thellusson, Sothebys 1931. 517, 981, 1149.
Thorburn	P. Thorburn, better known as a collector of Islamic coins, died in the 1960s. 938.
Tranent	Coins from the Tranent hoard 1981 (see also Hunterian list) purchased through the Queen's and Lord Treasurer's Remembrancer. 257, 401, 430, 441, 476.
Tyssen	Samuel Tyssen of Narborough Hall, Norfolk, Sothebys 1802. 839.

University College	The collection formed by Horace Waddington was presented to University College by Mrs Waddington in 1932 and deposited on loan in the same year. 130, 166, 239, 459, 554, 1415, 1441, 1483, 1500, 1505, 1526, 1728.
Walters	F. A. Walters, Sothebys 1932. 515, 527, 626, 725, 831, 910.
Weber	Coins from the collection of Dr F. Parkes Weber. 314, 546.
Wertheimer	E. Wertheimer, Glendining 1945. 1343.
Whelan	Francis E. Whelan, d. 1907, London manager of Rollin and Feuardent from the 1880s. Whelan bought coins from Pollexfen and sold these in *c.*1905. 355, 440.
Wigan	E. Wigan's collection was bought by Rollin and Feuardent, *c.*1892. 827, 976, 989, 992, 1405.
Willis	Browne Willis, 1682–1760. (See *SCBI Ashmolean Museum, Oxford, Anglo-Saxon Pennies* (1967) pp. xiii–xiv). 1, 53, 56, 81, 86, 89, 93, 103, 134, 136, 157, 168, 301, 312, 317, 319, 323, 356, 372, 396, 404, 460, 484, 495, 501, 535, 672, 694, 744, 748, 752, 773, 779, 843, 849, 850, 932, 942, 948, 957, 1002, 1013, 1028, 1032, 1047, 1056, 1092, 1095, 1098, 1123, 1128, 1134, 1137, 1205, 1239–40, 1243, 1251, 1253, 1257, 1270, 1279, 1287, 1295, 1301, 1310, 1380, 1389, 1395, 1403, 1406, 1424, 1439, 1446, 1462, 1568, 1573, 1592, 1597, 1610, 1619, 1634, 1636, 1646, 1675, 1677, 1683, 1685, 1688, 1692, 1705, 1711, 1713, 1731, 1736, 1740, 1745, 1771, 1829, 1834.
Wills	R. D. Wills, Glendining 1938. 529, 628–9, 887, 1407.
Wingate	J. Wingate of Linnhouse, Hamilton (1828–77), Sothebys 1875. 507, 1153, 1407.
Wormser	? Charles M. Wormser of Woodmore, N.Y., Fellow of ANS from 1941. 908, 1143.
Yorkshire	Finds from: 973, 1031, 1072.

(b) The Hunterian Museum

THERE are 670 Scottish coins from the Hunterian Museum included in the present sylloge of which 417 are listed as belonging to Hunter's own late eighteenth-century cabinet. Only a few specimens were added to this series during the nineteenth century and most of the additional 253 non-Hunter pieces have been obtained since 1920. Among these are a group from the Coats collection as well as a few small groups from a number of other private collections. However the majority of the additions have come from coin hoards particularly the large 1963 Renfrew hoard of Edwardian and Alexandrian sterlings. There are a few stray finds and excavation finds, nearly all with Scottish provenances. Purchases, other than through treasure trove, are not numerous but include the unique Alexander III short cross penny of Glasgow. The original Hunter donation is dealt with first and then the remainder in more usual alphabetical order.

Hunter. Dr William Hunter (1718–83) was educated at the University of Glasgow but spent most of his life in London where he was a pioneer in the study and teaching of anatomy and obstetrics and Physician Extraordinary to Queen Charlotte. He nevertheless found the time to put together one of the best private museums which included a coin collection then second in importance only to the French Royal Collection. His account book shows that between 1770 and his death in 1783 Hunter spent over £20,000 on his coins alone. He bought extensively in England and on the Continent and preferred to buy complete cabinets from which he extracted only the coins he needed to fill gaps or improve condition. His collection thus includes very few duplicates. A more detailed account of the history of the Hunter Cabinet will be found in the introduction to volume 1 of Sir George Macdonald's *Catalogue of Greek Coins in the Hunterian Collection* (Glasgow, 1899) and in the introduction to the second volume of the present Sylloge series on the *Anglo-Saxon Coins in the Hunterian and Coats Collections* by Professor Anne Robertson.

Hunter's main numismatic interest was in classical coins, and in the medieval and 'modern' (i.e. to 1783) period he specifically excluded European coins. However he did build up a very good collection of the Anglo-Saxon and English series but despite being a Scot his Scottish (and Irish) coins have several outstanding gaps. While he did possess such rarities as the David II noble there was no specimen of a David I penny nor a crescent and pellet penny of William the Lion. The latter were perhaps difficult for a collector in the 1770s to acquire especially the crescent and pellet coinage which only became more available after the discovery of the Dyke hoard in 1780 but this does not explain the absence of relatively more common types and varieties of the sixteenth and seventeenth centuries.

Hunter's Scottish collection however was at one time more substantial for in 1781 he made a donation of 109 such pieces to the museum of the then recently founded Society of Antiquaries of Scotland. A list of these made up of 24 gold, 67 silver and 18 copper is given in William Smellie's *Account of the Institution and Progress of the Society of Antiquaries of Scotland* (Edinburgh, 1782) though a discrepancy in the number occurs in a letter written in 1781 by William Hunter accompanying his gift and published in the *Numismatic Chronicle* 9 (1846–7), 87. There the figures are 24 gold, 42 silver and 22 billon and copper. In any event the coins given to the Antiquaries appear to be further Hunter duplicates. Other Scottish coins had been disposed of in Hunter's two great auctions of his duplicates at Mr Gerard's in London over two days in 1775 and eight days in 1777. It is interesting that Hunter once owned no less than three of the Darien pistoles of 1701: that listed here (no. 1732), another sold in 1775 (lot no. 74 of the second day of his sale, sold for £3. 5s. 0d.) and a third donated to the Society of Antiquaries in 1781 (Smellie, *op. cit.*, 64, no. 24).

It is unfortunate that once Hunter bought a piece or had extracted it from a collection and integrated it into his own cabinet he did not make a note of its provenance. Hence there are no pre-Hunter pedigrees attached to his coins. Some information can be gleaned about his sources from the pages of his account book and to a lesser extent the small number of surviving numismatic letters and receipts all preserved in the University of Glasgow. The account book maintained between 1770 and 1783 generally records the sum of money paid and the vendor or agent but rarely describes the actual coins themselves and only in rare instances can the two be matched. As regards the Scottish series, however, there is almost no information at all and indeed only four vague references in the account book. On 16 July 1773 Hunter paid £15. 15s. 0d. for 'Scotch Gold, by Mr. [Charles] Coombe' and on 3 March 1774 a further £12. 12s. 0d. to 'Mr. Millar, for Scotch'. On 29 April of the same year 'An inedited Scotch by Mr. Coombe' cost 10s. 6d. The final reference is to the large payment of £21 on 10 March 1780 for 'A Scotch David' which presumably refers to the David II gold noble (sylloge no. 358) but alas no mention is made of the supplier. Charles Coombe obtained many of Hunter's coins for him, wrote the first and only volume of the proposed catalogue of Hunter's coins published in 1782 (the '*Descriptio*' on the coins of the Greek cities) and was one of the three trustees who compiled the manuscript catalogue of Hunter's coins after his death. No doubt among the many payments made to him and to others over the years lie hidden the majority of the Scottish pieces.

The earliest extant list of William Hunter's coins is in fact this one volume manuscript catalogue drawn up by his three trustees sometime after his death in 1783. Its basic detail however will be appreciated by the fact that since then nine volumes have been published on the Greek, Roman Imperial and Anglo-Saxon coins alone. The Scottish coins are not individually numbered and are recorded by reference to Anderson (1739) for the gold and Snelling (1774) for the silver, billon and copper. It is not always clear just how many specimens are meant but there are at least 392 indicated. This compares favourably with the 417 coins in the present trays noted as belonging to Hunter himself. It is possible that the trustees with such a large and varied collection overall did not include everything or did not see the odd parcel. There is indeed evidence to suggest that this is the case.

The collection did not come to Glasgow until 1807 and the Scottish portion seems to have been ignored for some decades. In 1870 the University moved from the site of the Old College in the centre of Glasgow to its new, and present, location on Gilmorehill. The coin cabinet was put into storage in a bank vault before being transferred to the new Hunterian Museum and then the newly-built coin room. In the period between 1882 and 1884 Professor John Young, Keeper, worked on the coins including making preliminary lists of some of the Scottish in particular those of William the Lion, Mary and James VI. These lists are commented upon by Edward Burns in a number of letters in a group of eighteen written by him during the same period when he was preparing his *Coinage of Scotland* and enquiring about various Hunter specimens. A more complete list of the Hunter Scottish series was made in 1946 by Professor Anne Robertson when the Scottish coins were being ticketed and transferred to a new cabinet. This work has been of great assistance in the compilation of the present sylloge.

For the most part the nineteenth- and twentieth-century acquisitions have not been integrated with the Hunter coins in the cabinets. The sources for these are listed below in alphabetical order along with the numbers in this sylloge.

Bryce	Found at Ballynaughton, Islay and donated 1944 by Professor Bryce. 471, 776.
Buchanan	A small collection of miscellaneous coins donated by Miss Elizabeth Buchanan in 1936. 1051, 1094, 1421, 1478, 1589, 1600, 1628, 1640, 1739.
Christian	Found on the sandhills at Sanna, Ardnamurchan, Argyll and donated by Miss S. Christian in 1971. 803.
Coats	The Scottish coins of Thomas Coats of Ferguslie, Paisley, are normally associated with the collections of the National Museum of Antiquities of Scotland to which they were presented after being used to form the basis of Edward Burns's *The Coinage of Scotland* (1887).

The Coats Cabinet however also contained an excellent collection of about 5,000 Greek, Roman and English coins. The collection was put together between 1871 and 1882 and indeed many of the pieces were obtained through Burns. In 1921 the Coats family decided to donate the non-Scottish portion of the collection to an institution in the West of Scotland and offered it to the University of Glasgow where it found a permanent resting place in 1924. A full account of the Coats Cabinet has already appeared in the Hunterian and Coats Anglo-Saxon Sylloge (Robertson, *op. cit.*, xiii–xiv).

Among the Coats Collection in the Hunterian Museum is, however, a single tray of Scottish coins, mainly groats of Robert III perhaps from the Fortrose hoard. Since all the Robert III groats listed by Burns can be equated with specimens in the National Museum of Antiquities or other named collections this Glasgow group seems to represent a parcel not examined by Burns or acquired after Burns had completed his work.

The Coats number given in the present sylloge refers to a manuscript catalogue prepared by Spinks as part of the agreement for the transfer of the coins to the University of Glasgow in 1924. 532, 534, 539, 544, 552, 556–7, 559, 561–4, 566–8, 570–1, 573–4, 578, 581, 584, 586–8, 590, 592, 594, 596–8, 603, 606 (Robert III); 1426, 1823–4.

Dun Lagaidh	During excavations at the fortified site of Dun Lagaidh, Lochbroom, Ross and Cromarty, in 1968, a hoard of 24 short cross pennies and cut halfpennies included two Scottish specimens (see Barlow and Robertson, 1974, 78–81). Presented by Q & LTR 1968: 67, 77.
Edzell	In a manuscript list of accessions to the Hunter Coin Cabinet after 1807 prepared by Professor Robertson there is for 'about 1900' a manuscript note in the coin cabinet recording the donation of three finds including 'Three billon and twelve Scottish copper coins found in the Parish of Edzell in the County of Forfar'. These are in fact all billon and, though the source is unrecorded, may form part of a hoard of billon coins recorded in *Proceedings of the Society of Antiquaries of Scotland* 1 (1851–4), 73 as having been found 'in the parish of Edzell, Forfarshire'. 853, 1077, 1110, 1318, 1323–33.
George	This Alexander III halfpenny was donated by Mr W. George of Glasgow in 1966 and was said to have come from a hoard found in Lanarkshire. This may be a stray from the 1963 Renfrew hoard though there would then be a discrepancy in the county. 289.
Innerwick	Four Scottish pieces were purchased through the Q & LTR out of the 259 found in the late fifteenth-century hoard discovered at Innerwick, East Lothian in 1979—see Caldwell 1982, 132–50. 742, 747, 763, 771.
Inverary	A hoard of 252 coins, mainly composed of specimens of the 1663 issue of turner, was unearthed in 1981 at Inverary, Argyll. It was purchased *in toto* through the Q & LTR for the Hunter Coin Cabinet (publication forthcoming, J. D. Bateson). However, the condition is such that it was decided not to include the hoard in the present sylloge except for one half merk of 1673, a variety not otherwise represented. 1605.
Lawrence	Two coins donated by L. A. Lawrence in 1937. 1490, 1515.
Linlithgow	A single muled plack was purchased in 1964 through the Q & LTR from the large mainly billon hoard of 378 coins concealed in Linlithgow, East Lothian, early in the sixteenth century and recovered in 1963 (Brown and Dolley 1971, S.M.6; Metcalf 1977, 208 but otherwise unpublished). 944.
Loch Doon	A hoard of 1,887 coins was found on the water's edge of Loch Doon, Ayrshire in 1966 and was composed mainly of Edwardian sterlings (see Woodhead, Stewart, and Tatler, 1969, 31–49). Two of the Scottish pieces were purchased through the Q & LTR: 191, 309.
Lockie	J. R. Lockie is best known for his work on Scottish communion tokens. During the 1960s and 1970s he presented large numbers of these, along

with trade tokens and modern coins, to the Hunter Coin Cabinet. Among these were sixteen Scottish coins of which only six were in reasonable enough condition to integrate into the main collection. 99, 267, 412, 642, 1049, 1760.

Lumsden

Two coins, one this Scottish piece, were presented by Mr George Lumsden, bookseller, Glasgow, in 1809. 374.

Magee

During 1984–5 Mr G. Magee found a series of coins in the vicinity of Cambuskenneth Abbey (see forthcoming, Bateson, J. D., 'Coin finds from Cambuskenneth Abbey, Stirlingshire', *Glasgow Archaeological Journal* 12 (1985)). The most important of these is the cut farthing of William the Lion which was donated by the finder: 76. A further coin of John Baliol was purchased: 303.

Marshall, M.

The Donation List to the Hunterian Museum records the following gift on 11 October 1813, '4 coins of Edward 1st of England and one of Alexander King of Scotland found in the Island of Bute, on the property of Archibald McArthur Stuart Esq. of Ascough about two miles from Rothesay in the month of August 1813 and presented to the museum by the Rev. Mark Marshall, Minister of Kingarth in Bute'. This is apparently a parcel from the huge Ascog hoard (Metcalf, 1977, 122). 223.

McLelland

In 1943 Mr W. McLelland presented 22 silver coins, mainly English, found at 129 Trongate, Glasgow, among which are two Scottish. 1473, 1474.

Millet

A single coin was donated by Mr Peter Millet, writer, Edinburgh, in November 1814. 1583.

Neilson

Dr George Neilson (1858–1923) was a Glasgow lawyer who also made a great contribution to Scottish history and archaeology. His miscellaneous collection of 698 coins was presented to the University of Glasgow by his widow's trustees in 1946. Among these were 212 Scottish coins, the majority being seventeenth-century copper issues in poor condition and not integrated here. It may be noted that many have the appearance of being finds rather than purchases though no provenances are attached. Among them is a group of seven 'Crossraguel' pennies, a type not represented in Hunter's own collection. Twenty-seven of Neilson's coins, in addition to another thirteen listed in the next entry, are included here. 13, 60, 224, 280, 424, 456, 472, 666, 806–12, 856, 877–8, 956, 1081, 1221, 1277, 1475, 1551, 1555, 1657, 1759.

Neilson Unknown Hoard

Among the Neilson coins is a group of 58 pieces all having a similar dull brittle appearance and several of these are broken or fragmentary. They undoubtedly form all or part of a previously unrecorded hoard probably of Scottish provenance but awaiting further research. It appears to be a sixteenth-century hoard composed of groats, and a few half-groats of Henry VIII and groats, including a single third, of James V. 912, 916–21, 923, 925–6, 931, 936, 940.

Purchases

Few of the Hunterian coins have been acquired by purchase apart from those finds, mainly bought through the Q & LTR, noted elsewhere in the *Sources* and the important group of Glasgow pennies purchased from Dr Stewart. Otherwise there are only seven purchases mainly acquired from London dealers: 9, 26, 139, 343, 1368, 1584, 1832.

Q & LTR	Treasure Trove in Scotland, which includes objects of any metal or material, is dealt with by the senior Treasury official known as the Queen's and Lord Treasurer's Remembrancer. Specimens from the following finds have been obtained from the Q & LTR, mostly upon payment to the finders: Dun Lagaidh, Edzell(?), Innerwick, Inverary, Linlithgow (1963), Loch Doon, Renfrew, Rigghead (Collin), Tranent.
Renfrew	The bulk of the 1963 Renfrew hoard mainly of Edwardian sterlings was acquired by the Hunter Coin Cabinet through the Q & LTR in 1967 (see Woodhead and Stewart 1966, 128–47). A total of 510 coins out of 674 was purchased and of these 46 are Scottish. 179–85, 189, 197–9, 203, 208–10, 225–37, 242–5, 251, 258, 262–3, 266, 274, 277–8, 281, 284–5, 287, 321, 326; no. 289 may be also from this hoard.
Rigghead	In 1963 a large hoard of gold, silver and billon Scottish, English and French coins hidden in the mid-sixteenth century was discovered in Rigghead sandpit, Collin, Dumfries (see *NCirc* 1970, 389). Thirty-nine Scottish (and fifteen English) pieces mainly bawbees of James V and Mary were purchased through the Q & LTR. 915, 928–30, 951–5, 962–8, 970–2, 975, 1021–7, 1029–30, 1034–7, 1041–3, 1048, 1055, 1058.
Slype	Among 63 long cross pennies purchased in 1914 from the Slype hoard there are two of Alexander III. 104, 129.
Smithers	The Donation List to the Hunterian Museum records for 18 November 1816, 'Gold coin of James 2nd of Scotland found in the Cathedral Church Glasgow and presented by Thos. Smithers, Esq.'. 688.
Spurway	J. W. Spurway of Leicester. 90.
Stewart	It is perhaps surprising that prior to 1981 the Hunter Coin Cabinet possessed no specimen of a Glasgow penny. Five different varieties, including the unique short cross penny of Robert, as well as a Renfrew coin have been acquired from Dr Ian Stewart, MP, by donation: 94 and purchase: 90, 122, 132, 139, 151.
Thomson	W. F. Thomson of Irvine presented a Scottish and a Polish coin in 1942. 1012.
Tranent	The 1981 Tranent, East Lothian, hoard consists of 149 coins of England, mainly Edwardian pennies, and Scotland, mainly of David II and Robert II (see J. D. Bateson and P. Scott, forthcoming). Twenty coins were purchased through the Q & LTR and of these 14 are Scottish: 337, 380–1, 389, 391, 397, 406, 411, 431, 439, 481, 486, 499–500.
Unknown	A small number of mainly nineteenth-century acquisitions are of unknown origin. 861, 1342, 1364–5, 1383, 1429, 1561, 1586.
Younger	A single medieval coin found during excavations of the Broch of Leckie in 1980 is on loan along with the remainder of the finds from Lord Younger of Leckie. 605.

SELECT BIBLIOGRAPHY

THE present short bibliography is confined to those works actually referred to in the text, and to recent relevant work on Scottish coinage published after 1980. For a comprehensive bibliography of Scottish numismatics up to 1980, students are referred to the invaluable bibliographical essay by Ian Stewart, 'Two Centuries of Scottish Numismatics', in *The Scottish Antiquarian Tradition*, ed. A. S. Bell (Edinburgh, 1981), 227–65.

In this Sylloge volume works are cited by the name of the authors and the date of publication. Reference to the list below will provide the full title and bibliographical details. Exceptionally Stewart's monograph 'Scottish Mints', is cited by its title, while Edward Burns's three-volume classic *The Coinage of Scotland*, which provides the framework on which this Sylloge is based is indicated throughout simply by the letter B.

Anderson, J. 1739	*Selectus Diplomatum et Numismatum Scotiae Thesaurus* (Edinburgh).
Archibald, M. M. 1981	*Department of Coins and Medals: New Acquisitions No 1 (1976–77)* (British Museum Occasional Paper No. 25), 54–5.
Barlow, E. and Robertson, A. 1974	'The Dun Lagaidh Hoard of Short Cross Sterlings' *Glasgow Archaeological Journal* 3 (1974), 78–81.
Blunt, C. E. 1976	'Personal reminiscences of some distinguished numismatists of a previous generation' *BNJ* 46 (1976), 64–75.
Boon, G. C. 1983	'Henry of Northumberland, Type I' *NCirc* 1983, 226.
Brown, I. D. and Dolley, M. 1971	*A Bibliography of Coin Hoards of Great Britain and Ireland 1500–1967* (London).
Burns, E. 1887	*The Coinage of Scotland* (Edinburgh).
Caldwell, D. 1982	D. Caldwell, J. E. L. Murray and M. Delmé-Radcliffe. 'Innerwick Hoard 1979' *BNJ* 52 (1982), 132–51.
Cochran-Patrick, R. W. 1875	'Unpublished and Rare Varieties of Scottish Coins' *NC²* 15 (1875), 157–66.
Holmes, N. M. M. 1983	'A Fifteenth-Century Coin Hoard from Leith' *BNJ* 53 (1983), 78–107.
Lindsay, J. 1845	*View of the Coinage of Scotland* (Cork). Also supplements 1859 and 1868.
Lockett, R. C. 1957	*Catalogue of Part V of the Celebrated Collection of Coins formed by the late Richard Cyril Lockett Esq.* Glendining 1957. (See also Part XI, 1960.)

Metcalf, D. M. 1969   *Sylloge of Coins of the British Isles: 12 Ashmolean Museum, Oxford*: Part II *English Coins 1066–1279.*

Metcalf, D. M. 1977   'The Evidence of Scottish Coin Hoards for Monetary History, 1100–1600' in *Coinage in Medieval Scotland (1100–1600)* ed. D. M. Metcalf (Oxford), 1–59.

Metcalf, D. M. and Oddy, W. A. 1980   *Metallurgy in Numismatics* (RNS Special Publication 13).

Murray, J. E. L. 1971   'The Early Unicorns and Heavy Groats of James III and James IV' *BNJ* 40 (1971), 62–96.

Murray, J. E. L. 1979   'The First Gold Coinage of Mary Queen of Scots' *BNJ* 49 (1979), 82–6.

Murray, J. E. L. and Van Nerom, C. 1983   'Monnaies "au globe et à la croix" appartenant à des collections belges' *RBN* 129 (1983), 91–118.

Murray, J. E. L. and Stewart, I. 1970   'Unpublished Scottish Coins V' *NC*[7] 10 (1970), 163–86.

Murray, J. E. L. and Stewart, I. 1983   'St. Andrews Mint under David I' *BNJ* 53 (1983), 178–80.

Murray, J. K. R. 1966   'Two Scottish Re-Used Dies' *NCirc* 1966, 94.

Murray, J. K. R. 1966 Bawbees   'The Stirling Bawbees of Mary, Queen of Scots' *NCirc* 1966, 306.

Murray, J. K. R. 1967   'The Scottish Coinage of 1560–1' *NCirc* 1967, 95.

Murray, J. K. R. 1968   'The Scottish Coinage of 1553' *BNJ* 37 (1968), 98–109.

Murray, J. K. R. 1969   'The Scottish Silver Coinage of Charles II' *BNJ* 38 (1969), 113–25.

Murray, J. K. R. 1970   'The Scottish Gold and Silver Coinages of Charles I' *BNJ* 39 (1970), 111–44.

Murray, J. K. R. 1972   'The Billon Coinages of James VI of Scotland' *NC*[7] 12 (1972), 177–82.

Murray, J. K. R. 1979   'The Scottish Gold Coinage of 1555–8' *NC*[7] 19 (1979), 155–64.

Murray, J. K. R. 1981   'The Scottish Testoons' *NCirc* 1981, 397.

Murray, J. K. R. and Stewart, I. 1972   'The Scottish Copper Coinages 1642–97' *BNJ* 41 (1972), 105–35.

Richardson, A. B. 1901   *Catalogue of the Scottish Coins in the National Museum of Antiquities Edinburgh* (Edinburgh).

Scottish Mints 1971   I. Stewart in *Mints, Dies and Currency*, ed. R. A. G. Carson, London, 165–289.

Snelling, T. 1774   *View of the Silver Coin and Coinages of Scotland* (London).

Stevenson, R. B. K. 1959   'The "Stirling" Turners of Charles I, 1632–9' *BNJ* 29 (1959), 128–51.

Stewart, I. 1955   'Some Unpublished Scottish Coins' *NC*[6] 15 (1955), 11–20.

Stewart, I. 1958   'Unpublished Scottish Coins: III' *NC*[6] 18 (1958), 1–7.

Stewart, I. 1958–9   'An Uncertain Mint of David I' *BNJ* 29 (1958–9), 293–6.

Stewart, I. 1958–9 Brussels   'The Brussels Hoard. Mr Baldwin's Arrangement of the Scottish Coins' *BNJ* 29 (1958–9), 91–7.

Stewart, I. 1958–9 Glenluce   'The Glenluce Hoard' *BNJ* 29 (1958–9), 363–81.

Stewart, I. 1967   *The Scottish Coinage* 2nd edn. (London, 1967). (1st edn. published 1955.)

Stewart, I. 1970   'The Long Voided Cross Sterlings of Alexander III Illustrated by Burns' *BNJ* 39 (1970), 67–77.

Stewart, I. 1971   'Scottish Mints' in *Mints, Dies and Currency*, ed. R. A. G. Carson (London), 165–289.

Stewart, I. 1974   'The Scottish Element' in the 1969 Colchester Hoard, *BNJ* 44 (1974), 48–61.

Stewart, I. 1977   'The Volume of Early Scottish Coinage' in *Coinage in Medieval Scotland (1100–1600)*, ed. D. M. Metcalf (Oxford), 65–72.

Stewart, I. 1981   'Two Centuries of Scottish Numismatics' *The Scottish Antiquarian Tradition*, ed. A. S. Bell, (Edinburgh), 227–65.

Stewart, I. 1983 Imitation   'Imitation in later medieval coinage: the influence of Scottish types abroad' in *Studies in Numismatic Method presented to Philip Grierson*, eds. C. N. L. Brooke and others (Cambridge), 303–25.

Stewart, I. 1983 Propaganda   'Coinage and Propaganda: an interpretation of the Coin Types of James VI' in *From the Stone Age to the Forty-Five*, eds. A. O'Connor and D. V. Clarke, 452–64.

Stewart, I. and Murray, J. E. L. 1967   'Unpublished Scottish Coins IV, Early James III' *NC*[7] 7 (1967), 147–61.

Woodhead, P. and Stewart, I. 1966   'The Renfrew Treasure Trove, 1963' *BNJ* 35 (1966), 128–47.

Woodhead, P., Stewart, I. and Tatler, G. 1969   'The Loch Doon Treasure Trove 1966' *BNJ* 37 (1969), 31–49.

PLATES

DAVID I (1124–1153)

Phase a (Burns Class III, Edinburgh, nos. 1–2)

Edinburgh

	Weight gr	gm	Die axis	
1/A	21.3	1.38	300	Erebald. [+]DAVIDREX [ ]EREBALD[ ] B.24(23), 24C, 24D, same obv. die as 2/A. Browne Willis.
2/A	20.5	1.33	180	Erebald. [ ]REX +EREBALD[O]NEDE[N] as 1/A. Hird.

Phase b (Burns Class III, ?Edinburgh. Nos. 3–4. Prince Henry, died 1152, Earl of Northumberland, ?Newcastle. No. 5)

(?Edinburgh)

3/A	20.5	1.33	90	[+DAV]IDREX [ ]:ON:EODO[ ] B.24C, cf. Lockett 12. P 1946, Dakers 280, Cochran-Patrick 109.
4/A	21.6	1.40	NA	[+DAV[IDREX] [ ]NO[ ]SN cf. B.24, 24C, 24D. P 1946, Marshall 89, Cochran-Patrick 110.

Prince Henry (died 1152), Earl of Northumberland (Newcastle. No. 5)

5/A	11.4 (cut halfpenny)	0.74	180	[STIEFИ]ER[E:] [+I]O[CEON:CA]2T see 'Scottish Mints', 188 and 196. D 1982, Stewart, Prestwich T. T.

See also *SCBI 12 Ashmolean Museum, Oxford* nos. 291, 292 for two pennies of Henry.

Phase c (Burns Class I, good workmanship and lettering. Berwick, Carlisle. Nos. 6–8)

Berwick

6/A	19.4	1.26	90	Folpalt. [+DA[VIT·REX·] [+FOLPALT·O]NBERV[I] B.1 (1) (same dies), Lockett 1 (same dies). Hird, Cochran-Patrick 99.
7/A	19.1	1.24	160	Folpalt. [+DAVITR]EX·ISOIIᴄ [+FOLPA]LT:ONB[ER]✱ B.4A (but there read as ᴄSOᴄIE) (same dies). Lockett 679 (same dies). Jesus College.

Carlisle (Stewart, 1958–9, 293–6, Scottish mints, p. 195.)

8/A	22.4	1.45	60	Riccart or Hildart?. +D[AV]IT:REX: [RICC]ART:OИhA[ ] B.6B (same dies), Stewart, op. cit. P 1954, Parsons 698.

Phase d (Burns Class II, local workmanship, legends blundered. ?Roxburgh. Nos. 9–13)

9/H	15.9	1.03	40	[ ]V[ ] +hV[ ]I B.14(13) obv., 14A rev. (same dies). P 1980.
10/A	22.2	1.44	0	AVIT·IAIT +hV^A[:N]:VN[ ] B.16(16) (same dies), Lockett 7 (same dies). Hird, Cochran-Patrick 106, Advocates.
11/A	19.9	1.29	NA	Illegible B.? P 1982, Stewart.
12/A	22.3	1.45	NA	ĀV[ITR] ᴇᴧᴧ[ ]V[ ]Vᴧ short stalks instead of pellets in two angles of reverse B. —, Stewart, 1955, 11, no. 1, pl. III, no. 1 (same dies). P 1982, Stewart.
13/H	4.3 (cut farthing)	0.28	NA	B.18(18). Neilson.

MALCOLM IV (1153–65)

(Bust of good style; legends retrograde and upside down. Uncertain mint No. 14)

14/A	23.5	1.52	NA	[+M]ALCOLM·[ ]· [ ]IV[ ] reading anti-clockwise B.8C (same dies), Lockett 18 (same dies). Hird, Duke of Northumberland.

[*continued overleaf*]

PLATE 1

1   2   3   4   5   6   7

8   9   10   11   12   13   14

15   16   17   18   19   20   21

22   23   24   25   26   27   28

Plate 1 (*cont.*):

WILLIAM I (1165–1214)

Second Coinage—Crescent and Pellet Coinage (Without mint name, Berwick, Edinburgh, Perth, Roxburgh. Nos. 15–47)

Without Mint Name (colons between letters)

	Weight		Die	
	gr	gm	axis	
15/A	23.0	1.49	110	potent sceptre head. Folpolt. +[ ]AME +[ ]O:L:T: B. see i, 51, Lockett 691a. Hird.

Without Mint Name (Raul Derling and Radulfus)

16/A	22.5	1.46	80	pommée sceptre head. Raul Derling [+]LEREIWILAM: +Ro[ ]LDERLIG: B.36(10) (same obv. die, but rev. die of Adam at Berwick, cf. B.38(18, 19)), cf. Lockett 691d, same obv. die as 17/A and 18/A. Hird, Cochran-Patrick 128.
17/A	22.0	1.43	320	pommée sceptre head. Raul Derling [+L]ERE[IW[ILAM:] [ ]RLIG[ ] As 16/A. P 1982, Stewart.
18/A	21.4	1.39	140	pommée sceptre head. Raul Derling [+L]ERE[IW]ILAM[:] [ ]LDE[ ] As 16/A. P 1982, Stewart.
19/A	22.8	1.48	90	? sceptre head. Raul Derling +LERE[IWIL]AM +[ ]LDERL[ ] B.38A (same obv. die). P 1982, Stewart.
20/A	22.3	1.45	200	pommée sceptre head. Raul Derling Obv. illegible [ ]V[ ]DERL[ ] B.38(18, 19). P 1982, Stewart.
21/A	22.8	1.48	150	potent sceptre head. Raul Derling [ ]W[ ]L[·]A.M.E[ ] +:R:A[V:]L[:D:]E.R: B. see i, p. 60 and for rev. p. 58, B29–29B, Lockett 26c (same dies), same obv. die as 36/A. P 1982, Stewart, Dakers 283a?
22/A	21.1	1.37	270	pommée sceptre head. Radulfus +VILLAM∵REID['E] [ ]RA:DVL:FVS:ON B.—. P 1982, Stewart.

Berwick

23/A	21.1	1.37	50	pommée sceptre head. Raul Derling [ ]IL[ ] +RAVLDERLIGBER B. see i, p. 61, Lockett 21b (same dies). E 1963, Stewart, Parsons 700.
24/A	22.7	1.47	90	pommée sceptre head. Willame +[L]EREIWILA[ME:] [+]WILAMBERE[W]I[Œ:] B.35(7) (same dies). Hird, Cochran-Patrick 116a, Antiquaries 1874.

Edinburgh

25/A	11.4	0.74 (cut halfpenny)	270	Adam [ ]EREIWI[ ] +ADA[ ]EBV: B.39(20), Lockett 22c or 690c (same dies). P 1980.
26/H	22.2	1.44	280	pommée sceptre head. Adam [+L]EREIWILL[AM] +A[DA]MONEDENEBV B.39(21). P 1981, MacPherson.
27/A	23.0	1.49	330	pommée sceptre head. Adam +LEREIWILLAM +ADAMON:ED: B.40(22) (same obv. die), Lockett 690d (same dies), same obv. die as 28/A. P 1982, Stewart, Drabble (1943) 1162.
28/A	21.5	1.39	90	pommée sceptre head. Hue +[L]EREIWILLAM +hVEONEDENEBV B.40(22) (same dies), Lockett 23 (same dies), same obv. die as 27/A. Hird.

	Weight		*Die*
	gr	gm	axis

Perth

29/A 23.3 1.51 270 potent sceptre head. Folpolt +WILLAMΘ[:RΘX] +FOLPO[LTDΘ]PΘRT: B.31(4), Lockett 24 (same obv. die and ? rev.), same obv. die as 30/A. Christ Church, 'Found in ye burying place of ye family of Brodie, Dyke Parish, Morayshire', i.e. Dyke Hoard.

30/A 18.8 1.22 310 potent sceptre head. Folpolt +WI[LL]AMΘ:R[ΘX] +F[O]LPO[LT]DΘPΘR[T:] B.31(4), Lockett 24 (same obv. die), same obv. die as 29/A. P 1982, Stewart, R. Carlyon-Britton.

31/A 20.8 1.35 90 potent sceptre head. Folpolt [+LΘRΘIW]ILLAM: +FOLPOLT[DΘPΘR]: B.30(2) (same dies), Lockett 688 or 689 (same rev. die), same obv. die as 32/A. P 1963, Stewart.

32/A 22.0 1.43 70 (potent) sceptre head. Folpolt [+] L[ΘR]ΘIWILLA[M:] [ ]OLPOLTDΘPΘR[ ] B.30(2) (same obv. die), same obv. die as 31/A. P 1982, Stewart, Marshall 161 (part), Brushfield.

33/A 22.5 1.46 45 potent sceptre head. Folpolt [+L]ΘRΘIWILLA[ ] [ ]LPOLTDΘPΘ[RT.] B.30(2) obv./31(4) rev., Lockett 25 (same dies). Hird.

34/A 21.9 1.42 320 potent sceptre head. Folpolt [ ]LΘRΘI[ ]IL[ ] +FOLPO[LT]DΘPΘRT B.30. P 1982, Stewart, R. Carlyon-Britton.

Roxburgh

35/A 19.9 1.29 270 potent sceptre head. Raul +RΘIW[ ]M +RAVL:O[ ]:ROC B.—, cf. Lockett 26a. P 1963, Stewart.

36/A 12.9 0.84 0 potent sceptre head. Raul +[ ]:Θ·[ ] +[ ]AV[ ]Q· B.—, same obv. die as
(cut 21/A. D 1982, Stewart.
halfpenny)

37/A 21.3 1.38 100 potent sceptre head. Raul [ ]·AM:ΘRX +·R[ ]·V[ ]N·R·Q· B.—. P 1982, Stewart, Drabble (1943) 1163.

38/A 23.0 1.49 310 potent sceptre head. Raul +RΘI[W]ILL[A]M· +[R]A·V·L:[ ]N·RO B.33(11) (same dies). P 1982, Stewart.

39/A 9.7 0.63 NA (potent) sceptre head. Raul [RΘ]IWILLA[MΘ] [RA]VL:ON:R[OQ] B.—, Lockett 26a (same dies).
(cut D 1982, Stewart.
halfpenny)

40/A 22.8 1.48 180 potent sceptre head. Raul +··RΘIW[ILL]AM [+]RAVLDΘROQΘ[BVRG] B.—, see 'Scottish Mints', die link 3c, pl. XV, 3 (same obv. die). P 1982, Stewart, Cochran-Patrick 123.

41/A 21.9 1.42 180 pommée sceptre head. Raul +LΘRΘIWILLAM +RAVLONROQ· B.—. P 1963, Stewart, McFarlan, Napier 205a.

42/A 23.0 1.49 140 pommée sceptre head. Raul +[L]ΘRΘIWILAM +RAVLD[ΘR]OQΘBV B.37(15), Lockett 26b (same dies). Hird, Cochran-Patrick 121.

43/A 23.8 1.54 310 pommée sceptre head. Raul [ ]LΘRΘIW[ ]LAM +RAVLD[ ]V: B.37(15) P 1963, Stewart, 'Canadian Collection'.

44/A 20.7 1.34 90 pommée sceptre head. Raul [ ]RΘI[ ]AMΘ +RAVLDΘRO[ ]B[ ]R B.37(15). P 1963, Stewart.

45/A 22.5 1.46 220 pommée sceptre head. Raul +L[Θ]ΘIWILAM +R[A]VL[DΘR]LIGRO B.38A (same dies), Lockett 27a (same dies). E 1966, Stewart, Cochran-Patrick 127, Antiquaries.

46/A 21.8 1.41 90 pommée sceptre head. Raul +L[ ]ILLAM: +RAVLONR[ ] B.37(13). Hird.

47/A 22.5 1.46 230 pommée sceptre head. Raul [ ]WILLA[ ] [ ]DΘ[ ]QΘBVR[ ] B.37(15). P 1982, Stewart.

Third Coinage—Short Cross Coinage (Edinburgh, Perth, Roxburgh, without mint name. Nos. 48–78)

With Name of Mint

Edinburgh

48/A 20.7 1.34 90 Hue. +WILΘLMVSRX +hVΘOИΘDΘИBVR B.40D(1h) (same dies). Hird, Cochran-Patrick 134.
49/H 22.4 1.45 100 Hue. +WILΘLMVSRX +hVΘ:OИΘDИΘBVR B.41(2). Hunter.

[*continued overleaf*]

PLATE 2

Plate 3 (*cont.*):

Posthumous issue—Short Cross Coinage in William's name (Roxburgh. Nos. 79–84)

	Weight		Die	
	gr	*gm*	*axis*	
Roxburgh				
79/A	19.8	1.28	340	bust r., pellet behind neck, quatrefoil at end of obv. legend. Adam. +WIL[ ]GX [ ]ΛM:ON·ROϾG B.i, p. 72, 67C (same obv. die?). E 1966, Stewart, Dakers 289.
80/A	18.8	1.23	120	types as 79/A. Peris, Adam. +WILLGLMVSRGX ∴ +PGRISΛDΛMONRO B.67A(6b) (same dies), Lockett 32 (same dies). Bodleian.
81/A	21.8	1.41	140	bust r. Peris, Adam. +∴WILLGLMVSRGX +PGRIS·ΛDΛMON[ ]OϾ B.—. Browne Willis.
82/A	19.0	1.23	50	bust l. obv. legend retrograde. Peris, Adam. [+]Ϲ:XG[RSVMLGLLI]W: +P[GRIS·ADAM] DGROϾI: B.66C(5f) (same dies). Hird.
83/A	9.4 (cut halfpenny)	0.61	NA	Aimer, Adam. +WIL[ ]X [ ]GR·ΛDΛMO[ ] B.67C(6d) (same dies), *N.Circ.*, Oct. 1982, 270. P 1982, found at Great Bedwyn, Wilts.
84/A	22.7 (pierced and plugged)	1.47	310	bust l. Walter, Adam. +WILL[GLM]VS: +WΛLTG[R:Λ]DΛM B.66A(31b) (same dies), Lockett 700 (same obv. die). P. 1982, Stewart, Parsons 703 (part).

ALEXANDER II (1214-49)

Short Cross Coinage in own name (Roxburgh. Nos. 85-9)

	Weight		Die
	gr	gm	axis

Roxburgh

85/A 22.5 1.46 240 bust l. Alain, Andrew. +ALEXSANDEREX +ALAINANDRVON˜RO B.75(6) (same dies), Lockett 701 (same dies), same obv. die as 86/A. Hird, Drabble (1939) 768, Brussels Hoard.

86/A 22.7 1.47 90 bust l. Alain, Andrew. +ALEXSANDEREX +ALINANDRVVO[   ] B.75(6) (same obv. die), see also Bi, p. 116, Lockett 701 (same obv. die), same obv. die as 85/A. Browne Willis.

87/A 23.1 1.50 160 bust r. Pieres. +ALEXSA[MDERR]EX +PIERESO[NROERE] B.70(1) (same dies), Lockett 36 (same dies). Hird, Marshall 164.

88/A 17.7 1.15 110 bust l. Pieres. [   ]EXSANDERRECX +PIERESONROC B.72(3) (same obv. die), Lockett 702 (same dies). P 1946, Dakers 293.

89/A 18.8 1.22 0 bust l. Pieres. [   ]LE[   ]ERREX. +PIERE[   ]ROE B.71, 72(1, 2) (same obv. die B71?/ same rev. die B72?), Lockett 37 (same obv. die). Browne Willis.

ALEXANDER III (1249-86)

Transitional Coinage—Short Cross Coinage (Glasgow. No. 90)

90/H 19.3 1.25 270 bust r. Robert. +ALEXANDE˜R·REX +ROBERT·ON·GLA· B.—, Spurway 226 (see Appendix, p. 244). P 1984, Stewart, J. W. Spurway (Leicester) 226.

First Coinage—Long Cross Coinage (Various mints. Nos. 91-173)

Type I

91/A 23.1 1.50 180 Berwick, Robert. RO BE˜R ON BE B.77(1) (same dies), Lockett 40 (same dies). D 1981, Stewart.

Type II

92/A 21.5 1.39 190 Aberdeen, Andreas. [AN]D˜REA S:ON˜[AB] B.93A(42a) (same dies), Lockett 45 (same dies). D 1893, E. L. Hussey.

93/A 19.8 1.28 230 Berwick, Robert. RO BE RTO NBE B.79(3) (same dies), Lockett 46 (same obv. die). Browne Willis.

94/H 21.0 1.36 210 Glasgow, Walter. WA LT· ER'O NG B.92C(50a) D 1981, Stewart, Lockett 712, Brussels Hoard.

95/A 23.5 1.52 140 Glasgow, Walter. WA LT ER ON B.92C(50a) (same obv. die; Lockett 48A (same obv. die but wrongly numbered on Lockett Catalogue pl. II as 47)/Lockett 733, same rev. die i.e. class II/IV mule). P 1981, Stewart.

96/A 17.9 1.16 90 Perth, Ion Cokin, hooked cross ends. IO˜N COK IN O˜NP B.104, 104A (37, 37a), Lockett 49b (same dies). P 1981, Stewart, Marr.

Type III

97/A 18.8 1.22 350 Aberdeen, Alexander. ALE XO˜N A˜BI RD B.135(47) (same obv. die), Lockett 50a (same dies). Hird.

98/A 21.8 1.41 220 Aberdeen, Ion. IO˜N O˜N· AB ERD B.138(50) (same dies), Lockett 52a (same rev. die). Hird, Cochran-Patrick 156(part)?, Advocates.

99/H 19.2 1.24 300 Aberdeen, Ion. [ION] ON· AB E˜RD B.138(50). D 1964, J. R. Lockie.

100/A 21.9 1.42 0 Ayr, Simon. SIM ON ON AR B.106(33), Lockett 82 (= this coin but there class V), P 1957, Lockett, Brussels Hoard.

101/A 22.7 1.47. 0 Berwick, Robert. RO˜B ER O˜N˜B ER B.140A(21a), Lockett 54a. Hird, Cochran-Patrick 158b.

102/H 19.3 1.25 160 Berwick, Robert. RO˜B E˜RO NB ER B.140A(21a) (same dies). Hunter.

103/A 24.2 1.57 60 Berwick, Robert. RO˜B ER TO[ ]BE· B.140B(21b), Lockett 724b, 725c. Browne Willis.

104/H 16.1 1.04 170 Berwick, Robert. RO˜B ER' TO˜N BE˜R B.140B(21b). P 1914, Q & L T R, Slype Hoard.

105/A 22.8 1.48 250 Berwick, Robert. RO˜B E˜RT ON BE· B.107A(19a) (same rev. die). Ashmolean.

106/A 20.8 1.35 260 Berwick, Robert. RO˜B E˜RT ON BE B.107A(19a), Lockett 725b (same dies). Hird.

107/A 20.4 1.32 70 Berwick, Willem. WI [LL'] O˜N˜B ER B.139(20) (same dies), Lockett 728c, d (same obv. die). Ashmolean.

[*continued overleaf*]

PLATE 4

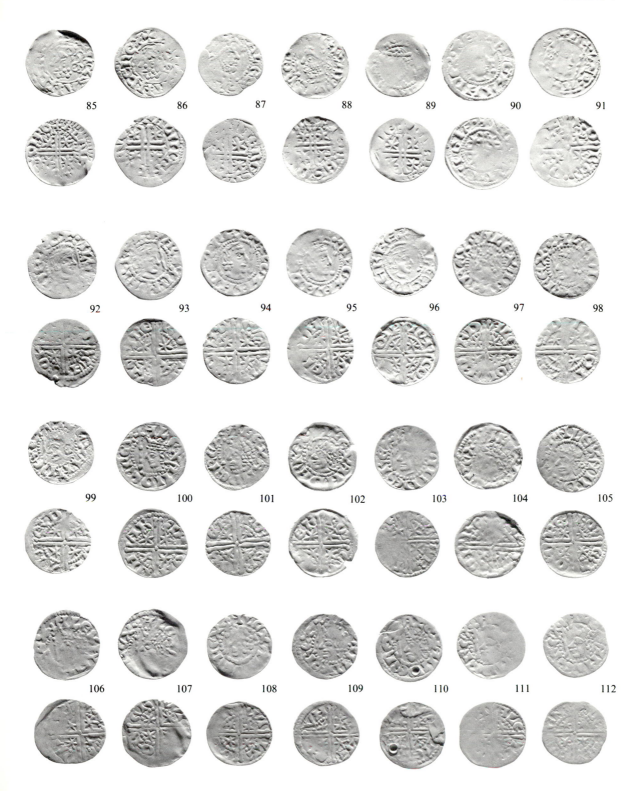

85 86 87 88 89 90 91

92 93 94 95 96 97 98

99 100 101 102 103 104 105

106 107 108 109 110 111 112

Plate 4 (*cont.*):

	Weight		*Die*
	gr	gm	axis

108/A   21.3   1.38   270   Berwick, Willem. **WI LL O^N^B ꓱR·** B.139, 139A (20, 20a), Lockett 55d (same dies). Hird, Brussels Hoard.

109/A   23.0   1.49   90   'Dun', Walter. **WA LTꓱ^R O^N^D VN** B.119A(54a) (same obv. die), Lockett 729b. Hird, Cochran-Patrick lot 146.

110/A   19.4   1.26   310   'Dun', Walter. **WA LTꓱ ^R[O]^N DV[N]** B.131A(60a) (same dies), Lockett 729c (same obv. die). Hird.
       (pierced)

111/A   21.6   1.40   30   'Dun', Walter. **ꓮLꓱ TꓱR O^[N^D V]N** B.132(61) (same dies), Lockett 730b (same rev. die), same obv. die as 112/A, see also 'Scottish Mints', p. 212 for connections with Edinburgh, die links 12, 64, 65. P 1981, Stewart.

112/A   20.7   1.34   270   Edinburgh, Alexander. **[ꓮ]Lꓱ XO^N ꓱD ꓱN:** B.134A(65a) (same obv. die), same obv. die as 111/A, Lockett 731b (same rev. die). P 1981, Stewart.
       (plugged)

	Weight		*Die*
	gr	gm	axis

113/A 19.3 1.25 20 Edinburgh, Alexander. ᴀL ᴇXO ˆNᴇD ᴇN B.134A(54a) (same rev. die), Lockett 58a (same dies). Hird, Brussels Hoard.

114/A 21.9 1.42 230 Edinburgh, Wilam. WI LᴀM·O ˆN·ᴇD B.94B(64b), Lockett 58d (same dies). Hird, Drabble (1939) 776c.

115/A 17.7 1.15 270 Forfar, Simond. [SI]M O ˆND ON [FO ˆR] B.116(62) (same dies), Lockett 65b (same obv. die 65a, same rev. die), same obv. die as 116/A. P 1981, Stewart.

116/A 22.5 1.46 120 Forfar, Wilam. WI LᴀM ˆ ON FO ˆR B.116(62) (same obv. die), Lockett 61a (same dies), same obv. die as 115/A. P 1981, Stewart.

117/A 16.1 1.04 130 'Fres', Walter. W[ᴀ ˆL] Tᴇ ˆR O ˆNF RᴇS B.129(58) (same dies), Lockett 62 (same dies), same obv. die as 119/A, 121/A, 126/A, see 'Scottish Mints', pp. 278–9, no. 11. Ashmolean.

118/A 20.4 1.32 120 ? 'Fres', Wilam. WI Lᴀ MO NFR B.114C (same obv. die), see 'Scottish Mints', pp. 276–7, no. 9. P 1957, Lockett 72b, Brussels Hoard.

119/A 19.6 1.27 300 Glasgow, Walter. Wᴀ LT ᴇR O ˆNG B.127(56) (same dies), same obv. dies as 117/A, 121/A, 126/A. P 1957, Lockett 61c, Brussels Hoard.

120/A 23.5 1.52 90 Glasgow, Walter. Wᴀ ˆL Tᴇ RO ˆNG· B.118A(53a), Lockett 66b (same rev. die). Hird, Brussels Hoard.

121/A 20.7 1.34 40 Glasgow, Walter. Wᴀ LTᴇ ˆRO ˆN GLᴀ ˆ B.128(57) (same obv. die), same obv. die as 117/A, 119/A, 126/A. P 1957, Lockett 67, Brussels Hoard.

122/H 20.1 1.13 290 Glasgow, Walter. Wᴀ LT ᴇ ˆRO ˆ GLᴀ B.128(57). P 1981, Stewart.

123/A 22.1 1.43 70 Inverness, Gefrai. GᴇF Rᴀ [ION] INV B.122B(67b) (same obv. die), Lockett 68b (same dies). E 1966, Stewart.

124/A 23.1 1.50 180 Kinghorn, Wilam. WIL ᴀM O ˆN·K ING B.108(66) (same dies), P 1981, Stewart, Lockett 758, Brussels Hoard.

125/A 23.0 1.49 180 Lanark, Wilam. WI Lᴀ MO ˆN·L· B.—, Lockett 72a (same obv. die). Hird, Brussels Hoard.

126/A 19.8 1.28 340 Montrose, Walter. Wᴀ LTᴇ ˆRO ˆN ˆMV ˆN B.131(60) (same dies), same obv. die as 117/A, 119/A, 121/A. See 'Scottish Mints', pp. 278–9, no. 11. P 1957, Lockett 73, Brussels Hoard.

127/A 18.1 1.17 110 Perth, Ion. IO ˆN ON Pᴇ ˆR Tᴇ B.—, Lockett 74b (same obv. die). Hird, Cochran-Patrick 159?

128/A 22.4 1.45 70 Perth, Ion. IO ˆN ON Pᴇ ˆR Tᴇ: B.—, Lockett 740a, b (same obv. die). P 1981.

129/H 23.0 1.49 190 Perth, Ion Cokin. ION ᴄ[O KIN ONP] B.111(38). P 1914, Q & LTR, Slype Hoard.

130/A 19.9 1.29 180 Perth, Ion Cokin. ION [ᴄO KIN] O ˆNP cf. B. 111–14(38–41), rev. die not in Lockett. University College, Waddington.

131/A 21.6 1.40 170 Renfrew, Walter. W ˆ ᴀL Tᴇ ˆR O ˆNR [IN] B.93B (same rev. die), Lockett 71, 738 (same rev. die). Ashmolean.

132/H 22.1 1.43 10 Renfrew, Walter. W ˆ ᴀL Tᴇ ˆR O ˆNR IN B.93B. P 1981, Stewart, Dakers.

133/A 19.1 1.24 70 Roxburgh, Adam. ᴀD ᴀM ON RO B.121(23) (same dies), Lockett 75a (same rev. die). Ashmolean.

134/A 23.6 1.53 90 Roxburgh, Andrew. ᴀN DR ᴇV· O ˆNR B.122(26) (same obv. die), Lockett 743d (same dies). Browne Willis.

135/A 19.6 1.27 160 Roxburgh, Michel. MI ᴄhᴇL O ˆNR B.—, Lockett 76 (but same rev. die as Lockett 91 (class VI)).
(plugged) P 1981, Stewart, Dakers.

136/A 23.1 1.50 220 St. Andrews, Tomas. TO ˆM ᴀS: ON [ᴀ]N B.115C(69c) (same dies), Lockett 747a (same dies). Browne Willis.

137/A 19.6 1.27 170 Stirling, Henri. hᴇ ˆN ˆ ˆRON ST ˆR IV['] B.110B(69h), Lockett 748d (same obv. die)/749b (same rev. die). Hird, Cochran-Patrick 160c.

138/A 20.7 1.34 30 Uncertain, Wilam. WI Lᴀ ˆN ˆ ᴇR Tᴇ ˆR B.110C (same dies), see 'Scottish Mints', pp. 278–9, no. 13. P 1957, Lockett lot 72c, Brussels Hoard.

141/H 21.3 1.38 0 St Andrews, Tomas. TO ˆM ᴀ[S:] ON ᴀN B.115C(69c). Hunter. (Misplaced on Plate 6 with Type IV coins.)

Type IV

139/H 24.7 1.60 150 Glasgow, Walter. Wᴀ LT ᴇR ON B.118B(53b), P 1981.

140/H 18.8 1.22 140 Glasgow, Walter. Wᴀ LT ᴇR ON B.118B(53b), P 1981, Stewart.

PLATE 5

113   114   115   116   117   118   119

120   121   122   123   124   125   126

127   128   129   130   131   132   133

134   135   136   137   138   139   140

Weight   *Die*
gr gm   axis

141/H   See text to pl. 5.

142/A 21.1 1.37 50   Stirling, Henri. hЄ^N RIO N·S TR B.94D(69e) (same dies), Lockett 81b (same dies). P 1981, Stewart.

Type V

143/A 21.6 1.40 140   Edinburgh, Alexander. ᴁLЄ XO^N^ ЄD ЄN B.94A(64a) (same obv. die), Lockett 754c (same dies). Ashmolean.

Type VI

144/A 19.3 1.25 120   Kinghorn, Wilam. WIL ᴁM· ON· KIN^ B.93C (same obv. die), P 1957. Lockett 87, Brussels Hoard.

145/A 21.0 1.36 40   Roxburgh, Michel. MI Gh ЄL O^NR B.—, Lockett 91 (same dies). P 1981, Stewart.

Type VII

146/A 18.5 1.20 270   Berwick, Ion. [I]Oh ᴁN ON BЄR B.93B,C, 94 (for type, not this mint/moneyer), Lockett 94a. P 1981, Stewart.

147/H 22.2 1.44 90   Berwick, Iohan. IOh ᴁN ON BЄ^R B.90(14). Hunter.

148/H 21.9 1.42 270   Berwick, Walter. WAL TЄ^R BЄ^R WI^h B.89B(13b) = this coin. Hunter.

149/A 20.5 1.33 350   Berwick, Willem. WI LL'O^N B Є^R B.—, Lockett 96b (same dies). P 1981, Stewart.

150/A 19.4 1.26 110   Edinburgh, Alexander. [   ]X:O ^NЄD ЄN B.—, Lockett 766a (same dies). P 1981, Stewart.

151/H 21.7 1.41 30   Glasgow, Walter. WA LT Є^R O^N^ GLᴁ B.102(51). P 1981, Stewart.

152/A 23.0 1.49 140   Perth, Ion Cokin. IO^N GO ON PЄR B.99(36), cf. Lockett 770a. P 1981, Stewart, Marr.

153/H 20.9 1.35 90   Perth, Rainald. [Rᴁl] Nᴁ^L DDЄ PЄR B.89A(33c) = this coin. Hunter.

154/A 17.0 1.10 0   Perth, Rainald. Rᴁl Nᴁ^L DDЄ PЄ^R B.101B (same dies), Lockett 99 (same rev. die). P 1981,
       (pierced)   Stewart.

155/A 24.5 1.59 320   Roxburgh, Andrew. ᴁN D^RЄ VO^N RO: B.96(22) (same dies), Lockett 100 (same dies). Hird, Brussels Hoard.

Type VIIIa

156/A 15.7 1.02 60   Berwick, Iohan. IOh ᴁN O^NB ЄR B.82(6), cf. Lockett 771a, same rev. die as 160/A. Hird, Cochran-Patrick 154c.

157/A 26.2 1.70 320   Berwick, Iohan. IOh ᴁN O^N·B ЄR[:] B.82(6), cf. Lockett 771a, same rev. die as 162/A. Browne Willis.

158/A 24.7 1.60 0   Berwick, Iohan. IOh ᴁN ON^B ЄR' B.82(6), cf. Lockett 771a. D 1915, Cozens.

159/A 17.7 1.15 110   Berwick, Iohan. IOh ᴁN ON BЄ^R B.83(7), cf. Lockett 101c. P 1981, Stewart.

160/A 23.1 1.50 40   Berwick, Iohan. IOh ᴁN O^NB ЄR B.82(6), cf. Lockett 771a, same rev. die as 156/A. P 1981, Stewart.

161/A 24.5 1.59 150   Berwick, Iohan. I[Oh] [ᴁN] BЄ^R ON B.—, Lockett 771c (same dies). P 1981, Stewart.

162/A 18.2 1.18 70   Berwick, Iohan. IOh ᴁN O^N·B ЄR: B.82(6), Lockett 771a (same obv. die?), same rev. die as 157/A. P 1981, Stewart.

163/A 18.7 1.21 60   Berwick, Walter. WA^L TЄ^R BЄ^R WIK B.89(13), Lockett 772a (same dies). P 1981, Stewart.

164/A 22.4 1.45 200   Berwick, Walter. WA LTЄ RO^N BЄ^R B.—, Lockett 772e (same obv. die). Hird.

165/A 22.2 1.44 90   Berwick, Walter. Wᴁ [   ] [   ] BЄR B.—, cf. Lockett 772e. P 1981, Stewart.

166/A 19.3 1.25 320   Berwick, Walter. Wᴁ^R [TЄR] BЄ^R WIK B.89(13) (same dies), Lockett 101d (same dies). University College, Waddington.

167/A 23.9 1.55 40   Berwick, Walter. Wᴁ LTЄ RO^N BЄ^R retrograde. B.87(11) (same dies), Lockett 103b (same dies). P 1981, Stewart.

168/A 22.5 1.46 270   'Fres', Walter. [Wᴁ] LTЄ RO^N FRЄ B.103(52) (same dies), Lockett 84 (same dies where given as class V but see Stewart 1958–9 Brussels, 93–4). Browne Willis.

PLATE 6

141 142 143 144 145 146 147

148 149 150 151 152 153 154

155 156 157 158 159 160 161

162 163 164 165 166 167 168

	Weight		*Die*	
	gr	*gm*	*axis*	
169/A	21.3	1.38	210	Perth, Rainald. RAI NAˆL DDE PEˆR B.103A (same dies), Lockett 776a (same dies), see 'Scottish Mints', pp. 278–9, no. 19. Hird, Brussels Hoard.
170/A	16.5	1.07	0	Perth, Rainald. [ ]A[ ] N[ ] DDE PEˆR B.103A, cf. Lockett 104a, 776a. Hird.

Type VIIIb

| 171/A | 22.1 | 1.43 | 180 | Berwick, Walter. WAˆL TEˆR ON BEˆR B.85(17) (same obv. die), Lockett 105 (same dies). P 1981, Stewart. |
| 172/A | 21.1 | 1.37 | 340 | Berwick, Walter. WAL [ ] ON BEˆR B.84A(9a) (same obv. die). Lockett 106b, c (same obv. die), same obv. die as 173/A. P 1981, Stewart. |

Type VIIId

| 173/A | 21.1 | 1.37 | 160 | Berwick, Walter. WAL TEˆR' ON BEˆR' B.84A(9a) (same dies), Lockett 106b, c, same dies, same obv. die as 172/A. P 1981, Stewart. |

Second Coinage (Without mint name. Penny, nos. 174–286; Halfpenny, 287–90; Farthing 291–3)

Penny

Group I, reverse 4 mullets of 6 points

Class I, Stewart B

174/A	21.1	1.37	280	B.142(2). Hird.
175/A	20.5	1.33	180	B.141(1). Hird.
176/A	18.4	1.19	270	B.142(3). Hird.
177/A	21.1	1.37	130	B.142(2). Hird.
178/A	20.2	1.31	60	B.142(3). Christ Church.
179/H	20.2	1.31	30	B.142(2). Renfrew Hoard 525.
180/H	21.1	1.37	220	B.142(2). Renfrew Hoard 527.
181/H	21.6	1.40	60	B.141(1). Renfrew Hoard 529.
182/H	20.7	1.34	230	B.142(3). Renfrew Hoard 531.
183/H	21.4	1.39	120	B.142(2). Renfrew Hoard 532.
184/H	19.7	1.28	260	B.142(3). Renfrew Hoard 533.
185/H	19.6	1.27	270	B.142(3). Renfrew Hoard 534.

Class I obv., III rev., Stewart B/C

186/A	21.6	1.40	330	B.144(17). Christ Church.
187/A	20.5	1.33	250	B.146(19). D 1912, A.C. Kay.
188/A	17.9	1.16	320	B.146(19). Keble College.
189/H	21.3	1.38	90	B.146(19). Renfrew Hoard 538.

Class II, Stewart A

190/A	20.8	1.35	40	rev. Escossie Rex B.148(7) but variant stops. D 1957, Executors of R. C. Lockett, Lockett 107, Roth, Murdoch (1904) 1018.
191/H	20.2	1.31	350	rev. Escossie Rex B.148(8). P 1969, Q & LTR, Loch Doon Hoard 1810.
192/A	19.3	1.25	350	B.147A(6a) (= this coin). P 1982, Spink Auction 20, 106, Grantley 1698, Murdoch 34, Richardson.
193/H	22.2	1.44	90	B.148A(8a) (= this coin). Hunter.
194/H	20.5	1.33	220	B.148B(8b) (= this coin). Hunter.

Class III, Stewart C

195/A	21.5	1.39	270	B.151(13). Hird.
196/A	19.0	1.23	200	B.151(—). Christ Church.
	(pierced)			

PLATE 7

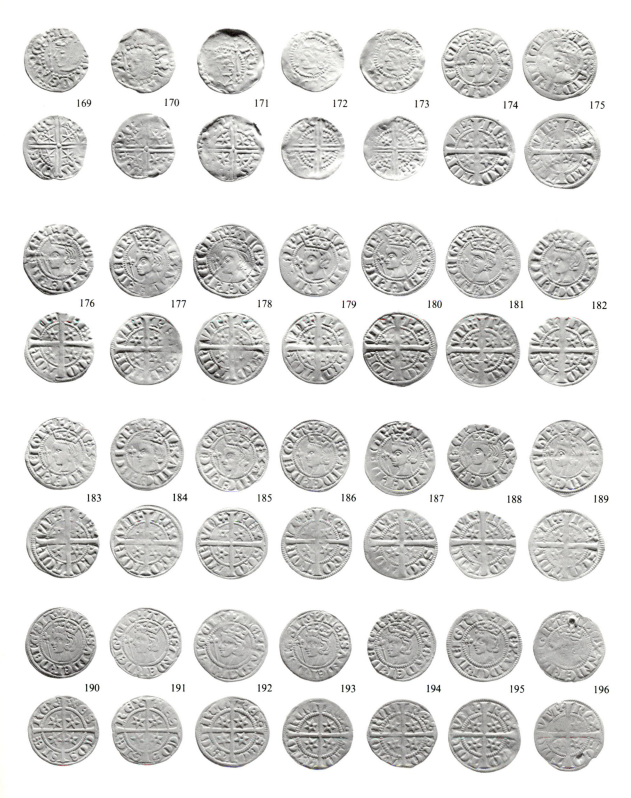

	Weight		*Die*	
	gr	*gm*	*axis*	
197/H	20.5	1.33	30	B.151(13) but no **:** after **DEI**. Renfrew Hoard 542.
198/H	21.4	1.39	20	B.151(13). Renfrew Hoard 544.
199/H	20.5	1.33	170	B.151(13). Renfrew Hoard 546.

Group II, various reverses

Reverse of 4 mullets of 6 points Class I, Stewart D

200/A	19.0	1.23	330	B.158A(27a). D 1975, H. de S. Shortt.
	(chipped)			
201/A	19.8	1.28	210	B.158A(27a). Lincoln College.

Class I obv., II rev., Stewart D/E

202/A	19.9	1.29	70	B.161(54). D 1975, H. de S. Shortt.
203/H	20.2	1.31	340	B.161(54). Renfrew Hoard 551.

Class II, Stewart E

204/A	21.9	1.42	0	B.169(37). St. John's College.
205/A	20.8	1.35	30	B.169(37). Hird.
206/A	15.6	1.01	200	B.169(37). Radcliffe.
207/A	16.0	1.04	250	B.169(37). Christ Church.
208/H	22.5	1.46	180	B.169(37). Renfrew Hoard 557.
209/H	19.9	1.29	250	B.169(37). Renfrew Hoard 558.
210/H	21.9	1.42	0	B.169(37). Renfrew Hoard 559.

Class II obv., III rev., Stewart E/FG

211/A	16.8	1.09	10	B.176(63). Christ Church.
212/A	19.9	1.29	60	B.176(63). Christ Church.

Class III, Stewart FG

213/A	21.5	1.39	330	1st, 2nd head B. 178, 184. P 1972.
214/A	17.1	1.11	320	3rd head B.198. Hird.
215/A	20.8	1.35	170	As 214/A. Ashmolean.
216/A	21.0	1.36	70	1st, 2nd head B.178, 184. Hird.
217/A	20.5	1.33	260	As 216/A. Christ Church.
218/A	21.1	1.37	280	As 216/A. Christ Church.
219/A	21.9	1.42	40	As 216/A. Christ Church.
220/A	20.7	1.34	170	As 214/A. Christ Church
221/A	21.3	1.33	140	1st, 2nd head B.198. Christ Church.
222/H	18.8	1.22	330	1st head B.178(44). Hunter.
223/H	21.1	1.37	340	As 222/H. D 1813, Revd M. Marshall (Ascog Hoard).
224/H	20.5	1.33	70	As 222/H. D 1946, Neilson.

PLATE 8

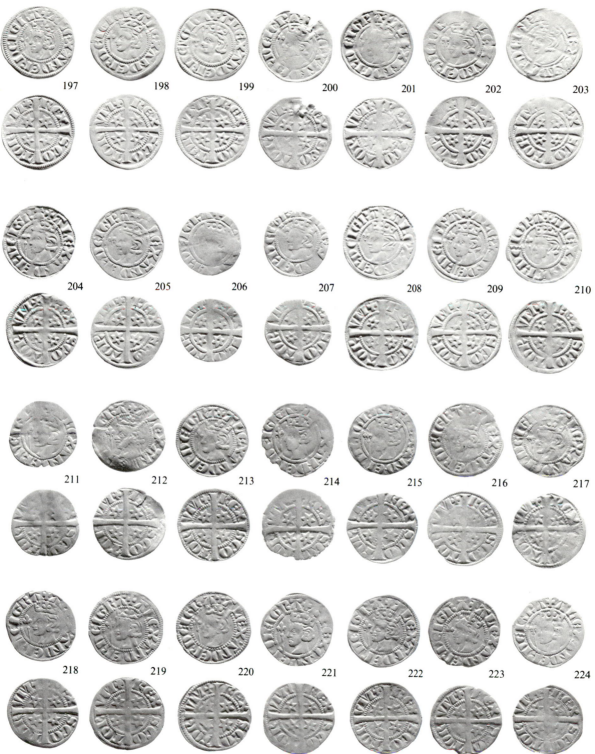

197   198   199   200   201   202   203

204   205   206   207   208   209   210

211   212   213   214   215   216   217

218   219   220   221   222   223   224

	Weight		*Die*	
	gr	gm	axis	
225/H	21.1	1.37	20	As 222/H. Renfrew Hoard 566.
226/H	21.9	1.42	20	As 222/H. Renfrew Hoard 568.
227/H	20.1	1.30	230	As 222/H. Renfrew Hoard 570
228/H	20.7	1.34	150	As 222/H. Renfrew Hoard 571.
229/H	21.0	1.36	270	As 222/H. Renfrew Hoard 572.
230/H	20.3	1.32	340	As 222/H. Renfrew Hoard 573.
231/H	17.4	1.13	90	As 222/H. Renfrew Hoard 574.
232/H	19.0	1.23	0	2nd head B.184(46). Renfrew Hoard 577.
233/H	21.0	1.36	40	3rd head B.198(50). Renfrew Hoard 579
234/H	18.2	1.18	180	3rd head B.198(50). Renfrew Hoard 581.

Class III obv., I rev., Stewart FG/D

235/H	20.7	1.34	200	1st, 2nd head B.182, 187. Renfrew Hoard 587.
236/H	21.1	1.37	350	As 235/H. Renfrew Hoard 588.
237/H	21.3	1.38	110	As 234/H. Renfrew Hoard 589.

Class III obv., II rev., Stewart FG/E

238/A	19.4	1.26	70	1st, 2nd head B.183, 189. Bodleian.
239/A	14.6	0.95	0	As 238/A. University College, Waddington.
240/A	19.8	1.28	270	3rd head B.203. Bodleian.
241/A	19.8	1.29	0	As 238/A. Bodleian.
242/H	21.1	1.37	280	As 238/A. Renfrew Hoard 592.
243/H	21.6	1.40	180	As 238/A. Renfrew Hoard 594.
244/H	20.3	1.32	270	3rd head B.203(74). Renfrew Hoard 596.
245/H	20.3	1.32	40	As 244/H. Renfrew Hoard 597.

Reverse of 4 mullets of 5 points. Class II, Stewart E

246/A	21.1	1.37	40	B.165. D 1975, H. de S. Shortt.
247/A	21.5	1.39	90	one pellet in 2nd quarter, 2 in 4th B.165–6. Bodleian.
248/A	21.5	1.39	140	one pellet in 2nd quarter, 2 in 4th. B.166. Ashmolean.
249/A	21.5	1.39	290	one pellet in 2nd quarter, 2 in 4th. B.165–6. Christ Church.
250/H	20.2	1.31	0	one pellet in 2nd quarter, 2 in 4th. B.166(34). Hunter.

Reverse of 1 mullet of 5 (in 4th quarter), 3 of 6 points. Class II, Stewart E

251/H	17.6	1.14	340	B.168(36). Renfrew Hoard 606.
252/A	20.8	1.35	230	B.168(36). Keble College.

PLATE 9

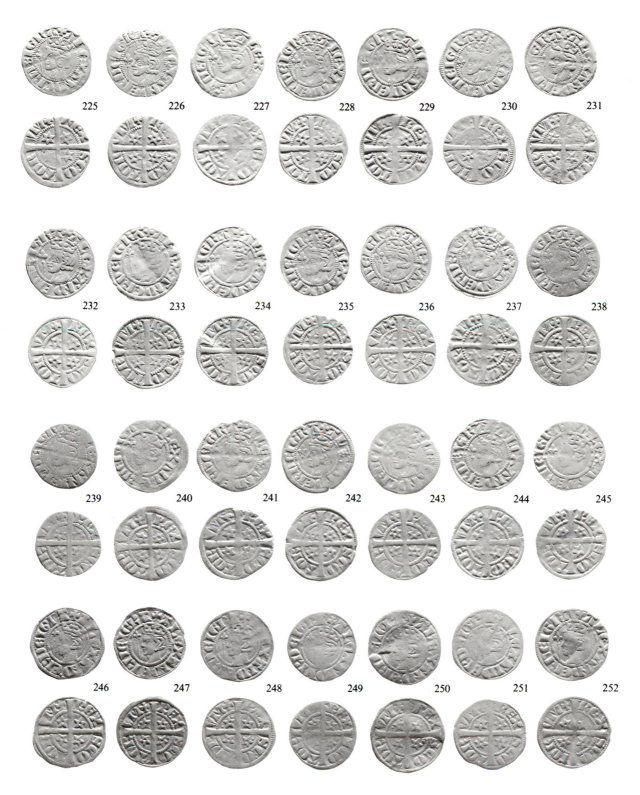

225 226 227 228 229 230 231

232 233 234 235 236 237 238

239 240 241 242 243 244 245

246 247 248 249 250 251 252

	Weight		*Die*	
	gr	*gm*	*axis*	
253/A	20.2	1.31	290	B.168(36). Bodleian.
254/A	18.8	1.22	110	B.168(36). Christ Church.
255/A	18.4	1.19	210	B.168(36). Christ Church.
256/A	13.7	0.89	330	B.168(36). Christ Church.
257/A	19.7	1.28	0	B.168 but obv. leg has stop after D. P 1982, Q & LTR, Tranent Hoard.

Reverse of 3 mullets of 6 points, 1 star of 7 points (in 4th quarter) Class I, Stewart D

258/H	20.8	1.35	230	B.159(29). Renfrew Hoard 610.

Class II obv., III rev., Stewart E/FG

259/A	21.3	1.38	180	B.177(64). P 1972.
260/A	22.1	1.43	30	B.177(64). Hird.

Class III, Stewart FG

261/H	22.2	1.44	300	B.179(45). Hunter.
262/H	21.9	1.42	270	1st, 2nd head B.179(45). Renfrew Hoard 615.

Class III obv., I rev., Stewart FG/D

263/H	20.5	1.33	240	1st, 2nd head B.188(68). Renfrew Hoard 619.

Class III obv., II rev., Stewart FG/E

264/A	20.8	1.35	240	B.190(72). Hird.

Reverse of 2 mullets of 6 points, 2 stars of 7. Class I, Stewart D

265/A	16.3	1.06	240	B.160(30–1). Hird.
266/H	21.1	1.37	110	B.160(31). Renfrew Hoard 626.
267/H	21.6	1.40	180	B.160(31). D J. R. Lockie.

Class I obv., II rev., Stewart D/E

268/A	21.5	1.39	250	B.162(55). P 1972.
269/A	18.4	1.19	270	B.162(55). Hird.
270/A	20.8	1.35	170	B.162(55). Hird.

Class II, Stewart E

271/A	21.0	1.36	240	B.170(38). Bodleian.
272/A	19.8	1.28	170	B.170(38). Bodleian.
273/H	21.7	1.41	200	B.170(38). Hunter.
274/H	20.8	1.35	260	B.170(38). Renfrew Hoard 634.

Class II obv., I rev., Stewart E/D

275/A	15.4	1.00	140	B.174(60). Bodleian.
276/A	16.2	1.05	70	B.174(60). L 1976, Aberdeen Art Gallery, Aberdeen Upperkirkgate Hoard (1886).
277/H	21.9	1.42	90	B.174(60).Renfrew Hoard 638.
278/H	21.6	1.40	90	B.174(60). Renfrew Hoard 639.

Class II obv., III rev., Stewart E/FG

279/A	20.7	1.34	310	B.177A(64a). Hird.

Class III obv., I rev., Stewart FG/D

280/H	13.7	0.89	270	2nd head B.188A(69a). Neilson.

PLATE 10

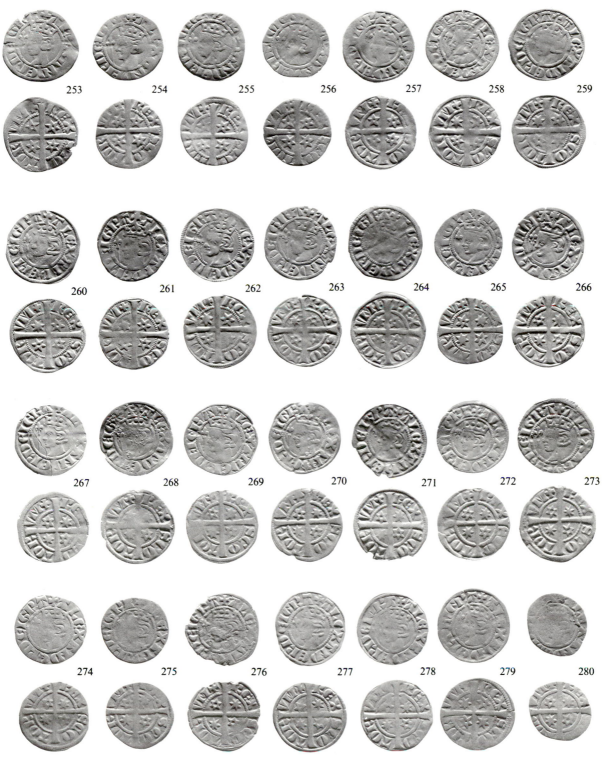

253 254 255 256 257 258 259

260 261 262 263 264 265 266

267 268 269 270 271 272 273

274 275 276 277 278 279 280

	Weight		Die	
	gr	gm	axis	
281/H	21.1	1.37	0	2nd head B.188A(68a). Renfrew Hoard 643.
282/A	19.1	1.24	250	3rd head B.202. Hird.

Class III obv., II rev., Stewart FG/E

283/A	17.4	1.13	340	B.191(73). Bodleian.
284/H	21.0	1.36	150	B.191(73). Renfrew Hoard 646.
285/H	20.8	1.35	70	B.204(75). Renfrew Hoard 648.

Anomalous Group with Baliol Types, Stewart I

| 286/A | 20.2 | 1.31 | 130 | B.209(79). P 1963, Stewart. |

Halfpenny

287/H	9.5	0.62	240	B.193(2). Renfrew Hoard 654.
288/H	10.7	0.69	150	B.193(2). Hunter.
289/H	9.9	0.64	140	B.193(2). D 1966, W. George, found Lanarkshire (? stray from Renfrew Hoard).
290/A	8.6	0.56	350	B.193–5(2–4). P 1953, found in a garden in Clive Road, Oxford.

Farthing

291/H	5.6	0.36	150	B.196(1). Hunter.
292/A	7.7	0.50	10	B.196(1), same dies as 293/A. P 1957, Lockett lot 113, Longstaffe, Bearman.
293/A	4.6	0.30	260	B.196(1), same dies as 292/A. D 1962, found at Chalgrove, Oxon.

JOHN BALIOL (1292–6)

Class I—Rough Surface Issue (St Andrews, without mint name. Penny, nos. 294–304)

St Andrews (2 mullets of 5 points, 2 stars of 6)

294/A	19.0	1.23	60	B.218(15) same obv. die but rev. also of rough type, same obv. die as 295/A. Hird.
295/A	18.4	1.19	170	B.218(15) same obv. die, same obv. die as 294/A. P 1982, Stewart.
296/A	19.3	1.25	30	mullets in 2nd and 4th quarters. B.214(11). P 1982, Stewart.
297/A	19.6	1.27	70	B. see i, pp. 224–5. P 1982, Stewart.

Without mint name (? Berwick. +REX SCOTORVM, 4 mullets of 6 points)

298/A	20.2	1.31	180	cross at end of rev. legend (from die of Alexander III). B.211A (same dies). P 1982.
299/A	21.1	1.37	40	B.213(8). Hird.
300/A	15.8	1.02	270	B.210(1a) same obv. die. Hird.
301/A	19.3	1.25	120	B.210–210B(1–1b) but normal Ns and pellet beside sceptre. Browne Willis.
302/A	22.2	1.44	130	with large mullets. B.210–12 (1–7) with large mullets. P 1982, Stewart.
303/H	21.3	1.38	50	B.210(1) but normal Ns. P 1984, G. Magee, found in the vicinity of Cambuskenneth Abbey, Stirlingshire, 1983.
304/H	21.0	1.36	270	B.211(2). Hunter.

Class II—Smooth Surface Issue (St Andrews, without mint name. Penny, nos. 305–14; Halfpenny, nos. 315–17)

Penny

St Andrews (2 mullets of 5 points, 2 stars of 6)

| 305/A | 17.6 | 1.14 | 140 | B.216(13). E 1949, Baldwin, Shand 217b. |

Without mint name (? Berwick—normally 4 mullets of 5 points)

306/A	20.5	1.33	30	2 mullets of 5 points, 2 stars of 5. B.221(18) same obv. die. Christ Church.
307/A	16.0	1.04	300	B.219(16) same obv. die, same obv. die as 308/A. Hird.
308/A	18.1 (pierced)	1.17	70	As 307/A. Bodleian.
309/H	20.3	1.32	320	B.219(16). P 1966, Q & LTR, Loch Doon Hoard no. 1847.

PLATE 11

281 282 283 284 285 286 287

288 289 290 291 292 293 294 295

296 297 298 299 300 301 302

303 304 305 306 307 308 309

JOHN BALIOL (*cont.*)

	Weight gr	gm	Die axis	
310/H	22.6	1.46	180	B.219(16) but 3 pellets after I of IOhANNES. Hunter
311/A	19.4	1.26	140	B.220(17) but 3 pellets after I of IOhANNES and SCOTORDA same dies as 312/A. Hird.
312/A	22.2	1.44	180	As 311/A. Browne Willis.
313/A	21.1	1.37	320	B.220(17). Hird.
314/A	19.6	1.27	50	B.220(17) same rev. die. D 1906, Dr F. P. Weber.

Halfpenny (2 mullets of 6 points)

315/A	9.0	0.58	340	mullets in 1st and 3rd quarters. B.222(1) same obv. die. P 1946, Dakers 331.
316/H	8.8	0.57	270	mullets in 1st and 3rd quarters. B.222(1). Hunter.
317/A	7.4	0.48	240	mullets in 2nd and 4th quarters. B.224(2) same obv. die. Browne Willis.

ROBERT I (1306–29)

Coinage starting c.1320 (Without mint name. Penny, nos. 318–21; Halfpenny, nos. 322–3; Farthing, nos. 324–6)

Penny

318/A	21.9	1.42	230	B.225(1) same dies. Hird.
319/A	17.4 (pierced)	1.13	50	B.225(1). Browne Willis.
320/H	20.2	1.31	270	B.225(1). Hunter.
321/H	18.8	1.22	180	B.226(3). Renfrew Hoard 663.

Halfpenny (2 mullets of 5 points in 2nd and 4th quarters)

322/A	8.1	0.53	270	B.227(1) same dies, same obv. die as 323/A. P 1946, Dakers 333, Cochran-Patrick 177a, Advocates 30.
323/A	8.6	0.56	250	B.227(1) same obv. die, same obv. die as 322/A. Browne Willis.

Farthing (4 mullets of 5 points)

324/A	4.9	0.32	200	B.228(1). Corpus Christi College.
325/H	3.7	0.24	160	B.228(1) but stop before obv. legend. Hunter.
326/H	3.1	0.20	180	B.228(1) but no stops after ROBERTVS and DEI. Renfrew Hoard 671.

DAVID II (1329–71)

First Coinage (*before 1357*)

Second issue penny 1351–7 (Without mint name. Nos. 327–56)

327/A	17.1	1.11	130	B.231(4) same obv. die/B.229(1) same rev. die. D 1937, the family of Peter Carruthers.
328/A	16.6	1.08	40	B.235(10) same obv. die/B.231(5) same rev. die, same obv. die as 329/A. Hird.
329/A	17.7	1.15	60	B.235(10) same dies, same obv. die as 328/A. Hird.
330/A	15.8 (pierced)	1.02	90	B.244–6(22–6) but bar across sceptre and DAVID DEI:GRACIA. P 1931.
331/A	13.4	0.87	40	B.244(23). Hird, Daniels.
332/A	15.9	1.03	70	B.234(8) same obv. die, same obv. die as 333/A. Hird, Daniels.
333/A	16.5	1.07	260	As 332/A. Hird, Daniels.
334/A	14.3	0.93	30	B.241(18) same dies?, same obv. die as 335/A and 336/A. Hird, Daniels.
335/A	14.2	0.92	150	As 334/A. D F. Pierrepont Barnard.
336/A	16.6	1.08	210	B.241(18) same obv. die?, same obv. die as 334/A and 335/A. Hird, Daniels.
337/H	14.4	0.93	90	B.241(18). P 1982, Q & LTR, Tranent Hoard.

PLATE 12

310   311   312   313   314   315   316

317   318   319   320   321   322   323

324   325   326   327   328   329   330

331   332   333   334   335   336   337

	Weight		*Die*	
	gr	gm	axis	
338/A	16.0	1.04	300	B.242(20) same obv. die. Hird, Daniels.
339/A	16.0	1.04	340	B.246(26) but **DAVID DEI·GRACIA**. Hird, Daniels.
340/A	16.3	1.06	120	B.236(11) same obv. die/237(12) same rev. die. P 1963, Stewart.
341/A	17.4	1.13	270	B.244(22), same obv. die as 342/A. P 1963, Stewart, Parsons 712.
342/A	14.3	0.93	270	As 341/A. P 1963 Stewart, Spufford.
	(pierced)			
343/H	14.6	0.95	150	B.244(22). P 1982.
344/A	17.1	1.11	330	cf. B.247(29) but colon after DEI. P 1963, Stewart, Bute 221 (part).
345/A	15.6	1.01	0	B.245(24) same dies. P 1963, Stewart.
346/A	14.3	0.93	20	B.247(29). P 1963.
347/A	17.6	1.14	200	B.240(16), same rev. die as 348/A. P 1963.
348/A	13.7	0.89	90	B.238(14) same obv. die, same rev. die as 347/A. P 1963.
349/A	14.3	0.93	120	B.237(13) same obv. die, same obv. die as 350/A. P 1963.
350/A	18.5	1.20	160	double-struck. B.237(12) same obv. die, same obv. die as 349/A. P 1963.
351/A	17.5	1.13	240	B.233(7) same dies. P 1963.
352/A	15.7	1.02	90	B.246(26) but colons between words on obv. P 1963.
353/A	16.6	1.08	120	B.246(26) same obv. die. P 1963.
354/A	16.6	1.08	330	B.238(14). P 1963.
355/A	17.6	1.14	160	B.244(23). P 1963, Whelan, Pollexfen.
356/A	13.1	0.85	200	B.243(21) same obv. die. Browne Willis.

Second Coinage (1357–67)

From this point, when the stops become more varied, all stops of whatever kind when mentioned in the text are indicated by a single mid-line stop.

GOLD

Noble (Jesus autem transiens per medium illorum ibat. Without mint name. Nos. 357–8)

357/A	118.8	7.70	0	B.285(1) same rev. die, see B.i, p. 268. Hird, Brand, Murdoch (1903) 58, Richardson, Addington, Hastings 576, Martin 422, Hawkins.
358/H	119.9	7.77	290	B.285(1) see B.i, p. 268 but not same dies. Hunter.

PLATE 13

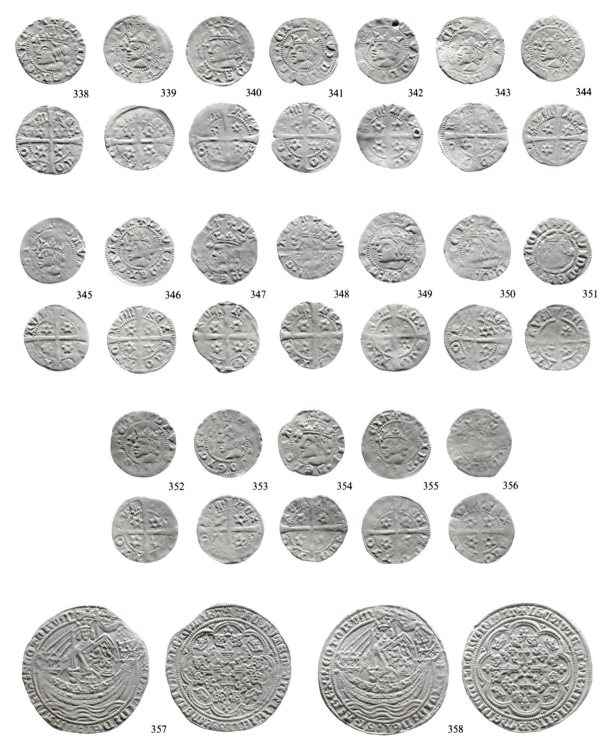

338   339   340   341   342   343   344

345   346   347   348   349   350   351

352   353   354   355   356

357   358

SILVER

Groat (Dominus protector meus et liberator meus. Edinburgh, Aberdeen. Nos. 359–90)

Stewart group A (*Burns small head*)

Edinburgh

	Weight		Die	
	gr	gm	axis	
359/A	72.3	4.69	340	B.250(2) but rev. reads **MS Ƶ LIB'**, same obv. die, same obv. die as 360/A, Stewart A1. Hird, Stuart-Menteth.
360/A	71.4	4.63	130	B.250(2) obv., same die/251(3) rev. but no saltire before **ЄD**, same obv. die as 359/A, Stewart A1. D 1964, Baldwin.
361/A	48.7	3.16	180	B.251(3) same obv. die, Stewart A1. Ashmolean.
362/H	54.9	3.56	40	sl. double-struck. B.251(3) but saltire stops obv., Stewart A2. Hunter.
363/A	64.1	4.15	50	B.252(4), Stewart A3. D 1964, Baldwin.
364/A	69.1	4.48	100	B.254(8) but saltire before **ЄD**, same obv. die, Stewart A5. D 1921, F. L. Griffith.
365/A	59.7	3.87	310	B.256(9) but rev. reads **DΠS·P** with saltire before **ЄD**, same obv. die, Stewart A5. Hird.
366/A	56.4 (chipped)	3.66	50	B.262B(15a) same obv. die, same obv. die as 367/A and 368/A, Stewart A5. D 1964, Baldwin.
367/A	62.3	4.04	350	B.262B(15a) same dies, same obv. die as 366/A and 368/A, Stewart A5. Provenance unknown.
368/A	66.9	4.34	300	B.262B(15a) but rev. with open, unbarred, ornamental **A** (see Bi, p. 245), same obv. die, same obv. die as 366/A and 367/A, Stewart A5. Hird.
369/A	60.3	3.91	120	B.257(10) but rev. has **·Ƶ·**, same obv. die, Stewart A6. Hird.
370/A	73.1	4.74	130	B.259(12) same dies, same obv. die as 371/A and 372/A, Stewart A7. P 1982, Stewart.
371/A	69.6	4.51	270	B.259(12) but rev. reads **DΠ⁻S·P**, same obv. die, same obv. die as 370/A and 372/A, Stewart A7. Hird.
372/A	65.7	4.26	150	B.260(13) same obv. die, same obv. die as 370/A and 371/A, same rev. die as 373/A, Stewart A7. Browne Willis.
373/A	66.2	4.29	20	B.260(13) but tressure of six arcs and segment and initial cross fourchy, same rev. die as 372/A, Stewart A7. Hird.

PLATE 14

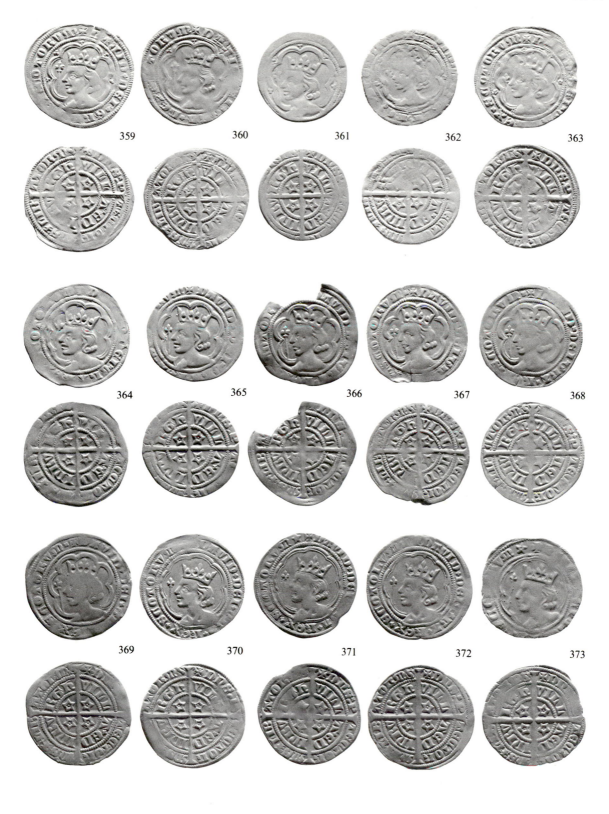

359   360   361   362   363

364   365   366   367   368

369   370   371   372   373

	Weight		*Die*	
	gr	*gm*	*axis*	
374/H	67.3	4.36	270	B.262(15) but *recte* no ‡ after R€X, Stewart A8. D 1809, G. Lumsden.
375/A	65.7	4.26	0	B.250(1) but plain tressure, no saltires by Ƶ and ornamental U in UILLA (see *BNJ*, 26, 1949–51, p. 157), Stewart A–. D 1925, Miss E. C. Hatchett Jackson.

Aberdeen

376/A	65.2	4.23	40	B.255(16) same dies, Stewart A6. Hird.

Stewart group B (Burns intermediate head—first and second varieties)

Edinburgh

377/A	59.8	3.88	330	B.279(19) same dies, Stewart B1. Bodleian.
378/A	54.3	3.52	90	B.279A(19a) same obv. die, same obv. die as 379/A, Stewart B3d. D 1966, Stewart.
379/A	66.8	4.33	310	B.279A(19a) same obv. die/271A same rev. die, same obv. die as 378/A, Stewart B3d. P 1982, Stewart.
380/H	64.2	4.16	70	B.280(21), Stewart B3d. P 1982, Q & LTR, Tranent Hoard.
381/H	63.8	4.13	340	B.281(22), Stewart B3d. P 1982, Q & LTR, Tranent Hoard.

Aberdeen

382/H	61.8	4.00	20	B.275(28) but *recte* add ·P after DNS to rev. reading, Stewart B1. Hunter.

Stewart group C (Burns intermediate head—third variety)

Edinburgh

383/A	66.5	4.31	80	B.286(24) but ornamental A in GRA, same obv. die as 384/A, Stewart C1. Hird.
384/A	64.5	4.18	40	As 383/A. P 1982, Stewart.
385/A	64.5	4.19	270	B.287(25), Stewart C1. Hird.
386/A	56.6	3.67	90	B.288–9(26–7) but small and large crosses at end of obv. legend, Stewart C2. Bodleian.

Stewart group D (Burns Robert II head)

387/A	62.1	4.02	310	B.297(36) but *recte* second coinage, same dies, Stewart D3. Stewart, Napier 213 (part).
388/A	62.8	4.07	320	B.297(36), Stewart D3. Hird.

PLATE 15

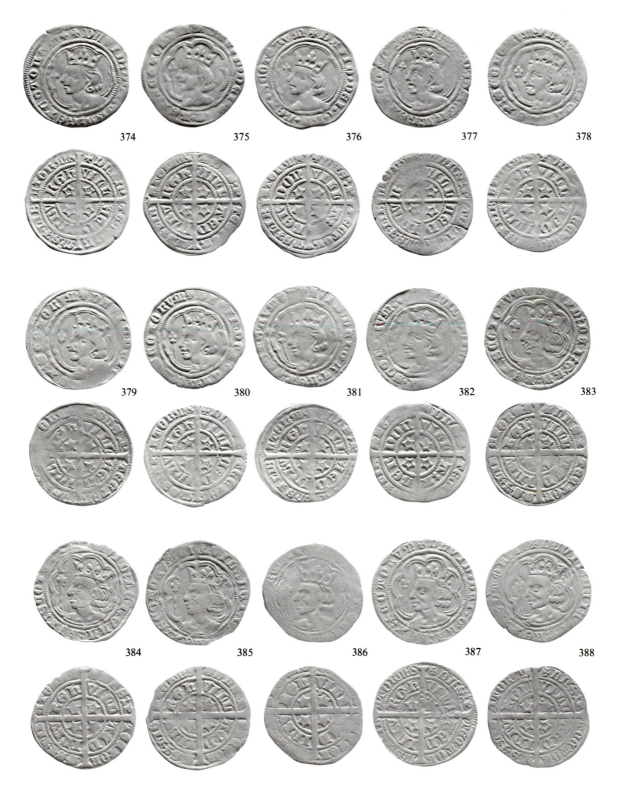

374 375 376 377 378

379 380 381 382 383

384 385 386 387 388

	Weight		*Die*
	gr	*gm*	*axis*
389/H	58.9	3.82	280	B.297(36), Stewart D3. P 1982, Q & LTR, Tranent Hoard.

2nd or 3rd Coinage

390/A 61.1 3.96 70 Star behind bust and between ₢ and D. See B.i, p. 257 and Lindsay 1845, pl. IV, no. 94, Stewart 1967, p. 32, group 1, where assigned to third coinage. Mrs J. E. L. Murray comments 'This is perhaps 3rd intermediate head (i.e. Stewart group C). I suspect these varieties with star behind head and between ₢ and D on rev. may belong before May 1366, and that those with pellet on sceptre handle (and Robert II head) were the result of the Act of that date, being approximately of the English weight'. Hird.

Halfgroat (Dominus protector meus. Edinburgh, Aberdeen. Nos. 391–402)

Edinburgh (*groups/heads as for groats*)

391/H 32.1 2.08 270 Stewart A5 (small head). B.263(1) but *recte* insert GRA obv. reading, but SCOTORVM. P 1982, Q & LTR, Tranent Hoard.
392/A 34.8 2.26 310 Stewart A (small head). B.263(2). Bodleian.
393/A 32.8 2.13 270 Stewart B1 (intermediate head 1/2). B.269(8). P 1963.
394/A 32.7 2.12 230 Stewart B1 (intermediate head 1/2). B. 269(9). P 1963.
395/A 32.2 2.09 120 Stewart B2b (intermediate head 1/2). B.269 but small cross in last quarter of rev., see B.i, p.261 re similar in Carruthers Collection, Lindsay, 1st *Sup.Des.Cat.*, no. 35. Hird, McCallum.
396/A 31.0 2.01 40 Stewart B2a (intermediate head 1/2). B.269(8) but small and large cross at end of obv. legend and small cross in third quarter of rev. (see 395/A for refs). Browne Willis.
397/H 30.9 2.00 240 Stewart B3a (intermediate head 1/2). B.272(10) but SCOTORV. P 1982, Q & LTR, Tranent Hoard.
398/A 32.7 2.12 160 Stewart C1 (intermediate head 3). B.290(14) but on rev. no D in quarters, legend reads +DNS PROT ₢CTOR M₢VS with small distinctive lettering, same obv. die, same obv. die as 399/A. Christ Church, D 1786, William Thomson MB.
399/A 31.9 2.07 270 Stewart C2 (intermediate head 3). B.290(14) same dies, same obv. die as 398/A. P 1982, Stewart.
400/A 32.7 2.12 90 Stewart C3 (intermediate head 3). B.299(19) same rev. die. P 1982, Stewart, Parsons 714 (part).

Aberdeen

401/A 31.5 2.04 40 Stewart A6 (small head). B.265(6) same obv. die. P 1982, Q & LTR, Tranent Hoard.
402/H 33.5 2.17 270 Stewart A6 (small head). B.265(6). Hunter.

Penny (Edinburgh, Aberdeen. Nos. 403–14)

Edinburgh (*groups/heads as for groats*)

403/A 17.4 1.13 120 Stewart A (small head). B.266(1) same dies, same dies as 404/A. Ashmolean.

PLATE 16

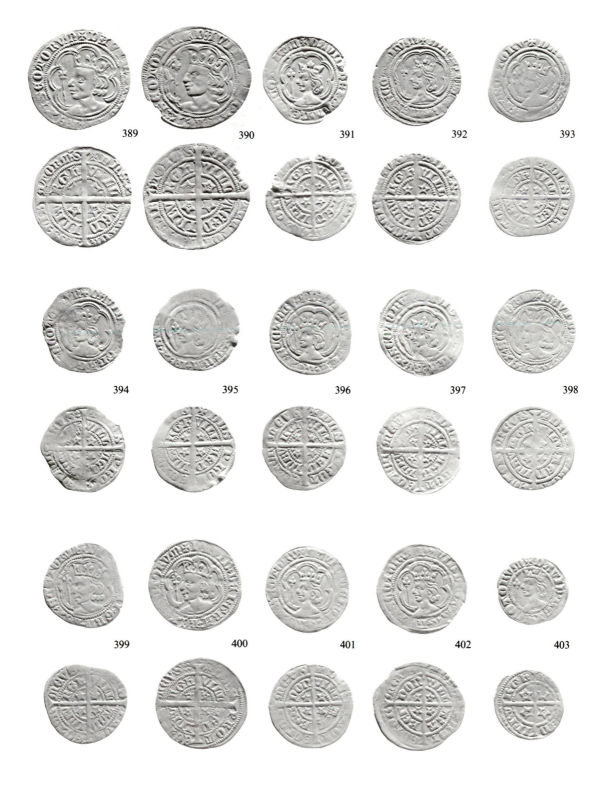

389 390 391 392 393

394 395 396 397 398

399 400 401 402 403

	Weight		*Die*	
	gr	gm	axis	
404/A	14.3	0.92	270	As 403/A. Browne Willis.
405/A	15.6	1.01	90	Stewart A (small head). B.266(1) but saltire at end of obv. legend. P 1982, Stewart.
	(chipped)			
406/H	16.7	1.08	330	Stewart A (small head). B.266(1). P 1982, Q & LTR, Tranent Hoard.
407/A	15.9	1.03	90	Stewart B1 (intermediate head). B.270(5) but unbarred plain A in DAVID. P 1963, Lockett 129 or 131.
408/A	15.4	1.00	180	Stewart B1 (intermediate head). B.270 but RER not REX, see B.i, p. 264 for example from Montrave Hoard. D 1912, A. C. Kay.
409/A	15.6	1.01	270	Stewart B1 (intermediate head). B.283(8) but no cross in 3rd quarter of rev. P 1982, Stewart.
410/H	16.4	1.06	180	Stewart B3b (intermediate head). B.274(6). Hunter.
411/H	14.8	0.96	40	Stewart D1 (Robert II head). B.294(10). P 1982, Q & LTR, Tranent Hoard.
412/H	15.5	1.00	90	Stewart D1 (Robert II head). B.294(10). D J. R. Lockie.
413/A	16.3	1.06	330	Stewart D1 (Robert II head). B.295(11). Hird.

Aberdeen

414/H	15.2	0.98	20	Stewart A (small head). B.267(4). Hunter.

Third Coinage (*1367–71*) ('Robert II' head and star on sceptre handle)

Groat (Edinburgh. Nos. 415–28)

415/A	61.2	3.97	320	B.301(38) but ornamental As, same obv. die 416/A. St John's College.
416/A	64.3	4.17	130	As 415/A. Christ Church.
417/A	50.7	3.29	90	B.301(38–9). Bodleian.
	(pierced)			
418/A	59.2	3.84	300	B.301(38). Hird.
419/A	50.3	3.26	40	B.301(38) same dies. Bodleian.
420/A	59.2	3.84	270	B.301(38–9). P 1982, Stewart.
421/A	47.5	3.08	230	B.302(41). Bodleian.
422/A	56.6	3.67	40	B.302(41). Bodleian.

PLATE 17

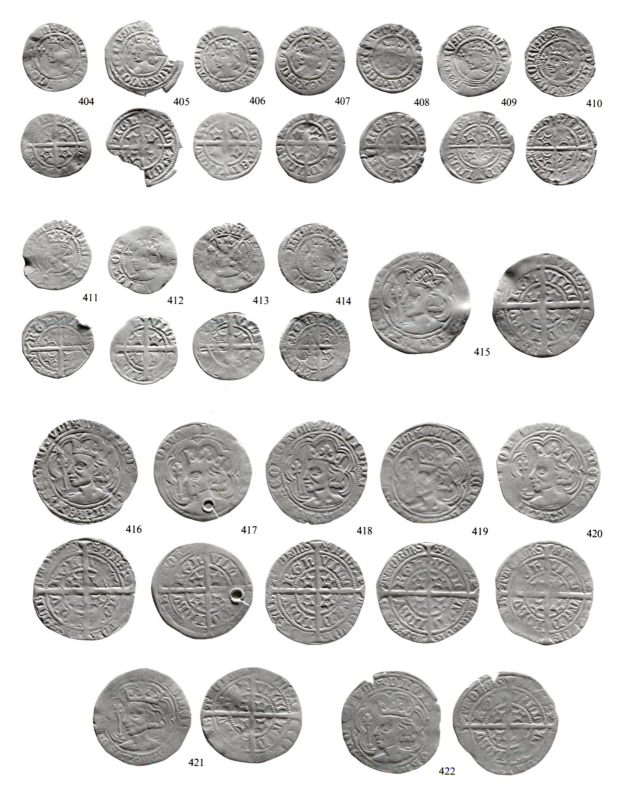

404   405   406   407   408   409   410

411   412   413   414   415

416   417   418   419   420

421   422

	Weight		*Die*	
	gr	*gm*	*axis*	
423/H	59.3	3.84	0	B.302(41). Hunter.
424/H	53.7	3.48	250	B.302(41). Neilson.
425/A	54.3	3.52	110	B.301(38) but two stars after DNS and saltire stops on rev. (as B.305–7). Radcliffe.
426/A	62.5	4.05	120	B.305(42). D 1903, J. G. Milne.
427/A	49.5	3.21	20	B.306(43). Stewart.
428/A	59.4	3.85	200	B.306(43) but VILL AED INB VRGh. Hird.

Halfgroat (Edinburgh. Nos. 429–38)

429/A	31.3	2.03	10	B.303(21). P 1982, Stewart.
430/A	28.8	1.87	170	B.303(21). P 1982, Q & LTR, Tranent Hoard.
431/H	29.8	1.93	0	B.303(21). P 1982, Q & LTR, Tranent Hoard.
432/H	30.1	1.95	60	B.303(21). Hunter.
433/A	30.8	2.00	0	B.303(22). P 1963, Stewart.
434/A	29.9	1.94	140	B.303(22). P 1982, Stewart.
435/A	26.8	1.74	160	B.303(22). P. 1963, Stewart.
436/A	26.5	1.72	40	B.303(22). P 1963? Stewart.
437/A	29.4	1.91	30	B.303 but double saltire stops, plain unbarred As and rev. reading +DNS PTEC TORM LATOR. Hird.
438/A	29.4	1.91	50	B.308 but tressure of six arcs and rev. reading +DNS· PTECT ORMS · Ƶ LIBA. P 1982, Stewart.

PLATE 18

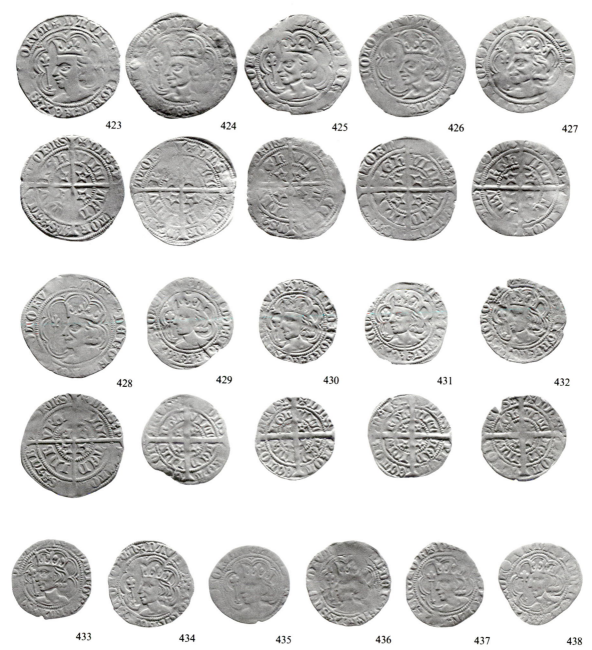

423 424 425 426 427

428 429 430 431 432

433 434 435 436 437 438

DAVID II (*cont.*)

Penny (Edinburgh. Nos. 439–42)

	Weight		*Die*	
	gr	*gm*	*axis*	
439/H	17.2	1.11	270	B.304(12). P 1982, Q & LTR, Tranent Hoard.
440/A	13.3	0.86	340	B.304(13) but double saltire stops obv. P 1982, Stewart, Drabble (1943) 1191, Whelan, Pollexfen.
441/A	14.5	0.94	90	B.304(13). P 1982, Q & LTR, Tranent Hoard.
442/H	13.3	0.86	160	B.304(13) but double saltire stops obv. Hunter.

ROBERT II (1371–90)

Coinage in silver only

Groat (Edinburgh, Perth, Dundee. Nos. 443–78)

Edinburgh

443/A	50.0	3.24	210	B.309(1). Bodleian.
444/A	60.5	3.92	200	B.309(1) same obv. die. Hird.
445/A	54.0	3.50	90	B.309(3). Christ Church.
446/A	61.2	3.97	180	B.309(3). Hird.
447/A	52.9	3.43	300	B.309(3) same obv. die as 448/A. Bodleian.
448/A	62.2	4.03	170	As 447/A. Bodleian.
449/A	59.4	3.85	270	B.309(3). Hird.
450/A	60.6	3.93	90	B.309(3). Bodleian.
451/A	58.0	3.76	300	B.309(3) but I not P in PROTECTOR. P 1982, Stewart.
452/A	47.7	3.09	120	B.309(3). P 1982, Stewart.
453/A	58.0	3.76	180	B.309(3). P 1982, Stewart.
454/A	56.9	3.69	180	B.309(3). P 1982, Stewart.

PLATE 19

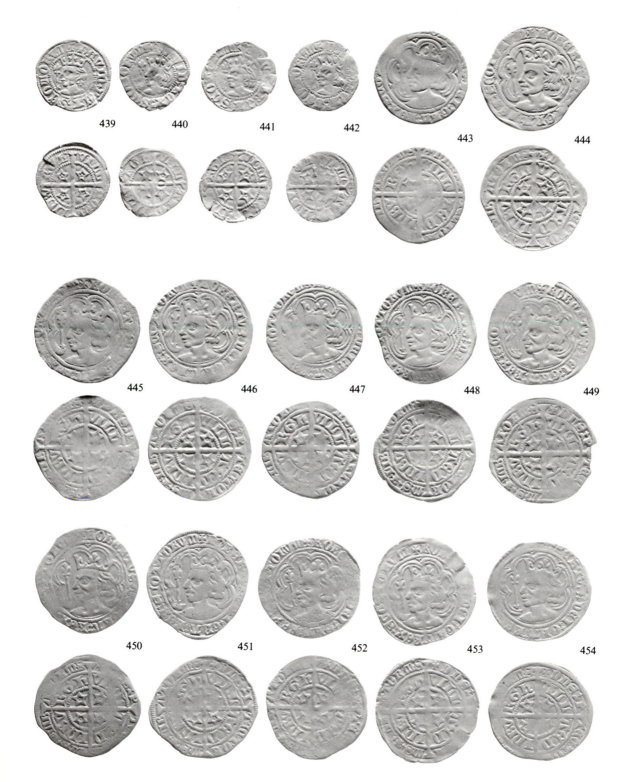

439   440   441   442   443   444

445   446   447   448   449

450   451   452   453   454

	Weight		*Die*	
	gr	gm	axis	
455/H	53.7	3.48	50	B.309(3). Hunter.
456/H	56.9	3.69	90	B.309(3). Neilson.
457/A	61.5	3.99	270	B.310(4). D 1903, J. G. Milne.
458/A	45.8	2.97	310	B.328(8) but without saltire after **VILLA** as on BM specimen noted B.i, p. 273, same obv. die as 459/A. P 1982, Stewart.
459/A	50.4	3.50	80	B.328(8) but rev. with later lettering, same obv. as 458/A; Mrs Murray has noted this die in NMAS without **B** behind head. University College, Waddington.

Perth

	gr	gm		
460/A	60.9	3.95	180	B.317(10). Browne Willis.
461/A	58.1	3.77	150	B.317(10) but **SCOTTSRVM**. Hird.
462/A	54.3	3.52	170	B.317(10). Hird.
463/A	51.5	3.34	60	B.317(10). D 1903, J. G. Milne.
464/A	61.1	3.96	180	B.317(10). P 1982, Stewart.
465/A	56.8	3.68	90	B.317(10). P 1982, Stewart.
466/A	46.4	3.01	0	B.317(10). P 1982, Stewart.
467/A	60.8	3.94	330	B.317(10). P 1982, Stewart.
468/A	60.3	3.91	120	B.317(10). P 1982, Stewart.
469/A	50.7	3.29	10	B.317(10) but stops of single cross. P 1982, Stewart.

PLATE 20

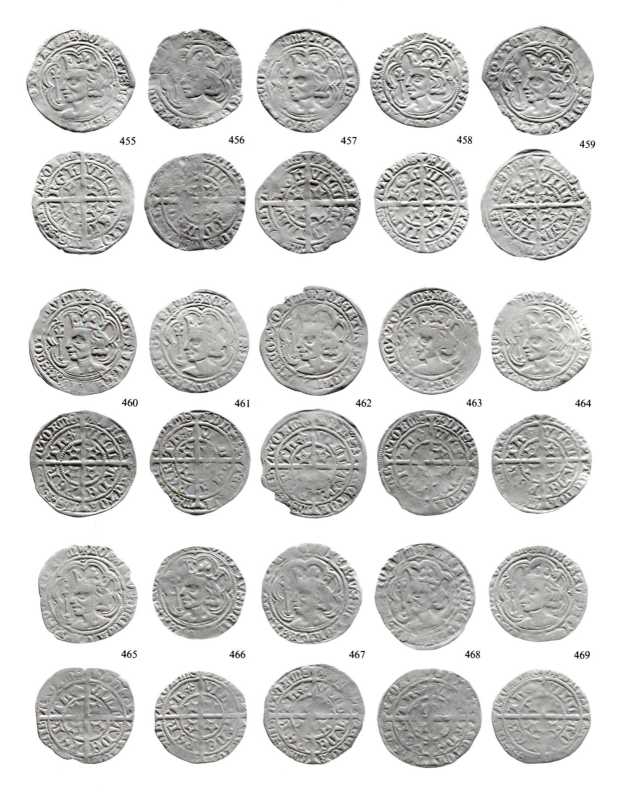

455 456 457 458 459

460 461 462 463 464

465 466 467 468 469

	Weight		*Die*	
---	gr	gm	*axis*	
470/H	61.1	3.96	140	B.317(10). Hunter.
471/H	38.3	2.48	300	B.317(10). D 1944, Professor Bryce, found at Ballynaughton, Islay.
472/H	53.1	3.44	320	B.317(10). Neilson.
473/A	59.5	3.86	310	B.318(11). Hird.
474/A	42.4	2.74	0	B.335(14) same obv. die? Hird.
475/A	55.2	3.58	90	B.335(14) but pellet behind head and SCOTTORVMX+. Bodleian.
476/A	62.0	4.02	0	B.335(14) but SEOTORVM. P 1982, Q & LTR, Tranent Hoard.

Dundee

| 477/A | 57.8 | 3.75 | 0 | B.332(15) but large **B** behind bust and on rev. double saltires stops and initial cross in inner legend askew, same obv. die as B.327(6) for Edinburgh (die link not in 'Scottish Mints'). Hird, Cochran-Patrick 189c. |
| 478/H | 53.1 | 3.44 | 130 | B.332(15). Hunter. |

Halfgroat (Edinburgh, Perth. Nos. 479–92)

Edinburgh

479/A	22.2	1.44	90	B.313(2) (note Burns' figured coin = 312(5)), same obv. die as 480/A. Hird, McCallum.
480/A	25.7	1.67	180	B.313(2), same obv. die as 479/A. P 1982, Stewart.
481/H	26.6	1.72	180	B.312(5). P 1982, Q & LTR, Tranent Hoard.
482/H	34.1	2.21	300	B.325(6). Hunter.

Perth

483/A	26.0	1.69	340	B.320(9) but SCOTORVM. Hird, Stuart-Menteth.
	(chipped)			
484/A	29.1	1.89	300	B.320(9) but SCOTORVM. Browne Willis.
485/H	26.3	1.70	90	B.320(9). Hunter.

PLATE 21

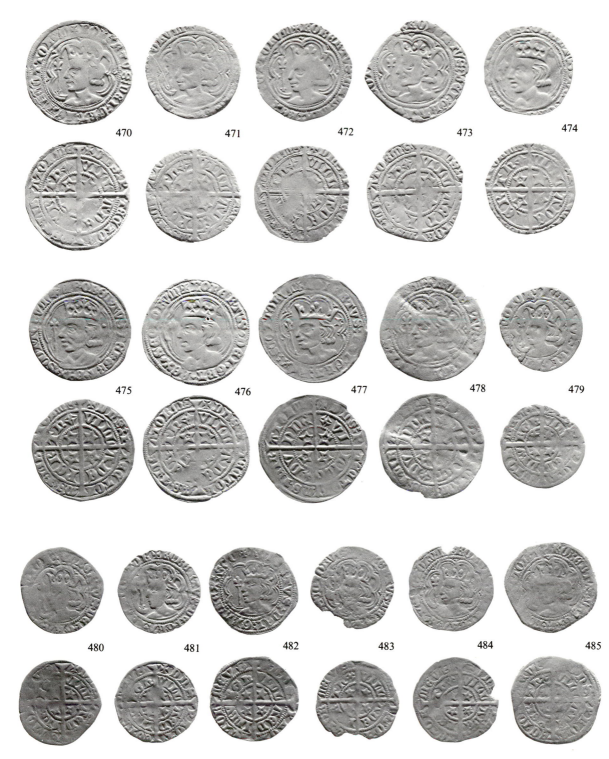

470   471   472   473   474

475   476   477   478   479

480   481   482   483   484   485

ROBERT II (*cont.*)

	Weight		Die	
	gr	gm	axis	
486/H	29.4	1.97	290	B.320(9). P 1982, Q & LTR, Tranent Hoard.
487/A	17.2	1.12	180	B.320(10) same obv. die 488/A. Hird.
488/A	26.2	1.70	270	B.320(10) same obv. die as 487/A, same rev. die as 489/A and 490/A. P 1982, Stewart.
489/A	26.7	1.73	40	B.320(9) same dies as 490/A, same rev. die as 488/A. Hird.
490/A	28.5	1.85	260	As 489/A. Bodleian.
491/A	28.1	1.82	260	B.320(10). P 1982, Stewart.
492/A	22.8	1.48	310	B.320(10). P 1982, Stewart.

Penny (Edinburgh, Perth. Nos. 493–501)

Edinburgh

493/H	15.9	1.03	300	B.313(1) but no stops and SΘOTO. Hunter.
494/A	11.7	0.76	270	B.313(2). Hird.
495/A	11.7	0.76	30	B.313. Browne Willis.
496/A	13.1	0.85	0	B.313A(4a) same obv. die, see, 'Scottish Mints', die link no. 36. Hird.
497/A	6.8	0.44	180	B.324 same obv. die but rev. reads VILL AΘD—presumably Edinburgh, die link not in 'Scottish Mints'. D 1982, Stewart.

Perth

498/A	12.0	0.78	280	B.322(8). Hird.
499/H	16.9	1.10	270	B.322(8). P 1982, Q & LTR, Tranent Hoard.
500/H	12.4	0.80	90	B.322(8). P 1982, Q & LTR, Tranent Hoard.
501/A	10.5	0.68	180	B.— ROBΘRTVS RΘX SCOTO, same form of R as B.331 usually associated with saltire stops, perhaps saltire on sceptre handle. Browne Willis.

Halfpenny (Edinburgh, Dundee. Nos. 502–6)

Edinburgh

502/A	6.6	0.43	130	B.315(2) but +ROBΘRTVSG RΘX, same obv. die as 503/A. Bodleian.
503/A	10.8	0.70	40	B.315 but +ROBΘRTVSG RΘX and VIL AΘI DIR RVR, same obv. die as 502/A. P 1957, Lockett 146, Mann 423 (part).
504/H	7.1	0.46	90	B.316(4a). Hunter.
505/H	7.4	0.48	40	B.316(4a). Hunter.

Dundee

506/A	6.8	0.44	330	B.333B(4b) = this coin, same obv. die as B.315(3), not figured, of Edinburgh mint. P 1957, Lockett 153, Cochran-Patrick 189g.

ROBERT III (1390–1406)

GOLD

First 'Heavy' Coinage c.*1390–1403. Second 'Light' Coinage* c.*1403–6*

Lion (Christus [XPC] regnat, Christus vincit, Christus imperat. Long Cross. Nos. 507–17)

507/A	59.8	3.88	10	B.341(1) same dies. Hird, Brand, Murdoch (1903) 76, Addington, Wingate 98.
508/A	60.8	3.94	210	B.349B(3a) but face *is* bearded with nimbus. Hird, Pollexfen 238.
509/A	58.6	3.80	180	B.351(5) but with lis and crescent stops sometimes punched over triple pellet stops on obv./rev. lacks nimbus and beard and reads XPΘRΘ ΘNATXPΘ· VIN ΘITXPΘI, same obv. die as 510/A. Hird, Newcomer.

PLATE 22

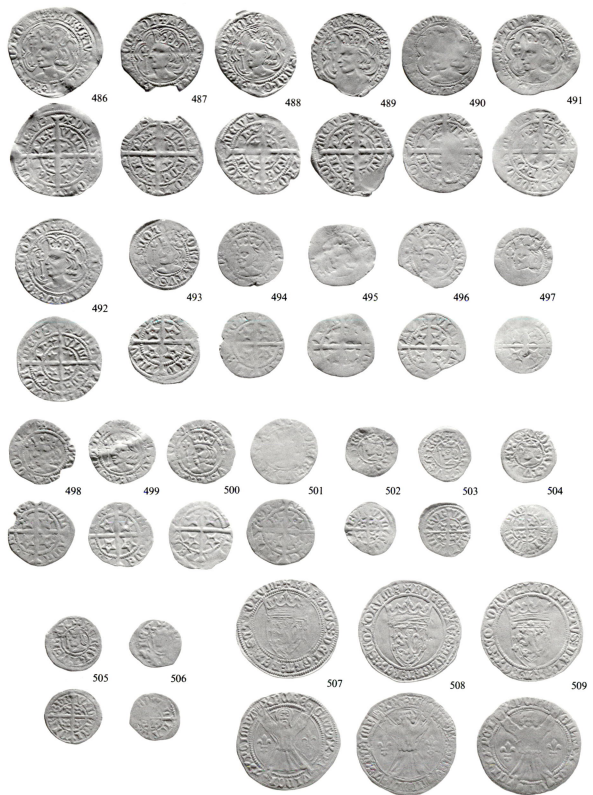

486   487   488   489   490   491

492   493   494   495   496   497

498   499   500   501   502   503   504

505   506   507   508   509

	Weight		*Die*	
	gr	gm	axis	
510/A	60.6	3.93	280	B.351(5) same obv. die as 509/A. Hird.
511/A	60.3	3.91	280	B.351(4) same dies. Hird.
512/A	60.2	3.90	140	B.351(4) but obv. with hairline circle and stops vary/same rev. die. Hird.
513/H	59.6	3.86	240	B.351(4) same dies. Hunter.
514/H	59.2	3.84	50	B.351(4) same obv. die but rev. legend distributed as BM specimen noted B.i, p.346. Hunter.
515/A	58.0	3.76	270	B.356(6) same dies. Hird, Walters 601.
516/A	60.8	3.94	120	B.359A(8a) same dies, same rev. die as 517/A. Hird.
517/A	60.8	3.94	110	B.359(8) same dies, same rev. die as 516/A. Hird, Thellusson 155 (part).

Lion (Short Cross. Nos. 518–19)

518/A	59.8	3.88	270	B.377(9) same rev. die. Hird, Brushfield.
519/A	59.5	3.86	280	B.383(10) same dies. Hird.

'Light' Lion (with same types and legends as on heavy lions. No. 520)

520/A	40.1	2.60	280	B.— unusual style, obv. reads +ROBERTVS·DEI·GRA·REX·SCOTOR' with uncertain stops which appear to be a lis over pellet/rev. reads XPCR GNAT·[ ] MP. and has St Andrew, without beard or nimbus, on cross with large fleurs of similar style to Burns' Aberdeen type (see B.i, p. 349); obv. of much better style. Hird.

'Light' Lion (Dominus protector meus et liberator meus. Nos. 521–4)

521/A	32.5	2.11	130	B.419(14) same dies. Hird, Duke of Atholl.
522/A	31.4	2.04	340	B.420 but rev. reads +DN S·P·TECTOR ·MS ·Z·LIBERA, same obv. die, same obv. die as 523/A. Hird, Duke of Atholl.
523/A	35.0	2.27	180	B.420 but rev. reads +DNS ·P·TECTOR· MS ·Z·LIBERA, same obv. die, same obv. die as 522/A. Hird.
524/H	43.4	2.81	170	B.421A(19a). Hunter.

Heavy Demi-Lion (Christus regnat etc. Nos. 525–9)

525/A	28.2	1.83	100	B.342A(1a) same dies, same rev. die as 526/A. Hird, Cochran-Patrick 8, Advocates Duplicates Sale 1873 151.

PLATE 23

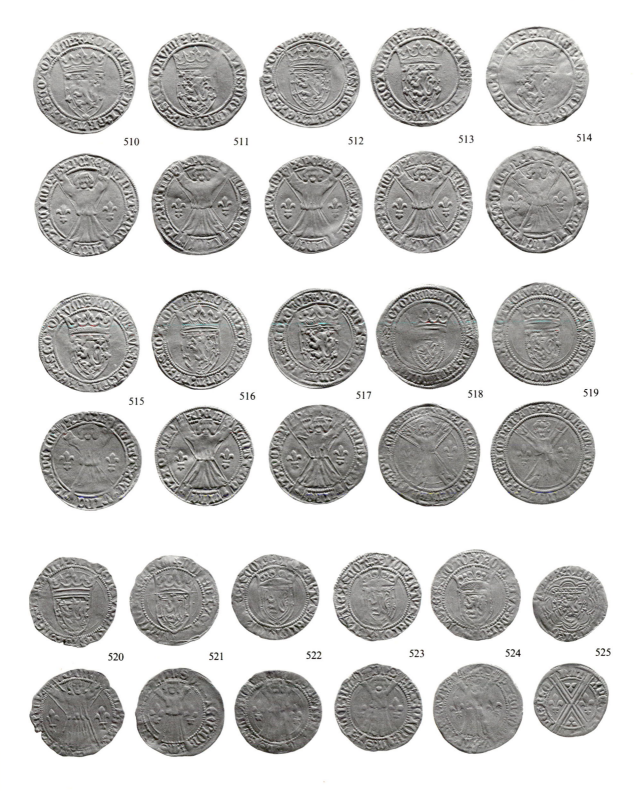

510   511   512   513   514

515   516   517   518   519

520   521   522   523   524   525

	Weight		Die	
	gr	gm	axis	
526/A	31.1	2.02	90	B.370(6) same dies, same rev. die as 525/A. Hird.
527/A	30.8	2.00	160	B.352(4) same die as 528/H, same obv. die as 529/A. Hird, Walters 602.
528/H	28.9	1.87	200	As 527/A. Hunter.
529/A	24.7	1.60	90	B.352(5) same obv. die as 527/A. Hird, Wills 168, Duke of Atholl.

Light Demi-Lion (Christus regnat etc. or Dominus protector etc. Nos. 530–1)

530/A	28.2	1.83	180	B.—, see B.i, p. 360 re weight, obv. as B.406A but legend ends :SCOTORV, rev. reads XPC REGNAT (?)XP VINCIT·. Hird.
531/A	24.0	1.56	50	B.406B but obv. reads SCOTO, same rev. die. Hird.

SILVER

Heavy Groat (Edinburgh, Perth, Aberdeen. Nos. 532–601)

532/H	41.7	2.70	0	B.337(1a) but MS · 7 · LIB ATORMS. Coats 2056.
533/A	41.2	2.67	60	B.340(2) but reads +DNS · P ·. Hird.
534/H	36.4	2.36	150	B.340(3). Coats 2049.
535/A	42.7	2.77	220	B.344(4) but *recte* rev. reads ATORMS same dies. Browne Willis.
536/A	43.3	2.81	220	B.344(4). P 1982, Stewart.
537/A	43.0	2.79	50	B.344(4) but SM · Z · LIB, same obv. die as 538/A. P 1982, Stewart.
538/A	46.1	2.99	310	B.344(4) but · ZL and ATORMS and RGh ·, same obv. die as 537/A. P 1982, Stewart.
539/H	35.8	2.32	240	B.344(4) but SCOTORVM and double saltires before MS and LIB. Coats 2048.
540/A	40.4	2.62	290	B.348(5). Hird.
541/A	45.2	2.93	270	B.348(5). P 1982 Stewart.

PLATE 24

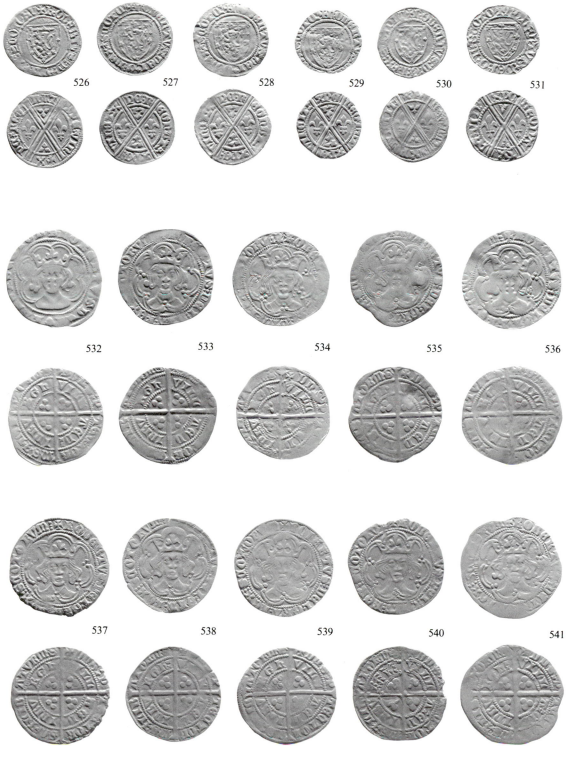

526   527   528   529   530   531

532   533   534   535   536

537   538   539   540   541

	Weight		Die	
	gr	gm	axis	
542/A	34.7	2.25	110	B.348(5). P 1982, Stewart.
543/A	42.6	2.76	270	B.348(5). P 1982, Stewart.
544/H	43.9	2.84	40	B.348(5) but no stop after ꓱ. Coats 2053.
545/H	35.8	2.32	240	B.348(5) but no stop before and after ꓱ. Hunter.
546/A	34.2	2.22	180	B.348(6). D 1906, F. P. Weber.
547/A	42.7	2.77	260	B.348(5) but no stop after ꓱ, same obv. die as 548/A. D 1930, E. S. Bouchier.
548/A	43.0	2.79	50	B.348(5) but no stop after ꓱ, same obv. die as 547/A. P 1982, Stewart.
549/A	43.8	2.84	60	B.348(5) but no stops inner rev. legend. P 1982, Stewart.
550/A	46.4	3.01	200	B.350 but stops vary obv. and rev. and TꓱꓫTOR, same obv. die as 551/A. Hird.
551/A	42.2	2.74	320	B.350 obv. but stops vary/B.353 rev., same obv. die as 550/A. P 1982, Stewart.
552/H	41.1	2.66	270	B.350(8) but obv. stops vary and TꓱꓫTOR. Coats 2046A.
553/A	43.9	2.85	330	B.353(10) same obv. die. Hird.
554/A	35.9	2.33	140	B.353(10). University College, Waddington.
555/A	45.2	2.93	270	B.353(10). P 1982, Stewart.
556/H	40.6	2.63	180	B.353(10). Coats 2045.

PLATE 25

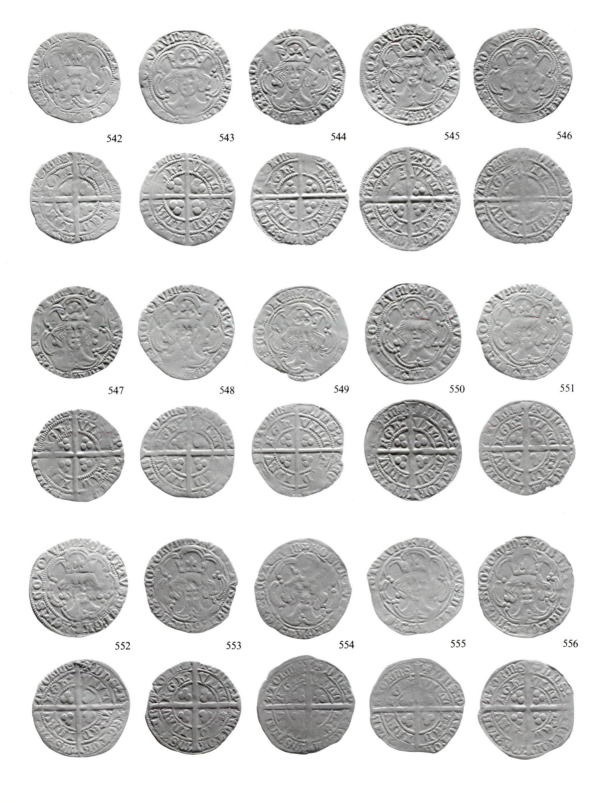

542 543 544 545 546

547 548 549 550 551

552 553 554 555 556

	Weight		*Die*	
	gr	gm	axis	
557/H	37.5	2.43	0	B.353(10) but **M**. Coats 2046.
558/A	44.6	2.89	130	B.355 but **SCOTORVM** as the common examples of this nine arc tressure type in the Fortrose hoard as noted B.i, p. 291. Hird.
559/H	44.8	2.90	270	B.355(13) but as last but rare variety with stop after **SCOTORVM**. Coats 2047.
560/A	37.8	2.45	160	B.357(14) but initial cross obv. Lockett 167 same dies. D 1971, J. K. R. Murray.
561/H	44.2	2.86	30	B.357(14). Coats 2044.
562/H	44.6	2.89	200	B.358(15). Coats 2055.
563/H	43.9	2.84	210	B.380(34) but **A TORMS** and **VILL A**. Coats 2052.
564/H	34.6	2.24	290	B.371(36). Coats 2054.
565/A	41.8	2.71	20	B.381(37) same dies. P 1982, Stewart.
566/H	43.7	2.83	130	B.381(37). Coats 2057.
567/H	43.5	2.82	200	B.372(38). Coats 2051.
568/H	42.3	2.74	200	B.373(39). Coats 2050.
569/A	31.9	2.07	80	B.391(40) same dies, same obv. die as 572/A. P 1982, Stewart.
570/H	41.9	2.72	25	B.391(40) but **MDNS ··**. Coats 2059.
571/H	44.5	2.88	0	B.391(40) but **+DNS · P · TECTOR MS · Z · LIB A TORMS**. Coats 2058.

PLATE 26

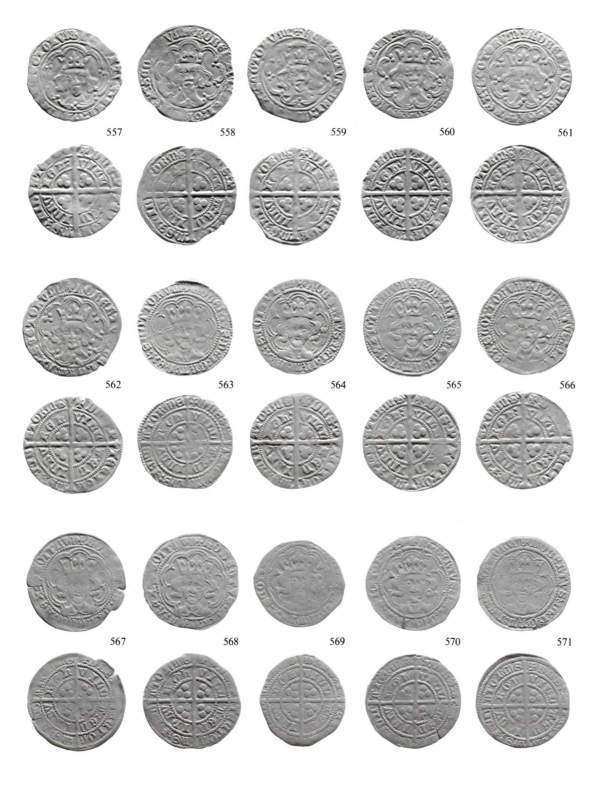

557   558   559   560   561

562   563   564   565   566

567   568   569   570   571

	Weight *gr*	*gm*	Die *axis*	
572/A	41.9	2.72	50	B.391(41) same obv. die, same obv. die as 569/A. Hird.
Perth				
573/H	39.1	2.53	10	B.360(16) but inner rev. legend begins in second quarter. Coats 2062.
574/H	43.0	2.78	180	B.361(17). Coats 2061.
575/A	43.8	2.84	80	B.361(18) but smaller lettering on rev. which reads **MS · Z · LIB** and **PER**. same obv. die, same rev. die as 576/A. Hird.
576/A	40.2	2.61	330	B.361(19a) but trefoil on breast and rev. reading varies, same obv. die as 577/A, same rev. die as 575/A. Hird.
577/A	41.2	2.67	290	B.361A(19a) obv., same obv. die / B.360(19) rev., but stops in inner legend vary, same obv. die as 576/A but without trefoil on breast. Hird.
578/H	43.1	2.79	190	B.362(20) but stops vary after **TECTOR** and **PER ThX**. Coats 2063.
579/H	40.2	2.60	130	B.362(20) but two saltires and pellet in stop after **P** and no stop before **LIB**. Hunter.
580/A	38.1	2.47	280	B.364(21) same dies. Radcliffe.
581/H	33.7	2.18	190	B.364(21) but no pellets in **B**s where used as **R**s (**BOBEBTVS**). Coats 2064.
582/A	43.0	2.79	90	B.366(24) same dies, same rev. die as 583/A. Hird.
583/A	39.0	2.53	340	B.366(24) but tressure and trefoil on breast vary, same rev. die, same rev. die as 582/A. P 1982, Stewart.
584/H	42.4	2.73	90	B.374(25) but double stops after **ROBERTVS**. Coats 2066.
585/A	38.1	2.47	250	B.— obv. tressure of seven arcs and trefoil on breast, **ROBERTVS · DEI · GRACIA · REX · SCOTORVI**/B.389 rev. but **A · DE · PER**. P 1982, Stewart.
586/H	45.4	2.94	190	B.389(26). Coats 2065.

PLATE 27

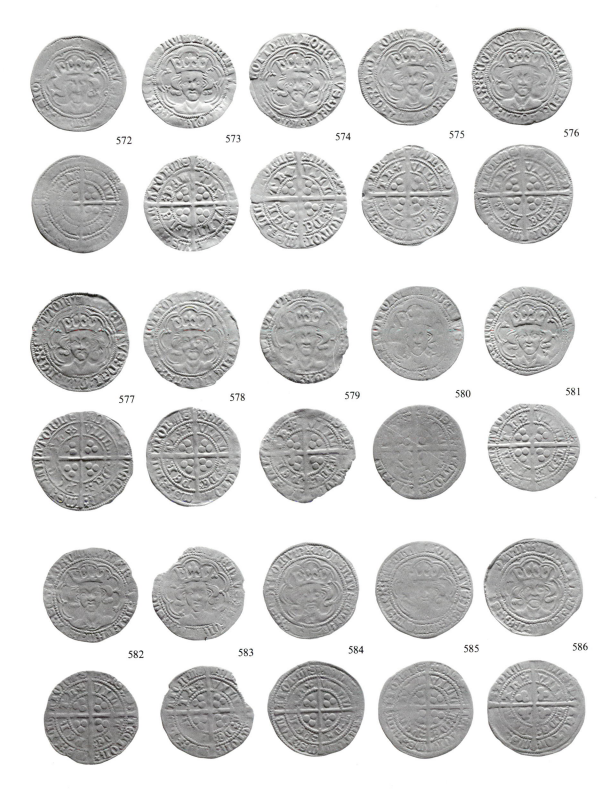

572   573   574   575   576

577   578   579   580   581

582   583   584   585   586

	Weight		Die	
	gr	gm	axis	
587/H	44.0	2.85	310	B.390(27). Coats 2067.
588/H	33.8	2.19	0	B.390(27). Coats 2069.
589/A	45.0	2.92	130	B.394(29) same dies. P 1982, Stewart.
590/H	39.8	2.58	160	B.394(29). Coats 2070.
591/A	43.3	2.81	350	B.396(31) but *recte* · DEI GRA ·, same dies. Somerville College.
592/H	42.6	2.76	300	B.396(31). Coats 2068.
593/A	44.1	2.86	200	B.394–7? ROB [ ] · DEIG [ ] REX · SCOTOR [ ] / +DNS [ ] TATOR MS · ƶL IDATO · and VILL ADE · PER ThX. P 1982, Stewart.
594/H	40.2	2.60	210	B.398E(32b) but lis after GRACIA. Coats 2060.

Aberdeen

595/H	37.1	2.40	90	B.393A(42a). Hunter.
596/H	41.4	2.68	45	B.393A(42a) but *recte* ATORMS, same rev. die, same obv. die? Coats 2043.
597/H	37.8	2.45	220	B.401(47). Coats 2041.
598/H	42.0	2.72	0	B.401(47a). Coats 2042.
599/A	43.0	2.79	180	B.401–2 but reads SCOTORV with double crescent stops on obv. and rev. reads +DNS [ ] TATOR · MS · ƶ LIB TORMS and VILL A · DE ABER DENX. Hird.
600/A	37.5	2.43	160	B.398(43) but *recte* stop after TATOR on rev., same dies. Bodleian.
601/A	40.6	2.63	330	B.— tressure of seven arcs, obv. crescent stops and rev. crescent stops only after TATOR and possibly MS. P 1982, Stewart.

PLATE 28

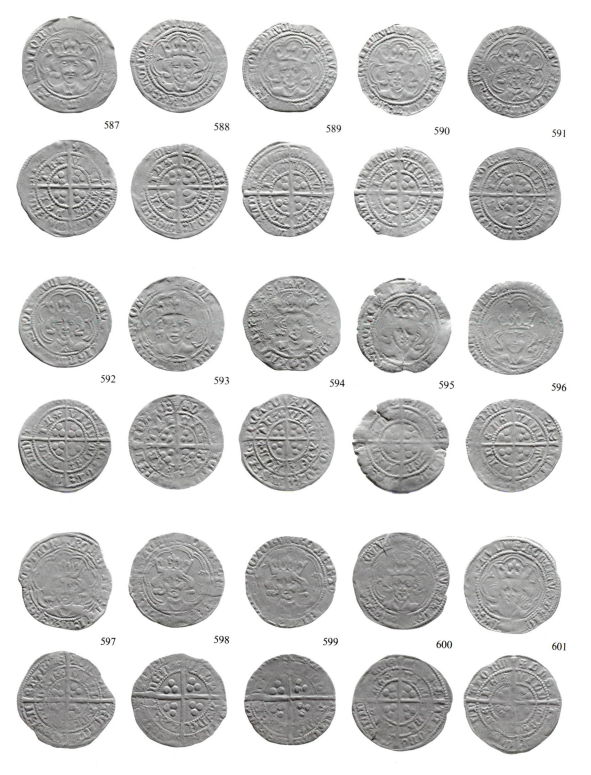

587   588   589   590   591

592   593   594   595   596

597   598   599   600   601

ROBERT III (*cont.*)

Half-Groat (Edinburgh, Perth. Nos. 602–6)

Edinburgh

	Weight		Die	
	gr	gm	axis	
602/A	23.1	1.50	330	B.346(5). E 1966, Stewart, Parsons 718 (part).
603/H	23.3	1.51	70	B.386(14). Coats 2071.

Perth

604/A	25.3	1.64	120	B.376(13) same obv. die but seven arcs in tressure?, stops on rev. visible only after DกꞨ. P 1982, Stewart.
605/H	19.8	1.28	90	B.376(13) with signs of overstriking on obv. as on specimen noted by Burns. L 1980, Lord Younger of Leckie, found during excavation of the Broch of Leckie, Stirlingshire 1980.
606/H	20.9	1.35	170	B.376(13). Coats 2072.

Penny (Edinburgh, Aberdeen. Nos. 607–9)

Edinburgh

607/A	13.5	0.88	120	B.339(2) same rev. die, ?same obv. die. P 1982, Stewart.
608/A	12.6	0.82	270	B.—. Without mint name and no stops. ROBꞓRTVS DꞓI GRAꞒIA / RꞓX SꞒO TOR VM+. P 1982, Stewart, Grantley 1734 (part).

Aberdeen

609/A (clipped)	7.1	0.46	140	B.403–403A similar style of bust? but reads ROBꞓRTVS·DꞓI [ ]/VILL A·AB IRD Ꞓ[ ]. Bodleian.

Halfpenny (Edinburgh, Perth. Without mint name. Nos. 610–15)

Edinburgh

610/A	5.4	0.35	140	B.347 but reads +ROBꞓRTVS [ ]SꞒO/VIL [ ] VR [ ]. Bodleian.
611/A	6.8	0.44	90	B.399A late issue, but reads +ROBꞓRTVS · DꞓI [ ]/VILL AꞓD INBV RGh. P 1980.

Perth

612/A	6.0	0.39	110	B.376C but reads +ROBꞓRTVS · DꞓIG· / VIL [ ] PꞓR Th·. Christ Church.
613/H	9.9	0.64	50	B.— reads [ ] ROBꞓRTVS RꞓX · SꞒO [ ]/VILL A Dꞓ PꞓR ThX. Hunter.
614/H	7.1	0.46	270	B.— reads +ROBꞓRTVS RꞓX · SꞒO/V[ILL ADꞓ] PꞓR ThX. Hunter.

Without mint name

615/H	7.4	0.48	230	B.— without mint name, reads ROBꞓRTVS DꞓI GA /RꞓX [ ]R VM. Hunter.

Light Groat (Edinburgh, Dumbarton. Nos. 616–19)

Edinburgh

616/A	25.4	1.65	130	B.417–18? but nine arcs in tressure and reads ROBꞓRTVS · DꞓI · GRAꞒIA · RꞓX · SꞒ/DꞚS P TORꞘS · LIBꞓRA TORꞘS and VILL AꞓD INBV RGh·. P 1982, Stewart, McFarlan.
617/H	28.4	1.84	280	cf. B.417(50a) but MꞨ ꝅ LIBꞓ. Hunter.

Dumbarton

618/A	33.6	2.18	130	obv. mis-struck. B.— reads + · ROBꞓRTVS DꞓI · GRA · RꞓX · SVOTORVM but stops uncertain /+DꞚS · P TꞓꞒTO RꞘSLIB ATORꞘS with unusual S in RꞘSLIB and VILL ADV NBꞓR TAN·. Hird, Dakers 367.
619/A	21.6	1.40	20	B.416D(57a) same obv. die, rev. reads +·DꞚS·P TꞓꞒTOR· ꞘS · LIB ATORꞘS and VILL A · DV NBꞓR TAN·. P 1946, Dakers 368, Cochran-Patrick 193.

JAMES I (1406–37)
JAMES II (1437–60)

GOLD

Demy (Salvum fac populum tuum domine. Stops: saltire, lis, annulet. Nos. 620–36)

JAMES I

	Weight		Die	
	gr	gm	axis	
620/A	51.0	3.31	220	B.424(1) same dies. Hird, J. E. Cree.
621/A	51.7	3.35	210	B.429(2) same dies. Hird, Murdoch (1903) 94.
622/A	52.0	3.37	340	B.434(3) same dies. Hird, Browne 486.
623/A	46.7	3.03	260	B.454(8) but *recte* lis after GRAꞒIA same dies and same dies as 624/H, same obv. die as 625/A and 626/A. Hird.
624/H	51.7	3.35	160	As 623/A. Hunter.
625/A	49.8	3.23	320	B.456C(12b) same dies, same obv. die as 623/A, 624/H, and 626/A. Hird.

PLATE 29

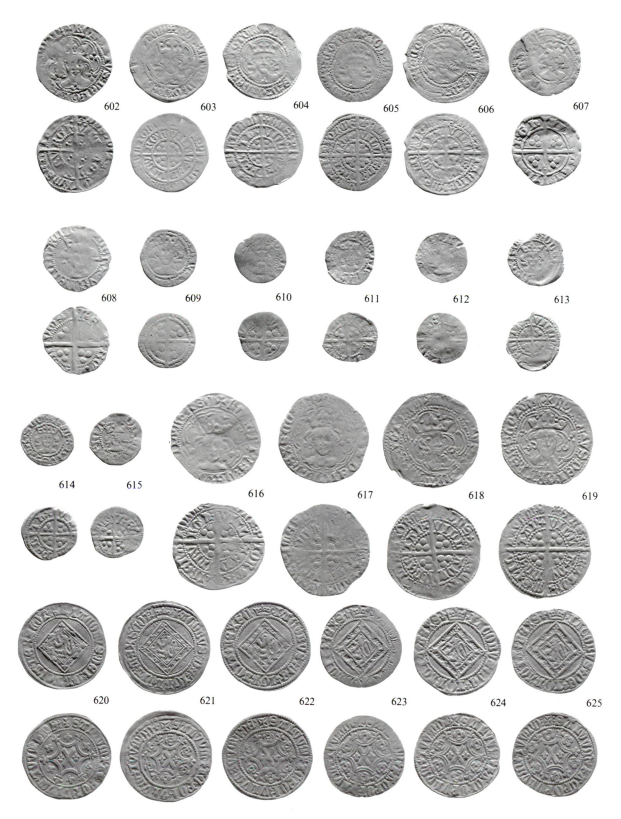

602 603 604 605 606 607

608 609 610 611 612 613

614 615 616 617 618 619

620 621 622 623 624 625

	Weight		Die	
	gr	gm	axis	
626/A	47.0	3.05	290	B.457(13) same dies, same obv. die as 623/A, 624/H, and 625/A. Hird, Walters 603.
627/A	52.0	3.37	200	B.455(11) same dies. Hird.
628/A	54.1	3.51	290	B.465B(8c) same dies. Hird, Wills 170–2?, Cochran-Patrick 20.
629/A	51.5	3.34	290	B.470(18) same dies, same obv. die as 630/A and 631/A. Hird, Wills 170–2?, Scott-Plummer 356.
630/A	52.1	3.38	60	B.471(19) but rev. reads +·SⱯLVVₘ·FⱯＱPOPVLVₘ·TVVₘ·, same obv. die, same obv. die as 629/A and 631/A. Hird.
631/A	52.6	3.41	340	B.471(19) but rev. ends TVVₘ··, same obv. die, same obv. die as 629/A and 630/A. P 1946, Tennant 49.
632/A	50.7	3.29	310	B.484(21) same dies. Hird.

JAMES II

633/A	50.1	3.25	240	B. — obv. IⱯＱOBVS·DⱭI·GRⱯＱIⱯ·RⱭX SＱOT / rev. annulet on centre of cross, +SⱯLVₘ·FⱯＱ·POPVLVₘ·TVVₘ·DIIⱭ. Hird.
634/A	51.0	3.31	130	B.499(3) same dies. Hird, Cochran-Patrick 25, Advocates.
635/A	51.7	3.35	150	B.513(7) same obv. die, and same obv. die as 636/A. P 1946, Tennant 50.
636/A	51.5	3.34	130	B.509(4) same dies and same obv. die as 635A. Hird.

Half demy (Nos. 637–8)

JAMES I

| 637/A | 25.9 | 1.68 | 220 | B.444(1) same dies. Hird, Brand. |
| 638/A | 25.1 | 1.63 | 180 | B.445(2) same dies. Hird, Cree. |

SILVER

Fleur-de-lis groat (Edinburgh, Linlithgow, Perth, Stirling. Stops: saltire, lis, annulet, crescent. Nos. 639–72)

Initial variety

Edinburgh

| 639/A | 32.7 | 2.12 | 40 | B. —, see Stewart, 1967, p. 43, rev. reads +D[   ]P TⱭＱTOR ·ₘSZLI·BⱯTOTₘ· and VILL·Ɐ·ⱭD IₙBV· RGh· P 1982, Stewart. |

First variety

Edinburgh

640/A	33.1	2.15	40	B.430(3) but *recte* SＱOTO· same obv. die and rev. reads +DₙS·P TⱭＱTOR ·ₘSZLI·BⱯTORₘ· and inner legend as B428B(2c) but different stops. Hird.
641/H	33.7	2.18	340	B.431(5) but +DₙS·P· TⱭＱTOR ·ₘSZLIB ATORₘ···. Hunter.
642/H	33.8	2.19	70	B.437B(9a) but IACOBVS and no saltire to right of crown or behind sceptre, rev. reads [+Dₙ]S·P· and VILL A·ⱭD· IₙBV ·RGh· with saltire either side of lis in first quarter and to right of lis in third quarter. D J. R. Lockie.
643/A	43.5	2.82	180	B.453(19) but rev. lis stops smaller than usual and points in first, second, and fourth quarters, +DₙS·P TⱭＱOTOR ₘS[ ]IB ⱯTOR·ₘ· and VILL[ ]ⱭD· IₙBV··RGh Hird.

PLATE 30

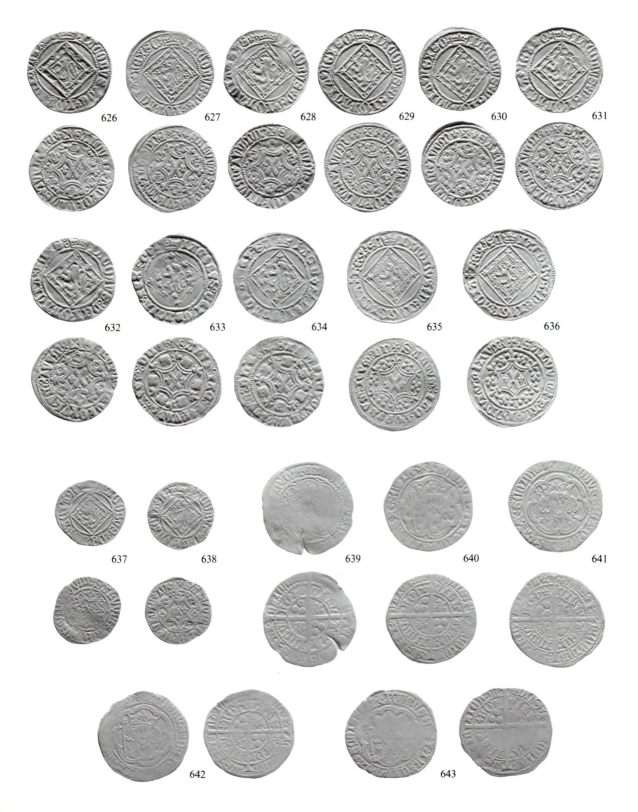

626   627   628   629   630   631

632   633   634   635   636

637   638   639   640   641

642   643

	Weight		Die	
	gr	gm	axis	
644/A	33.5	2.17	270	B.— + ·IꝐOBVS, lis on breast and to left of neck, saltire on shoulders, I to right of neck and on sceptre handle, ⁞ behind sceptre, unusual lis stops (both sides) / +DꝐS[ ] TEꝐOTOR MSZLI·BꝩTORM· and VILL ꝩ·ED· IꝐBV ·RGh·, point in each quarter and saltire in third, lis on centre of cross, same dies as 645/A. Hird.
645/A	27.0	1.75	100	As 644/A. Bodleian.
646/A	26.1	1.69	30	B.— ends SꝐOTO·, lis on breast, saltire on shoulders, to left of neck and right of crown, I to right of neck (? and on sceptre handle), lis stops / +DꝐS·P· TEꝐOTO· RMSZL· BꝩTORM and VILL ꝩ·ED· IꝐBV ·RGh, two points in third quarter, one in each of the other quarters; same obv. die as 647/A, same rev. die as 648/A. Hird.
647/A	31.3	2.03	220	B.— same obv. die as 646/A/ rev. +DꝐS[ ] TEꝐOTOR M[ ]LI[ ] BTORM· and VILL ꝩ·ED· IꝐBV ·RGh, point in each quarter. Hird.
648/A	31.8	2.06	230	B.— reads TRꝩꝐI·, lis on breast, saltire on shoulders and to right of neck, I on sceptre handle / rev. same die as 646/A. Hird, Stuart-Menteth.
649/H	30.1	1.95	110	B.446(15) but rev. points in each quarter and stops differ. Hunter.
650/H	33.5	2.17	340	B.449A(17a) but rev. stops differ and B of Edinburgh normal. Hunter.
651/A	30.5	1.98	90	B.453(19) but obv. legend ends with three lis and rev. stops differ with one point in first quarter, four in second, one point and one saltire in third, and three or four in fourth. Bodleian.
652/A	25.6	1.66	330	B.458(20) same obv. die, same obv. die as 653/A, but rev. reads +DꝐS·P EꝐOTOR MSZLI BꝩTORM and VILL ꝩ·ED IꝐBV ··RGh with one point in first quarter, four in second and fourth, and one point and one saltire in third. Hird.
653/A	35.3	2.29	310	B.458(20) same dies, same obv. die as 652/A. P 1982, Stewart.
654/A	34.5	2.24	150	B.458A(20a) same obv. die but rev. reads VILL ꝩ·ED· IꝐBV ·RGh· and single point in first, second, and fourth quarters, a small lis in the third. Same obv. die as 655/H. P 1982, Stewart.
655/H	35.2	2.28	330	B.458A(20a) but rev. reads DꝐS·PT EꝐOTO· RMSZL IB[ ] and ILL ꝩ·ED ·IꝐB· RG·V with point in each quarter. Same obv. die as 654/A Hunter.
656/A	31.9	2.07	130	B.473(25) same dies—this is a first variety Linlithgow obv. (same die as 658/A) and a second variety Edinburgh rev. Hird.

Linlithgow

657/A	35.8	2.32	0	B.463A(26a) same dies. P 1946, Dakers 389 (part).
658/A	31.4	2.04	200	B.464(28) same dies. Same obv. die as 656/A. P 1982, Stewart.

PLATE 31

644 645 646 647 648

649 650 651 652 653

654 655 656 657 658

	Weight gr	Weight gm	Die axis	
659/A	32.5	2.11	310	B.464A(28a) same obv. die/B.463A(27) rev. Hird.

Perth

| 660/A | 32.3 | 2.09 | 110 | B.467(33a) but rev. reads DNS·P· TEᴄOTO RMSZL IBᴧT[   ] and +VI LLᴧ· DEᴄ·PEᴄ RTh· where one of the stops may be from the same punch as that used for the cusps of the tressure, point in second and fourth quarters. Hird. |
| 661/A | 34.7 | 2.25 | 270 | B.465(31) but *recte* lis after final S of obv. same dies. P 1982, Stewart. |

Second variety (see Intro. pp. xiv—xv)

Edinburgh

662/A	31.8	2.06	90	B.476(38) but 'peculiar' L and additional ornaments in quarters as B.476(36) same obv. die, same obv. die as 663/A. Hird.
663/A	33.6	2.18	120	B.476(37) same obv die, same obv. die as 662/A. P 1982, Stewart.
664/H	33.1	2.15	150	B.478(41) same dies. Hunter.
665/H	33.1	2.15	320	B.487(43) but rev. reads +DNS P· TEᴄOT· RMS Z L IBᴧTOR and VILL ᴧ·EᴅD· INBV ··RGh with point in second and fourth quarters. Hunter.
666/H	33.9	2.20	270	B.488(45) but rev. reads +DNSP TEᴄOTO RMSZL BᴧTOR and VILL ᴧ·EᴅD INBV ·RGh with point in second, third, and fourth quarters and without lis centre of cross. Neilson.
667/H	29.9	1.94	120	B.488 obv. variety as noted top of p. 27 / B.488(46) rev. but no stop after EᴅD. Hunter.
668/A	27.3	1.77	230	B.— obv. reads +IᴧᴄOBVS·DEᴅI·TRᴧᴄI[·]REᴄX[·]SᴄOT with lis on breast, saltire on shoulders and to right of neck / rev. reads +DNSP TEᴄOTO RMSZL IBᴧTR and VILL ᴧ·EᴅD· INBV RGh with lis on centre of cross, point in second and fourth quarters and saltire in third quarter. Hird.
669/A	33.8	2.19	140	B.475(34) and 490A(48a) same obv. die, same obv. die as 670/A (of Linlithgow—this die link not noted in 'Scottish Mints' but see link no. 42 for the Perth–Edinburgh link) / B.— rev. reads +DNSP TEᴄOTR MSZLI BᴧTORM and VILL ᴧ·EᴅD· INBV ·RGh with lis on centre of cross and point in second and fourth quarters. Bodleian.

Linlithgow

| 670/A | 33.0 | 2.14 | 0 | B.475(34) and 490A(48a) same obv. die, same obv. die as 669/A (of Edinburgh—this die link not noted in 'Scottish Mints' but see link no. 42 for the Perth–Edinburgh link) / B.489(48) but +DNS·P TEᴄOTO RMSZL IBᴧTOR and VILL ᴧ·BEᴄ LIIL IThC' and no cross in third quarter. Hird, Cochran-Patrick 200. |

Stirling

| 671/A | 34.4 | 2.23 | 50 | B.492(50) but *recte* lis after SᴄO, rev. reads +DNSP TEᴄOTO RMSZLI BᴧTOR and VILL ᴧ·ST REᴄV· EᴄLVN with point in second and fourth quarters, same obv. die. Hird, Duke of Atholl. |
| 672/A | 24.5 | 1.59 | 50 | B.491(49) but rev. reads +DN[   ] TEᴄOTO· [   ]MSᴢL IBᴧTO and VILL ᴧST· REᴄV· EᴄLVI with (?)crescent on centre of cross, point in second and fourth quarters, point and crescent in third, same obv. die, note same rev. die as 43b in 'Scottish Mints'. Browne Willis. |

BILLON

Penny (Edinburgh, Aberdeen, Inverness. Stops: lis, crescent, cross, pellet, saltire. Nos. 673–6).

Stewart group A

Edinburgh

| 673/A | 14.5 | 0.94 | 270 | B.423 E–G (3b–d). P 1982, Stewart. |

PLATE 32

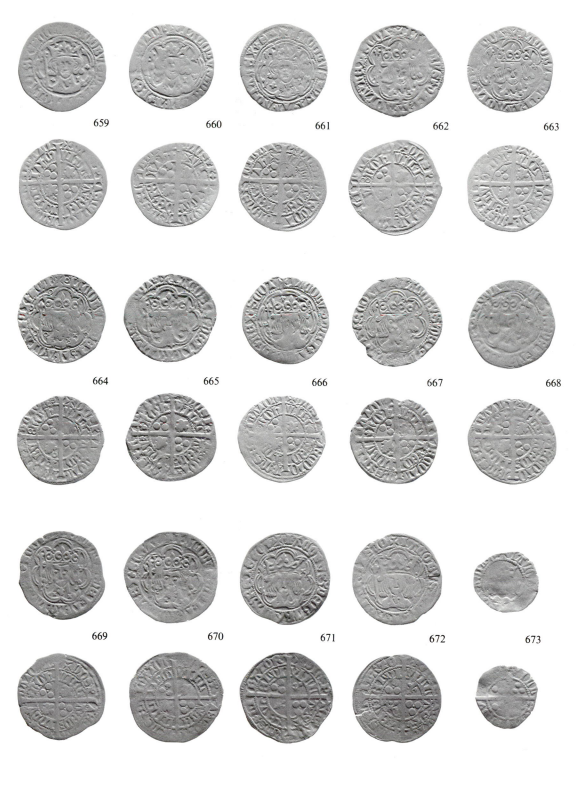

659   660   661   662   663

664   665   666   667   668

669   670   671   672   673

| | Weight | | Die |
| | gr | gm | axis |

Aberdeen

674/A 12.8 0.83 0 B.423C(2c) but SCOTOR. D 1982, Stewart.

Inverness

675/H 9.3 0.60 90 B.427 but upright S and lis after VILLA and cross at end of rev. legend. Hunter.

Stewart group C

Aberdeen

676/H 12.4 0.80 180 B.479(3) but +VIL · LADE ABE · [D]EN where stops differ. Hunter.

Halfpenny (Edinburgh. No. 677)

Stewart group C

677/A 5.7 0.37 120 B.479A(1b) this coin, Stewart 1967, pl. VI, 88 this coin. P 1946, Dakers 396 (part) (where catalogued perhaps correctly as James II), Cochran-Patrick 216.

Fleur-de-lis groat cont. (Edinburgh, Linlithgow. Nos. 678–82)

Third variety

Edinburgh

678/A 35.8 2.32 130 B.496B(3a) with +IACO·BVSDE·IGRACA·IAREX· on rev., same obv. die, Lockett 208 same dies. P 1957.

679/A 30.4 1.97 70 B.— obv. reads +IACOBVS·DEI·GRACIA·REX·SCO[T·] with pellets on cusps and eight arcs to tressure / rev. reads +DNS·P TECTOR MS·Z·L IB[ ]· and ·VIL LAE DIN·BVRG without additional marks in quarters, see die link no. 46 with Stirling in 'Scottish Mints'. Hird.

680/H 34.1 2.21 330 B.504(8) but +IACOBVS·DEI·GRACIA·REX·SCOTORVM· and +DIISPT ECTOR MSZLI· BERAT· and +VIL LAED IIIBV RGh·. Hunter.

681/A 33.4 2.17 0 B.506(10) same dies. D 1951, Mrs C. H. Fisher.

Linlithgow

682/A 31.4 2.04 350 B.502(14) but rev. reads +DNS· PTECTO R·MS·Z· LIBER and +VIL LA·L IN·L IThC', same obv. die, new rev. die—see die link no. 45 with Edinburgh, 'Scottish Mints'. Hird.

Penny (Stirling. No. 683)

Stewart group D

683/H 8.8 0.57 180 B.— obv. [ ]COBVSD IGR[ ] / rev. [ ]VIL LAST RIVE[ ]. Hunter.

Fleur-de-lis groat cont. (Edinburgh. No. 684)

Fourth variety

Edinburgh

684/A 29.9 1.94 .10 B.508(17) but *recte* two saltires after initial cross, same dies. P 1982, Stewart, McFarlan.

[*continued overleaf*]

PLATE 33

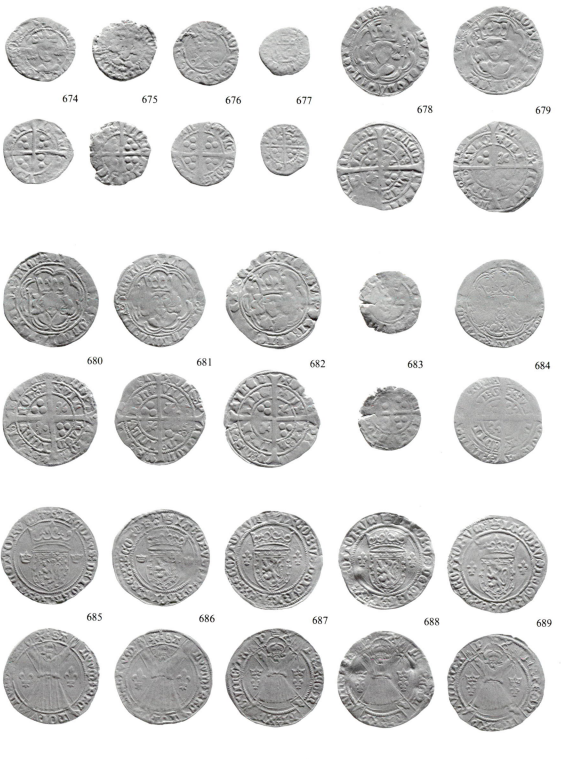

674   675   676   677   678   679

680   681   682   683   684

685   686   687   688   689

Plate 33 (*cont.*):

James II Second Coinage 1451–60
GOLD

Lion (Salvum fac populum tuum domine or Christus (XPC) regnat, Christus vincit, Christus imperat. Stops: cross, saltire, annulet. Nos. 685–91)

	Weight		Die	
	gr	gm	axis	
685/A	48.7	3.16	100	B.519(1) same dies, same rev. die as 686/A. Hird, Royal Scottish Museum, Lindsay-Carnegie.
686/A	52.9	3.43	210	B.519A(1a) same dies, same rev. die as 685/A. Hird, Murdoch, British Museum Duplicates.
687/A	52.9	3.43	310	B.525(3) same rev. die, same dies as 688/H, same rev. die as 689/A, 690/A, and 691/A. Hird.
688/H	53.3	3.45	40	As 687/A also same rev. die as 689–91/A. D1816, T. Smithers, Found in Glasgow Cathedral.
689/A	52.7	3.42	260	B.526(4) but *recte is* illustrated as 528, same dies, same rev. die as 687/A, 688/H, 690/A, and 691/A. Hird, Burton-Jones.

	Weight		*Die*	
	gr	gm	axis	
690/A	52.4	3.40	300	B.528(6) but *recte not* illustrated, same rev. die as 687/A, 688/H, 689/A, and 691/A. Hird, Cochran-Patrick 29, Advocates.
691/A	53.4	3.46	90	B.527(5) same dies, same rev. die as 687/A, 688/H, 689/A, and 690/A. Hird, Brand.

Half lion (No. 692)

692/A	26.2	1.70	150	B.529(1) same dies. Hird, Bute 151.

SILVER

Crown groat (Edinburgh, Aberdeen, Perth, Stirling. Stops: cross, saltire, annulet. Nos. 693–721)

First issue

Edinburgh

693/A	53.8	3.49	230	B.517(6) but rev. reads Z·LIBER ΛTOR·ME· DNS·PTE ETOR·ME·, same obv. die as 694/A and 695/A. Hird.
694/A	54.9	3.56	140	B.517(6) same obv. die, same obv. die as 693/A and 695/A. Browne Willis.
695/A	55.8	3.62	60	As 694/A. Bodleian.
696/A	50.0	3.24	130	B.516(3) but rev. reads DNS·P·TE ATORME· ZLIBER ΛTOR·ME·, same obv. die, same obv. die as 697/A. Bodleian.
697/A	54.1	3.51	10	B.516(3) but DNS and no stop before initial cross of inner legend, same obv. die, same obv. die as 696/A. P 1982, Stewart.
698/A	53.7	3.48	260	B.515(2b) same obv. die. Hird.

Second issue

Edinburgh

699/A	51.4	3.33	200	B.530(13) same obv. die (Stewart II—see Stewart and Murray 1967, 149–50). Hird.
700/A	47.3	3.07	20	B.531(15) but GRΛSIΛ and DNS·P· (Stewart II). Hird.
701/A	52.0	3.37	230	B.532(17) but DNSPRO, same obv. die (Stewart II). Hird, Cochran-Patrick 211C.
702/A	52.7	3.42	270	B.532(19b) but TECTRM, same obv. die (19a and b now in NMAS—Richardson 1901, addenda 157 and 158), (Stewart II). Hird.
703/A	51.0	3.31	110	B.524(11) but DNS·P·, same obv. die (Stewart II irregular). Hird.
704/H	50.5	3.27	130	B.534(22a) but double saltires before and after IΛCOBVS and rev. stops differ (Stewart II). Hunter.

PLATE 34

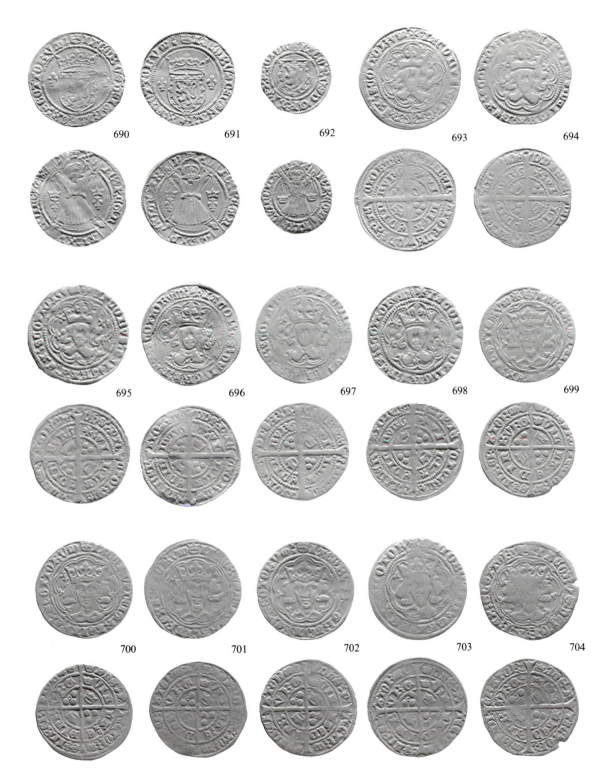

690   691   692   693   694

695   696   697   698   699

700   701   702   703   704

	Weight		*Die*
	gr	gm	axis
705/H	53.1	3.44	300
706/A	52.0	3.37	160
707/A	53.8	3.49	310
708/A	55.8	3.62	150
709/A	49.8	3.23	300
710/A	52.0	3.37	330
711/A	52.1	3.38	250
712/A	52.9	3.43	310
713/A	54.1	3.51	130
714/H	56.4	3.65	270

705/H B.534(22a) but rev. reads DNS[   ]ECTORM [   ]LIB [   ] and VIL LⱯED INB· ·VRG· (Stewart II). Hunter.

706/A B.538(24b) but rev. reading as B.533(21a), same obv. die (Richardson 1901 fig. 178; 'squashed annulet' stops as Stewart and Murray 1967, p. 152. (Stewart III obv./II rev.). Hird.

707/A B.542(26) but annulets between pellets and reads DNSP· TECTOR[M]? ?[S]ZLIBER ⱯTORM· and VIL LⱯED INB VRG, same obv. die as 708/A (Stewart III obv./II rev.). P 1982, Stewart.

708/A B.542(26) but ·VRG·, same obv. die as 707/A (Stewart III). P 1982, Stewart.

709/A B.— obv. saltire either side of neck, lis above and to right of crown, IⱯCOBVS·DEI·GRⱯ·REX· SCOTTORVM· / rev. nothing between pellets in first and third quarters, point below crown in fourth, DNS·P· TECTORM SZLIBER ⱯTORMS and VIL ·LⱯE· DINB V·RG· (Stewart III; Caldwell 1982, p. 142, and 149 n. 18 where suggested struck under James III). P 1982, Q & LTR, Innerwick Hoard no. 53.

710/A B.547A(33a) but no subsidiary marks rev. where stops also differ, same obv. die (Stewart III). P 1982, Q & LTR, Innerwick Hoard no. 50.

711/A B.548(40) = Roxburgh die, same obv. die, same obv. die as 717/A and 718/A (both Perth—see 'Scottish Mints', die link no. 51) / rev. no subsidiary marks and reads DNS·P· TECTORM SZLIBR ⱯTORMS and VIL ·LⱯE DINB VRG (Stewart III; suggested struck under James III as 709/A). P 1982, Q & LTR, Innerwick Hoard no. 52.

712/A B.542(25) same obv. die / B.542(27) (Stewart III). Hird.

713/A B.546(32) same rev. die, same obv. die as Richardson 1901 66 and no. 51 of Stewart and Murray 1967 (this obv. also combined with Roxburgh and Perth rev. see 'Scottish Mints' die link no. 52) (Stewart III). Somerville College.

714/H B.550(36) but stops differ rev. Hunter.

Aberdeen

715/A	56.1	3.64	180
716/H	50.0	3.24	140

715/A B.541(39) same obv. die / B.541A(39a) same rev. die, Lockett 217 this coin. P 1957, Lockett 217, Dakers 403, Cochran-Patrick 213, Antiquaries 50.

716/H B.541A(39a) but stops differ rev. Hunter.

Perth

717/A	54.0	3.50	170
718/A	51.5	3.34	30

717/A B.548(40). obv / B.549(41a) rev. (but *recte* B.549(41a) not same obv. die as B.548(40)), same obv. die, same dies as 718/A, same obv. die as 711/A, this obv. die combined with Edinburgh and Roxburgh reverses—see 'Scottish Mints', die link no. 51. Hird.

718/A As 717/A. Hird.

Stirling

719/A	52.0	3.37	170

719/A B.540A(38b) but rev. stops differ, same obv. die, same obv. die as 720/A (Stewart III). P 1982, Stewart.

PLATE 35

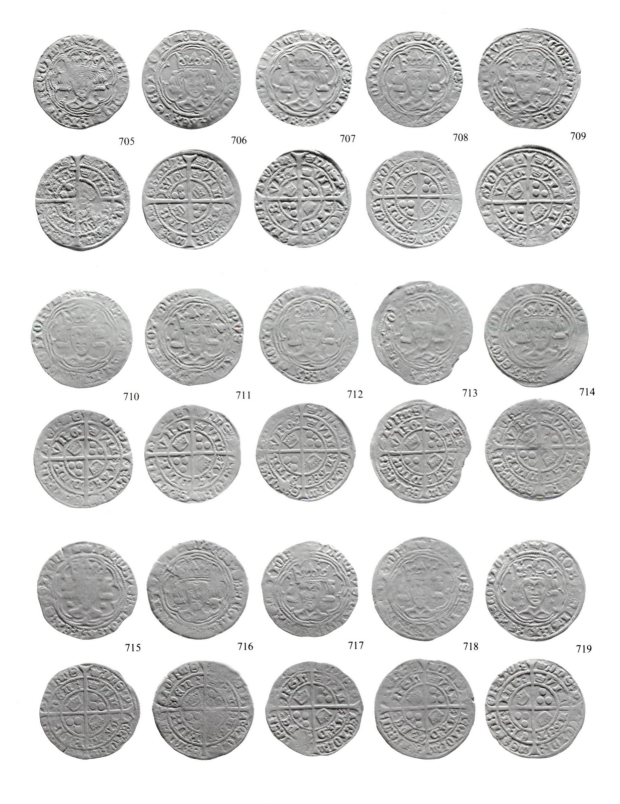

705 706 707 708 709

710 711 712 713 714

715 716 717 718 719

	Weight		Die	
	gr	gm	axis	
720/A	51.5	3.34	300	B.540A(38b) same dies, same obv. die as 719/A (Stewart III). P 1982, Q & LTR, Innerwick Hoard no. 54.
721/H	58.5	3.79	340	B.539(37) obv. but double saltires after DЄI / B.540A(38b) rev. Hunter.

BILLON

Penny (Edinburgh. Nos. 722–7)

722/A	7.3	0.47	210	B.518A(1b) but gives fuller reading of double saltire stop before R and after initial cross, same dies. P 1946, Dakers 396 (part).
723/A	8.5	0.55	240	B.522A(2a) same rev. die, see Stewart 1958–9 Glenluce, p. 378, no. 19. D.1962, Q & LTR, Glenluce Hoard no. 19.
724/A	8.5	0.55	240	B.— obv. reads IⴙCORЄIG[ ]RVⴔ / rev. reads VIL LⴙЄ D[ ] VRGh. P 1946, Dakers 396 (part).
725/A	9.4	0.61	270	B.555A(6a) but no initial mark and reads SCOTRVⴔ, double saltire stop after VIL. P 1946, Dakers 396 (part), Walters 641 (part).
726/A	8.8	0.57	0	B.— obv. reads IⴙCORЄIGRⴙRЄXXSV· / rev. reads VIL [ ] DIⴖR VR[ ]. P 1946, Dakers 396 (part).
727/A	10.0	0.65	0	B.555(5) but not saltires in quarters of rev. and reads VIL·LⴙЄ· DIⴖR VRG. P 1946, Dakers 396 (part).

JAMES III (1460–88)

GOLD

Rider (Salvum fac populum tuum domine. Stops: saltire, colon. Nos. 728–32)

First variety, king riding right.

728/A	78.2	5.07	50	B.599(1) same dies. Hird, Earl of Haddington.
729/H	75.6	4.90	80	As 728/A. Hunter.
730/A	77.7	5.04	60	B.600(2) but *recte* single saltire only after DЄI, same dies. Hird, Newcomer.
731/A	77.9	5.05	20	B.603(7)—the ⴙ below the horse and lis in front added to the obv. die of B. 601–2(3–6) same dies. Hird.

Second variety, king riding left

732/H	78.6	5.09	60	B.619A(7a) same dies, this specimen noted by Burns. Hunter.

Half Rider (second variety only. Nos. 733–6)

733/A	37.2	2.41	0	B.620(1) but note obv. illustration is of B.620(2). Hird, Brand.
734/A	37.8	2.45	90	B.620(2) but obv. stops as B.620(1). Hird, Duke of Atholl.
735/H	36.6	2.37	330	B.620(2) but colon and stop after POPVLVⴔ. Hunter.
736/A	37.3	2.42	320	B.621(3) same dies. E 1953, Hird.

Quarter Rider (second variety only. Nos. 737–8)

737/A	19.9	1.29	110	B.622(1) but colon after RЄX, same obv. die (rider side), same obv. die as 738/A. Hird, found on a new housing site at Selkirk 1946.
738/A	16.8	1.09	120	B.622(1) but reads IACOBV S:DЄI:G Rⴙ:RЄX SCOTOR, same obv. die, same obv. die as 737/A. Hird, Bute 170.

PLATE 36

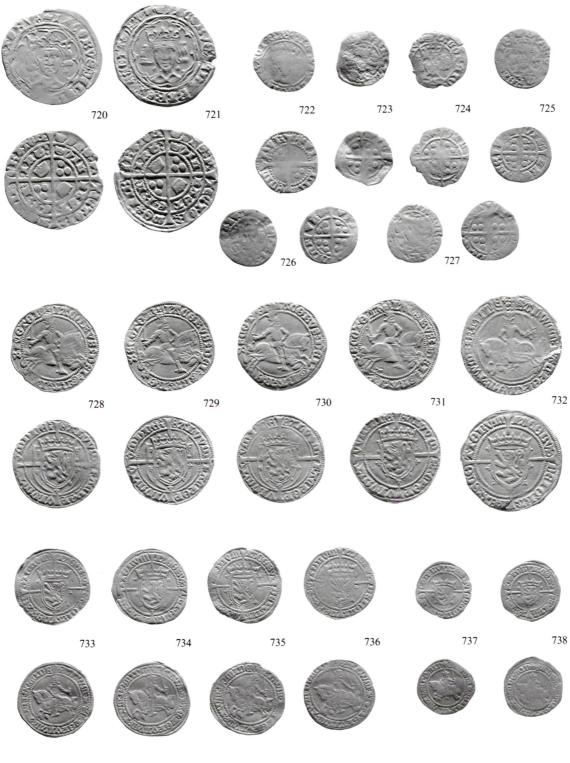

720   721   722   723   724   725

726   727

728   729   730   731   732

733   734   735   736   737   738

Unicorn (Exurgat Deus et dissipentur inimici eius. Stops: star. See Murray 1971, esp. p. 70. No. 739)

	Weight		Die	
	gr	gm	axis	
739/A	60.6	3.93	30	B.629(7), 630(8) but without **S** at end of tail, double stops throughout and obv. ends **ICI·C**. Murray 1971 type X(Ia). Hird, Browne 489.

SILVER

Group I

Groat (Edinburgh, Berwick. Stops: saltire, cross. Nos. 740–7)

Edinburgh

740/A	38.7	2.51	0	B.561(1) same dies, Innerwick 62. P 1982, Q & LTR, Innerwick Hoard.
741/A	40.3	2.61	30	B.567(2) same obv. die / B.568(3) same rev. die, same rev. die as 743/A and 744/A, Innerwick 64. P 1982, Q & LTR, Innerwick Hoard.
742/H	40.2	2.60	330	B.567(2), Innerwick 63. P 1982, Q & LTR, Innerwick Hoard.
743/A	36.8	2.39	50	B.568(3) same dies, same dies as 744/A, same obv. die as 746/A, same rev. die as 741/A ('Scottish Mints', die link no. 56). Hird.
744/A	39.9	2.59	170	As 743/A. Browne Willis.
745/A	37.3	2.42	10	B.569(4) same dies, Innerwick 68. P 1982, Q & LTR, Innerwick Hoard.

Berwick

746/A	37.0	2.40	260	B.570A(5a) same dies, same obv. die as 743/A and 744/A ('Scottish Mints', die link no. 56). P 1957, Lockett 234.
747/H	37.8	2.45	200	As 746/A. Innerwick 69. P 1982, Q & LTR, Innerwick Hoard.

Half Groat (Berwick. No. 748)

748/A	17.6	1.14	260	B.561A(1a) same dies ('Scottish Mints', die link no. 57). Browne Willis.

Group II

Groat (Edinburgh. Stops: saltire. See Metcalf and Oddy 1980, 182 and Murray and Stewart 1970, 178–80. Nos. 749–52)

749/H	27.5	1.78	140	B.577(6). Hunter.
750/A	31.9	2.07	30	B.578(8) but **SCOTORVM[**] and stop after **G** in rev. Hird.
751/A	31.1	2.02	240	B.578(8) but **SCOTORVM·** and stop after **VIL**. P 1963, Stewart.
752/A	30.2	1.96	70	B.579(9) but tressure of seven arcs and obv. stops saltires except after **GRA** and no stop at end, rev. ends **DIN BVR**. Browne Willis.

Half Groat (Edinburgh. No. 753)

753/A	14.0	0.91	0	B.584(1). P 1957, Lockett 237, Bearman, Murdoch (1904) 1036 (part).

PLATE 37

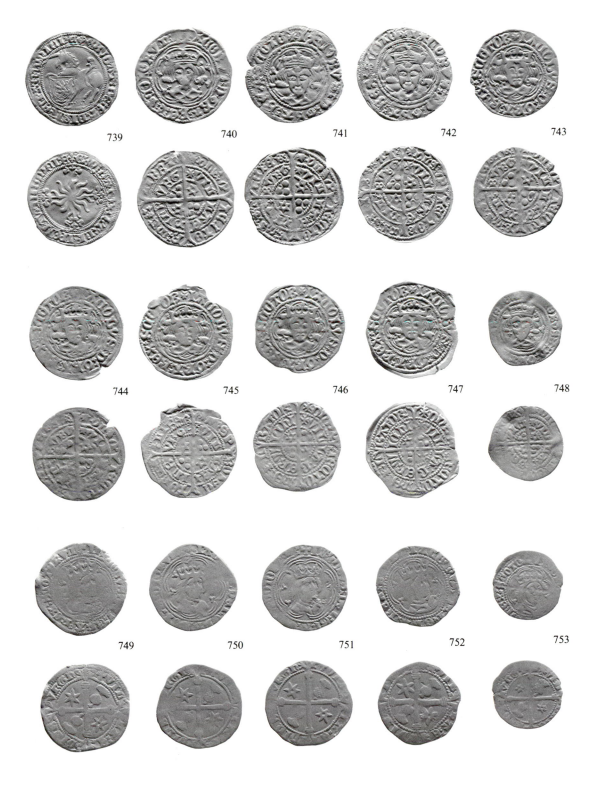

739 740 741 742 743

744 745 746 747 748

749 750 751 752 753

Group III

Groat (Edinburgh, Berwick. Stops: saltire. Nos. 754–61)

Edinburgh

	Weight		Die	
	gr	gm	axis	
754/A	34.8	2.26	0	B.588(15) same obv. die, same dies as 755/A. Hird, Cochran-Patrick 222(b).
755/A	40.2	2.61	220	As 754/A, Innerwick 70. P 1982, Q & LTR, Innerwick Hoard.
756/A	36.8	2.39	190	B.591(18) same dies, same obv. die as 761/A, 757/A, and 758/A ('Scottish Mints', die link no. 59). P 1982, Stewart.
757/A	38.1	2.47	260	B.591(19) same dies, same obv. die as 761/A, 756/A, and 758/A ('Scottish Mints', die link no. 59), same rev. die as 759/A, Innerwick 74. P 1982, Q & LTR, Innerwick Hoard.
758/A	38.2	2.48	150	B.592(20) same dies, same obv. die as 761/A, 756/A, and 757/A ('Scottish Mints', die link no. 59). P 1982, Stewart.

Mule—group IV obv. / group III rev.

759/A	37.5	2.43	180	B.604(21) same dies, same obv. die as 764/A, same rev. die as 757/A, Innerwick 77. P 1982, Q & LTR, Innerwick Hoard.

Berwick

760/A	37.3	2.42	200	B.589(16) same dies. Hird.
761/A	36.8	2.39	250	B.593(22) same dies, same obv. die as 756/A, 757/A, and 758/A ('Scottish Mints', die link no. 59), Innerwick 76. P 1982, Q & LTR, Innerwick Hoard.

Group IV

Groat (Edinburgh. Stops: pellet, colon. Nos. 762–6)

762/A	34.8	2.26	170	B.605(23) but *recte* single stop after REX, same obv. die, same obv. die as 763/H, but rev. reads ⅄TVRMS. Hird.
763/H	39.2	2.54	300	B.605(23) but *recte* single stop after REX, same obv. dies as 762/A, Innerwick 93. P 1982 Q & LTR, Innerwick Hoard.
764/A	38.7	2.51	30	B.605(24) but pellets in first and third quarters, same obv. die (= same obv. die as B.604), same obv. die as 759/A, Innerwick 82. P 1982 Q & LTR, Innerwick Hoard.
765/A	30.5	1.98	170	B.605(25). Hird.
766/A	34.8	2.26	340	B.606(27) same obv. die. Hird.

Half Groat (Edinburgh. No. 767)

767/A	18.5	1.20	270	B607(6) same dies. P 1982, Stewart.

PLATE 38

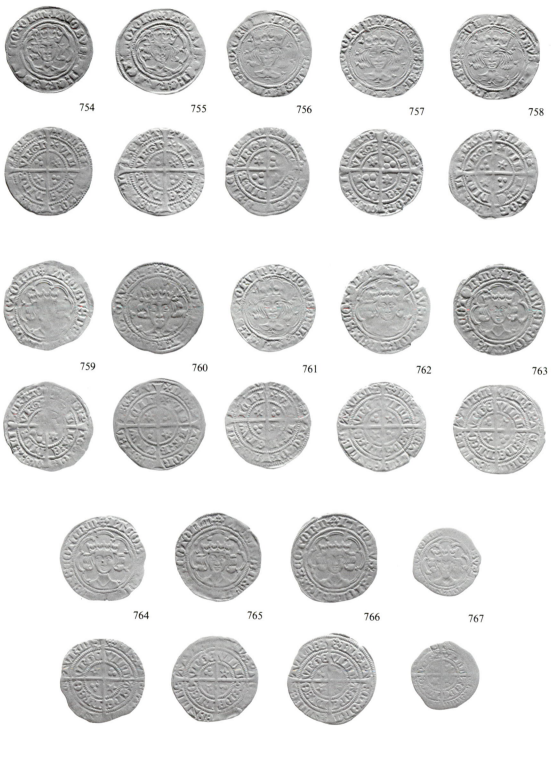

754   755   756   757   758

759   760   761   762   763

764   765   766   767

JAMES III (*cont.*)

Penny (Edinburgh. Nos. 768–71)

	Weight		*Die*	
	gr	*gm*	*axis*	
768/A	7.5	0.49	110	B.610(2) same obv. die. P 1982, Stewart.
769/A	10.1	0.66	40	B.611(3)? / 610(2), Innerwick 102. P 1982, Q & LTR, Innerwick Hoard.
770/A	7.8	0.51	270	B.609(1) same obv. die, Innerwick 100. P 1982, Q & LTR, Innerwick Hoard.
771/H	10.9	0.71	300	B.611(3) same obv. die, Innerwick 103. P 1982, Q & LTR, Innerwick Hoard.

Group VI

Groat (Edinburgh, Aberdeen, Stops: annulet, saltire, cross. Nos. 772–88)

Edinburgh

772/A	43.5	2.82	120	B.639(39) same dies, same dies as 773/A, same obv. die as 774/A. Hird.
773/A	43.6	2.83	220	As 772/A. Browne Willis.
774/A	42.6	2.76	270	B.638(34) but crowns in second and fourth quarters, and different stops outer legend, and same obv. die as B.639(39), same obv. die as 772/A and 773/A. Hird.
775/A	46.4	3.01	340	B.641(41) same dies. Hird.
776/H	38.1	2.47	0	B.641(41) but different stops outer legend. D 1944, Professor Bryce, found Ballynaughton, Islay.
777/H	46.2	2.99	290	B.641(41) obv. / B.641(42) rev. but different stops. Hunter.
778/A	41.5	2.69	130	B.641(42). P 1982, Stewart.
779/A	47.5	3.08	40	B.642(46) same dies, same dies as 780/A and 781/A. Browne Willis.
780/A	43.6	2.83	230	As 779/A. Radcliffe.
781/A	43.3	2.81	290	As 779/A. P 1982, Stewart.
782/A	45.5	2.95	310	B.643(48), same dies as 783/A. P 1982, Stewart.
783/A	46.7	3.03	310	As 782/A. P 1982, Stewart.

PLATE 39

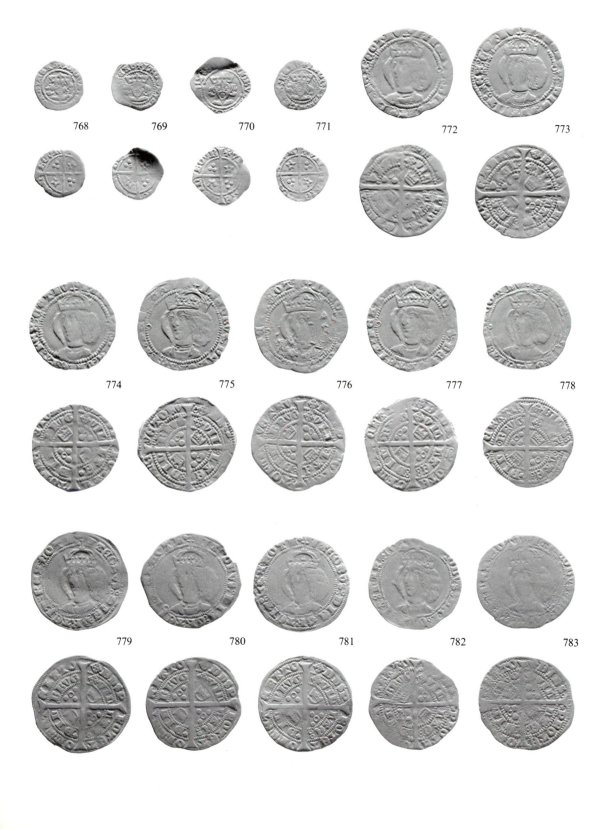

768   769   770   771   772   773

774   775   776   777   778

779   780   781   782   783

	Weight		*Die*	
	gr	gm	*axis*	
784/A	47.7	3.09	270	B 643(48a) same obv. die, same dies as 785/H. P 1982, Stewart.
785/H	45.4	2.94	340	As 784/A. Hunter.
786/A	41.9	2.72	0	B.644(52). P 1982, Stewart.

Aberdeen

| 787/A | 38.1 | 2.47 | 0 | B.646(55) same dies, same dies as 788/H. P 1982, Stewart, Dakers 421 (part). |
| 788/H | 42.8 | 2.77 | 180 | As 787/A. Hunter. |

Half Groat (Edinburgh. Nos. 789–90)

| 789/A | 19.9 | 1.29 | 130 | B.648(9a) same dies. P 1960, Lockett 868 (part), Bearman, Pollexfen 291 (part). |
| 790/A | 20.8 | 1.35 | 160 | B.649(13) but single annulet before RO₡T, Lockett 254 (this coin but *recte* Burns no. 13). D 1957, Executors of R. C. Lockett, Dakers 417 (part). |

BILLON

Plack (Edinburgh. Stops: saltire, cross. No. 791)

| 791/A | 31.8 | 2.06 | 180 | B.571(1) but rev. reads VIL·LⱯ·Dₑ ₑDIN·BVRGh. D 1982, Stewart. |

Half Plack (Edinburgh. No. 792)

| 792/A | 15.9 | 1.03 | 100 | B.573(1a) but single saltire after RₑX and also in ₑDIN·B ·VRGh. D 1982, Stewart. |

Penny (Edinburgh. Stops: none, saltire, cross, annulet. See Stewart 1958–9, Glenluce. Nos. 793–803)

793/A	5.8	0.38	270	Stewart Ai with rev. initial mark crown—see Murray and Stewart 1970, p. 171 but 1980 Leith Hoard, Holmes 1983, shows these not to be mules. P 1957, Lockett 257, Drabble (1943) 1195 (part) (where sold as James II).
794/A	6.3	0.41	220	Stewart Aii, Glenluce 29 (this coin). D 1962, Q & LTR, Glenluce Hoard.
795/A	7.5	0.49	260	Stewart Aii, cf. Glenluce 28. D 1957, Executors of R. C. Lockett, Lockett 278 (part).
796/A	9.2	0.60	140	Stewart Aiii. Ashmolean.
797/A	6.0	0.39	270	Stewart Cii, Glenluce 45 (this coin). D 1962, Q & LTR, Glenluce Hoard.
798/A	7.8	0.51	60	Stewart Cii, Glenluce 57 (this coin). D 1962, Q & LTR, Glenluce Hoard.
799/A	7.4	0.48	230	Stewart Cvb, cf. Glenluce 72, rev. reads VILLA·ₑ DINB VRG. P 1960, Lockett 871 (part).
800/A	6.6	0.43	30	Stewart Cvb, Glenluce 79 (this coin). D 1962, Q & LTR, Glenluce Hoard.
801/A	5.1	0.33	90	Stewart C. P 1982, Stewart.
802/A	5.7	0.37	260	Stewart C. P 1982, Stewart.
803/H	8.7	0.56	—	Stewart C. D 1971, Miss S. Christian, found in sandhills at Sanna, Ardnamurchan, Argyll.

PLATE 40

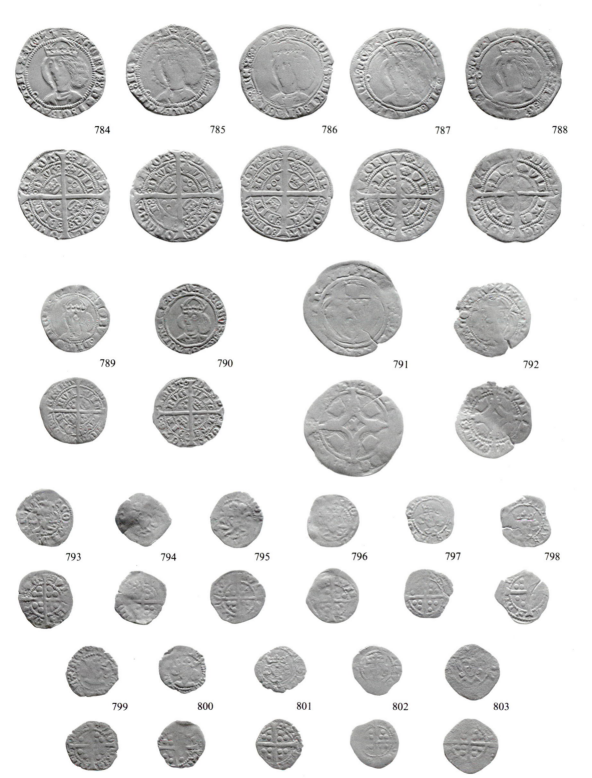

784   785   786   787   788

789   790   791   792

793   794   795   796   797   798

799   800   801   802   803

COPPER

Farthing (Edinburgh. Stops: none, saltire. No. 804)

	Weight		Die	
	gr	gm	axis	
804/A	2.6	0.17	—	Stewart 1967 *black farthing* first issue (p. 144 & fig. 113), Glenluce 112 (this coin). D 1982, Stewart, Glenluce Hoard.

Farthing (Moneta pauperum. No. 805)

805/A	4.9	0.32	—	Stewart 1967, 'ecclesiastical issues' type III (p. 141 & fig. 101). P 1982, Stewart.

Penny (Crux pellit omne crimen. Stops: saltire, annulet, star. See Stewart 1967, groups I–III, p. 141, Figs. 95–9. Nos. 807–14)

806/H	25.4	1.65	270	Stewart Ia (fig. 95), saltire stops. Neilson.
807/H	28.4	1.84	0	As 806/H. Neilson.
808/H	22.3	1.45	40	As 806/H. Neilson.
809/H	17.7	1.15	150	Stewart IIa (fig. 97), stops: none/annulet, pellet on cusps, annulets in spandrels. Neilson.
810/H	10.2	0.66	330	Stewart IIa (fig. 97), stops: ?/annulet, pellet on cusps. Neilson.
811/H	31.8	2.06	290	Stewart IIa (fig. 97), stops: annulet/annulet, annulet on all four cusps. Neilson.
812/H	19.3	1.25	270	Stewart IIa (fig. 97), stops: ?/annulet. Neilson.
813/A	22.4	1.45	140	Stewart III (fig. 99), stops: saltire/annulet. D 1961, J. K. L. Hartley.
814/A	24.8	1.61	340	As 813/A. P 1960.

JAMES IV (1488–1513)

GOLD

Unicorn (Stops: star, v-shape. See Murray 1971, 70. Nos. 815–29)

First Division (three lis on crown on unicorn)

815/A	58.1	3.77	260	B.632(10) same obv. die, same dies as 816/A; Murray Y(Ib)/X(Ia)—mule James IV obv./James III rev. Hird.
816/A	57.8	3.75	280	As 815/A. Hird.
817/A	57.4	3.72	320	B.627(3) same obv. die; Murray Y(Ib). Hird, Newcomer.
818/A	54.9	3.56	160	B.659(1) but weak initial marks and v-shaped stops irregularly aligned and reads SCOTO and +EXVRGAT·DS·ET·DISIPENT·INIMIA; Murray Q(Id). Hird, Duke of Atholl.
819/A	56.9	3.69	70	B.659(1) same dies, same dies as 820/A and 821/H; Murray Q(Id). Hird.
820/A	46.6	3.02	10	As 819/A. Christ Church.
821/H	56.8	3.68	340	As 819/A; Murray Q(Id), *op. cit.*, p. 70 and pl. V, 19 (this coin). Hunter.

PLATE 41

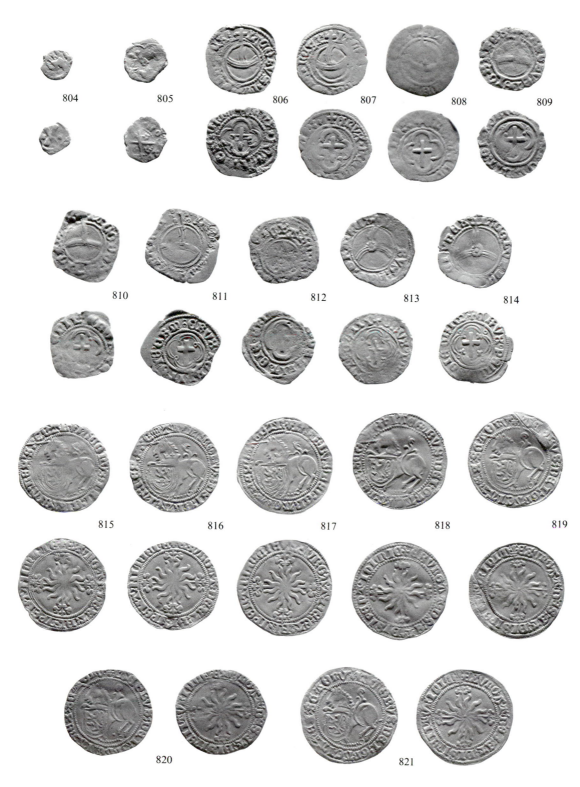

804   805   806   807   808   809

810   811   812   813   814

815   816   817   818   819

820   821

	Weight		*Die*	
	gr	gm	axis	
822/A	56.9	3.69	70	B.628(6) but reads SCOTORV and EXVRGAT·DES·ET·DISIPENT·INIMICI·E, same dies as Lockett 225; Murray Z(Ie). Hird.
823/A	58.1	3.77	110	B.628(6), Richardson 1901 fig. 81 same dies; Murray Z(Ie). Hird, Cree.

Second Division (five lis on crown on unicorn)

824/H	58.5	3.79	0	B.679(4) but stops differ slightly. Hunter.
825/A	58.6	3.80	230	B.679(5) but reads DEVS·DISSIPENT·INIMICI·EIVS, same obv. die. Hird, Earl of Haddington, Murdoch 153.
826/A	57.4	3.72	60	B.680A(6a) but *recte* add numeral to end of obv. legend, same obv. die. Hird.
827/A	57.4	3.72	10	B.687(7a) same obv. die. Hird, Cochran-Patrick 44, Wigan.
828/A	59.4	3.85	180	B.699(11) same dies. Hird, Bute 166.
829/H	58.2	3.77	310	B.699(11) but stops differ slightly. Hunter.

Half Unicorn (Nos. 830–7)

830/H	30.1	1.95	40	B.635(5); Murray y(Ib). Hunter.
831/A	28.7	1.86	220	B.663(4) same dies; Murray p(Ic). Hird, Walters 605.
832/A	28.7	1.86	80	B.660(1) same obv. die, same obv. die as 833/A and 834/A; Murray q(Id). Hird, Duke of Atholl.
833/A	27.2	1.76	180	B.660(1) same dies, same obv. die as 832/A and 834/A; Murray q(Id). Hird.
834/A	27.2	1.76	0	B.661(3) same dies, same obv. die as 832/A and 833/A; Murray q(Id). Hird.
835/A	28.7	1.86	200	B.633(1) same dies, same rev. die as 836/A; Murray z(Ie). Hird, Newcomer.
836/A	28.7	1.86	190	B.633(3) same rev. die, same rev. die as 835/A; Murray z(Ie). Hird, Duke of Atholl.
837/A	27.1	1.76	20	B.— no obv. initial marks and SCOTOR, rev. reads EXVRGAT·DS·ET·DISIPENT·INIMICI; Murray z(Ie). Hird.

PLATE 42

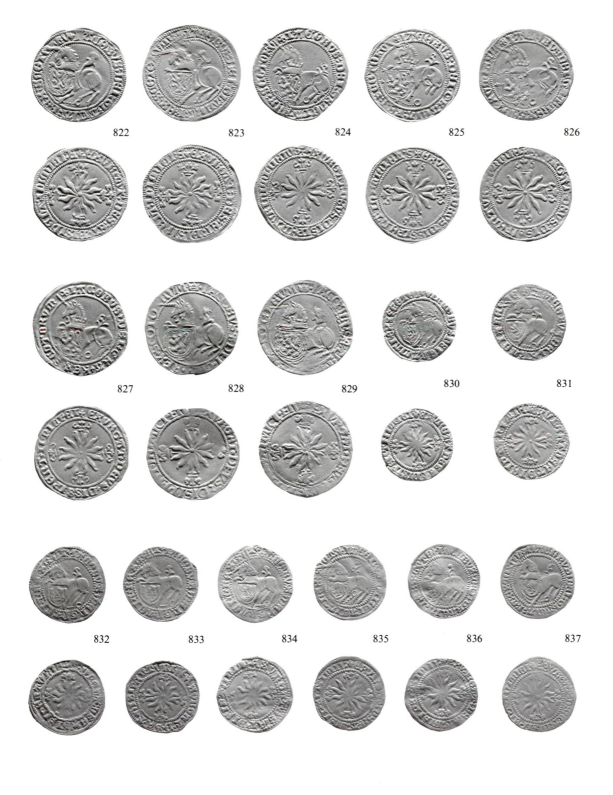

822   823   824   825   826

827   828   829   830   831

832   833   834   835   836   837

	Weight		Die
	gr	gm	axis

Lion (Stops: star. No. 838)

838/A 52.3 3.39 30   B.673(1) but no stop after IIII, same rev. die. Hird, Duke of Atholl.

Half Lion (Stops: star. No. 839)

839/A 25.9 1.68 210   B.672A(Ia) same dies. Hird, British Museum Duplicates, Barré Roberts, Samuel Tyssen.

SILVER

From the reign of James IV the mint may be presumed to be Edinburgh unless otherwise noted.

Groat (Murray 1971, 78. Nos. 840–51)

Heavy Coinage

I. (Murray B; crown and pellets on rev.; stops: annulet)

840/A 43.6 2.83 350   B.— 13 arc tressure and +IᴧꞒOBVS·DΘI·GRᴧꞒIᴧS·RΘX·ꞒOT / pellets with annulets in first and third quarters, no lis in centre of cross, reads +DNS·P ROTORᴍ ΘVᴍΘT ᴍΘVOR· and +VIL LᴧΘ DIN BRVG; Stewart fig. 123 (this coin). Hird, Mackenzie, Drabble (1943) 1196.

II. (Murray C; pellets, crown, and lis on rev.; stops: star)

841/A 41.0 2.66 350   B.623(28) but lis in first quarter and no stop after DIN, same obv. die (*recte* ꞒOT·) same dies as 842/H. P 1982, Stewart, Marr, R. Carlyon-Britton.
842/H 44.2 2.86 330   As 841/A. Hunter.
843/A 42.6 2.76 260   B.625(30) same dies. Browne Willis.

Light Coinage

III. (Murray ibid. p. 96; pellets and mullets on rev.; stops: v-shape, star)

844/A 35.8 2.32 160   B.657A(3a) same rev. die. P 1981.
845/H 36.9 2.39   40   B.658(5). Hunter.
846/A 38.4 2.49 300   B.665(8) but reads ·DΘIGRᴧRΘX·, Lockett 874 same dies, same dies as 847/A. Hird.
847/A 33.5 2.17 130   As 846/A. Douce.
       (chipped)
848/H 35.9 2.33 180   B.666(10) but ·SᴧLVV· FᴧꞒ·PP LVVᴍ·T VV·DNΘ. Hunter.
849/A 33.3 2.16 170   B.666(11) but stops differ. Browne Willis.
850/A 31.4 2.04 350   B.675(15) but stop at end of outer legend, same obv. die. Browne Willis.
851/H 36.8 2.38   60   B.675A(15a) but *recte* open ᴧ in GRᴧ, but no stop end of inner legend. Hunter.

PLATE 43

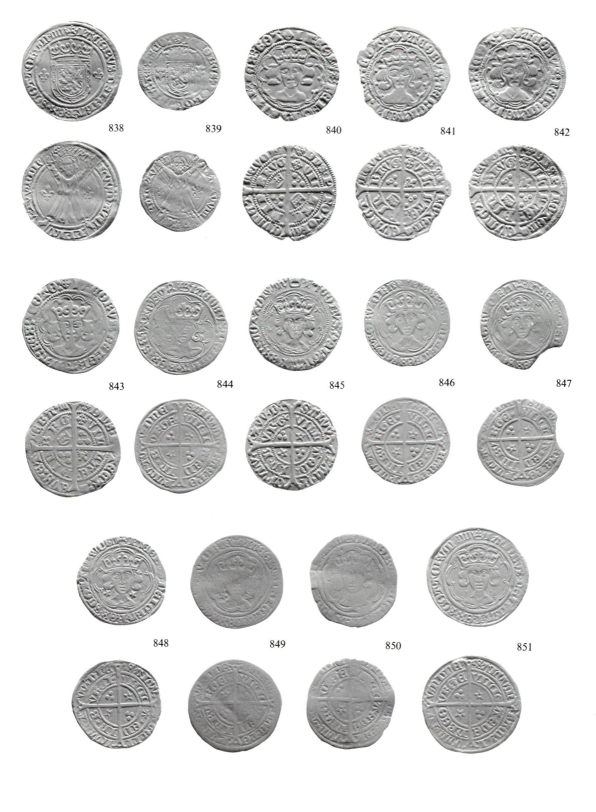

838   839   840   841   842

843   844   845   846   847

848   849   850   851

BILLON

Plack (Stops: trefoil, pellet, lis, star, fork. Nos. 852–61)

	Weight		Die	
	gr	gm	axis	
852/H	25.6	1.66	30	B.682A(4c) same dies. Hunter.
853/H	29.9	1.94	240	B.690(10), but obv. i.m. crown. Unknown, Edzell Hoard.
854/A	35.9	2.33	350	B.693(16) but no stops visible rev. D 1957, Executors of R. C. Lockett, Lockett 278 (part).
855/A	34.8	2.26	50	B.693 but details of legend unclear (star stop visible GRᴧCIᴧ·RℰX). Bodleian.
856/H	31.8	2.06	290	B.697(24) but *recte* Roman N rev. Neilson.
857/A	23.3	1.51	350	B.700 but reads IᴧⵦOBVS·4Dℰl·GRᴧ·RℰX·SⵦOTORVM. D 1957, Executors of R. C. Lockett, Lockett 278 (part).
858/H	32.8	2.13	180	B.700(27a) but stops differ slightly. Hunter.
859/H	30.2	1.96	0	B.700(28). Hunter.
860/A	26.8	1.74	300	B.700C(29a). D. F. Pierrepont Barnard.
861/H	23.3	1.51	0	B.700C(29a). Unknown.

Half Plack (stops: pellet, lis. No. 862)

862/H	12.4	0.80	320	B.691(1) but crowns at side of shield and ✠VIL [LAℰ D]IN BVRG. Hunter.

Penny (Nos. 863–81)

First Issue (cross and pellets, mint name. Stops: annulet, saltire. See Murray 1971, 90)

863/A	8.8	0.57	140	B.598(13) annulets in second and fourth quarters; Murray E/Stewart Ia (mule James III obv./James IV rev.). P 1960, Lockett 877 (part).
864/A	7.8	0.51	170	B. — annulets by neck; Stewart Ia/Murray E (mule James IV obv./James III rev.); points between pellets on rev. as Glenluce 96. D 1957, Executors of R. C. Lockett, Lockett 278 (part).
865/A	6.0	0.39	150	B. — annulets by neck; Stewart Ib; Glenluce 90 (this coin). D 1962, Q & LTR, Glenluce Hoard.
866/A	8.6	0.56	230	B. — annulets by neck; Stewart Ib. Ashmolean.
867/A	9.4	0.61	180	B.595(7) but reads ✠IᴧⵦOBVS·Dlℰ·GRᴧ·RℰX and ✠VI·Lᴧℰ·[DIⵝ]·BVR; Stewart IIa. D 1957, Executors of R. C. Lockett, Lockett 278 (part).

PLATE 44

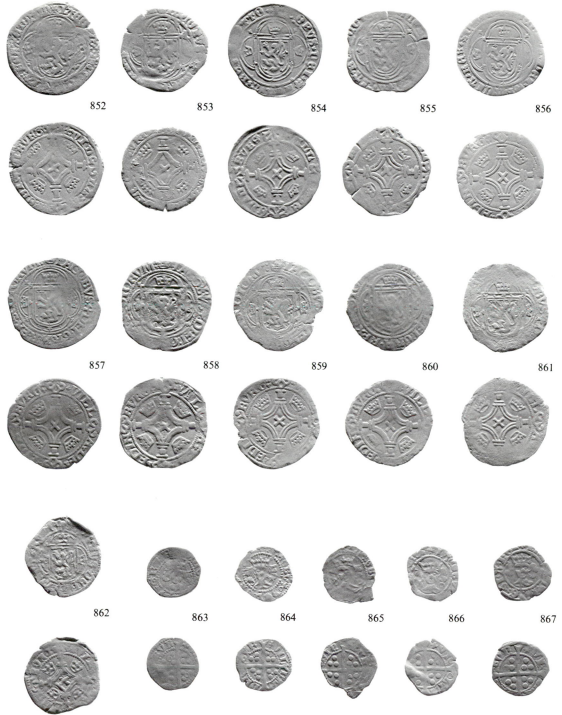

852   853   854   855   856

857   858   859   860   861

862   863   864   865   866   867

	Weight		*Die*	
	gr	gm	axis	
868/A	6.9	0.45	140	B.595(7), legends not legible; Stewart IIa; Glenluce 107 (this coin). D 1962, Q & LTR, Glenluce Hoard.
869/A	8.3	0.54	280	B.595(7) but reads [ ]OBVS·DЄI[ ]RΛRЄX and +VI LΛЄ DIⱤ BVR and stops uncertain; Stewart IIb. Ashmolean.

Second Issue (crowns and lis in alternate quarters, (I) Salvum fac populum tuum domine or (II–IV) mint name. Stops: star, pellet, saltire, trefoil, none)

870/A	10.9	0.71	310	B.678C(6f)? this coin same dies, Stewart II. P 1960, Lockett 877 (part)
871/A	11.7	0.76	250	B.678A(6c) but not all obv. stops clear; Stewart II. P 1960, Lockett 877 (part).
872/A	9.5	0.62	240	B.678(5) but reads [ ]L LΛЄD IⱤBV, same obv. die; Stewart II. P 1960, Lockett 877 (part).
873/A	13.7	0.89	0	B.682D(6h); Stewart III. P 1960, Lockett 877 (part).
874/A	11.7	0.76	10	B.682D(6g) but *recte* rev. initial mark pellet and reads RGGT; Stewart III. P. 1960, Lockett 877 (part).
875/A	10.8	0.70	180	B.684A(13a); Stewart IVc. P 1960, Lockett 877 (part).
876/A	8.6	0.56	30	B.685(14); Stewart IVd. P 1960, Lockett 877 (part).
877/H	5.9	0.38	90	As 876/A. Neilson.
878/H	8.1	0.52	170	B.685(17) but reads SCO; Stewart IVd. Neilson.
879/A	12.0	0.78	210	B.685(20a); Stewart IVd. P 1960, Lockett 877 (part).
880/A	12.0	0.78	120	B.685(20); Stewart IVd. P 1960, Lockett 877 (part).
881/A	11.7	0.76	180	B.686A(23a) this coin same dies (? contemporary forgery). Lockett 877 (part).

Mrs Murray suggests that it seems likely that 870, 871, 873–5, 879, and 881 are the Pollexfen coins mentioned by Burns.

JAMES V (1513–42)

GOLD

First Coinage (1518–26)

Unicorns (Stops: trefoil, pellet. Nos. 882–8)

I. with cinquefoil countermark rev.

882/A	58.8	3.81	140	B.726(1) same dies, same obv. die as 883/A; Mrs Murray notes probably James V/James IV mule. Hird, Duke of Atholl.

Ia. with countermark and mullet in centre of rev.

883/A	58.0	3.76	100	B.726(1) obv. only, same obv. die, same obv. die as 882/A /B— rev., unknown to Burns (ii, p. 241), reads EXVRGΛT·DЄVS·ET·DISIPENT·NIMICI·E, Cochran-Patrick 1875, pl. III, 6 (this coin). Hird, Cochran-Patrick (his ticket marked 'Bought at a sale in London. May, 1873. 12.0.0').

II. without countermark, mullet in centre of rev.

884/A	58.6	3.80	300	B.730(3) but *recte* no stop after DISIPENT same dies (without countermark or mullet). Hird, Bute 172.
885/A	59.1	3.83	310	B.732(4) same dies. Hird.
886/A	58.8	3.81	270	B.729(2b) but without lines between rays of star and reads EXVRGΛT·DE·ET·DISIPENT·NIMICI·EI, same obv. die. Hird, Cochran-Patrick 49, Advocates 191.
887/A	58.5	3.79	280	B.733(5) but *recte* figured as B.727, same obv. die / B.727(2) but *recte* not figured, same obv. die as 888/H. Hird, Wills 178.
888/H	59.8	3.87	50	B.733(5) but *recte* figured as B.727/B.734(6) but stops differ slightly. Same obv. die as B.727 and 887/A. Hunter.

PLATE 45

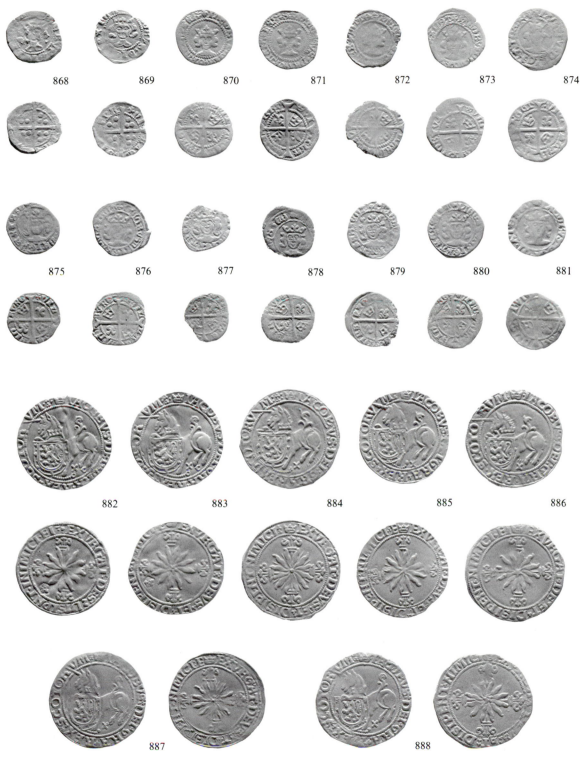

868   869   870   871   872   873   874

875   876   877   878   879   880   881

882   883   884   885   886

887   888

JAMES V (*cont.*)

Half Unicorn (As unicorns II. Nos. 889–90)

	Weight		Die	
	gr	gm	axis	
889/A	28.2	1.83	120	B.735(1) but *recte* reversed S on obv. and F for E on rev., same dies and same dies as 890/H; Cochran-Patrick 1875, pl. III, 5 (this coin); Stewart 1967, p. 201 suggests possibly James IV. Hird, Cochran-Patrick 51, Advocates 193.
890/H	29.2	1.89	150	As 889/A. Hunter.

Second Coinage (1526–38)

Crowns (I. Per lignum crucis salvi sumus. II–IV. Crucis arma sequamur. Nos. 891–900)

I. (large closed crown, shield with pointed base, annulet stops)

891/A	52.4	3.40	240	B.749(12) same dies. Hird, Cochran-Patrick, Advocates.

II. (smaller open crown, shield with pointed base, annulet stops)

892/A	52.4	3.40	120	B.747(10) same dies; this is a group II/III mule. Hird, Bute 175.

III. (smaller open crown, shield with rounded base, trefoil stops)

893/A	51.5	3.34	60	B.743(5) but SCOTOR V' and rev. stops vary. Hird, Cochran-Patrick 52.
894/H	52.5	3.40	100	B.743(6) but single pellet after DEI. Hunter.
895/A	52.7	3.42	100	B.745(8) but with seven pellets in crown. Hird.
896/A	53.1	3.44	300	B.743(6) same rev. die. Hird, Cree.
897/A	52.3	3.39	150	B.743(6), 745(8) with corded band to diamonded crown, five pellets at end of each arm of cross fleury and ·ᴀRM· Hird.
898/A	52.6	3.41	30	B.739(2) same obv. die / B.742(4a) same rev. die, same rev. die as 899/A; this is a group III/IV mule. Hird, Newcomer.

IV. (as III but colon stops)

899/A	53.2	3.45	140	B.742(4a) same dies, same rev. die 898/A. Hird, Brand.

V. (very small crown, shield with rounded base, colon stops)

900/A	52.1	3.38	0	B.— ; Stewart fig. 302 (this coin). Hird.

Third Coinage (1538–42)

Ducat (or 'Bonnet piece': Honor regis judicium diligit. Stops: pellet. Nos. 901–5)

901/A	87.3	5.66	140	1539. B.751(1) same dies, same dies as 902/A, same rev. die as 904/A. Hird, Advocates.
902/A	86.8	5.63	240	1539. B.752(2) same dies as 901/A, same rev. die 904/A. Hird.
903/H	87.5	5.67	110	1539. B.752(2). Hunter.

PLATE 46

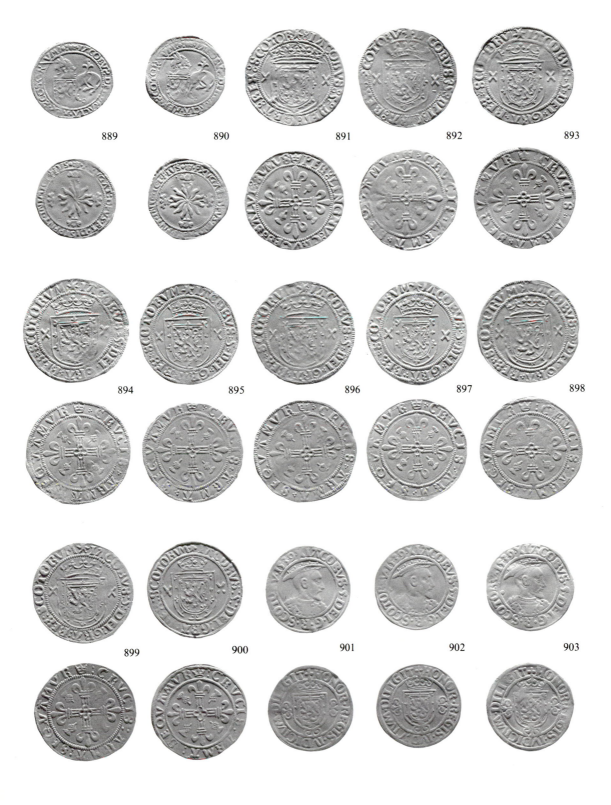

889 890 891 892 893

894 895 896 897 898

899 900 901 902 903

	Weight		*Die*	
	gr	gm	axis	
904/A	87.0	5.64	330	1540. B.753(3) same dies, same rev. die as 901/A and 902/A. Hird, Browne 492.
905/H	88.3	5.72	90	1540. B.754(4). Hunter.

Two Thirds Ducat (Nos. 906–7)

| 906/A | 57.7 | 3.74 | 300 | 1540. B.755(1) but *recte* obv. initial mark lis; same dies. Christ Church. |
| 907/H | 58.5 | 3.79 | 110 | 1540. As 906/A. Hunter. |

One Third Ducat (Nos. 908–9)

| 908/A | 28.2 | 1.83 | 80 | 1540. B.756(1). Hird, Wormser, Rees, Gaunt, Murdoch (1903) 185, Hastings 601, Cuff 2033. |
| 909/H | 28.7 | 1.86 | 80 | 1540. B.756(1) same dies. Hunter. |

SILVER

Second Coinage (1526–38)

Groat (Nos. 910–38)

I. (closed mantle, double-arched crown, pointed shield, annulet stops)

910/A	38.0	2.46	0	B.725(24). Hird, Walters 652 (part)?
911/H	33.8	2.19	130	B.725(24) same rev. die. Hunter.
912/H	34.1	2.21	180	B.725(24). Neilson, Unknown Hoard.

II. (closed mantle, single arched crown, pointed shield, annulet stops)

| 913/A | 41.3 | 2.68 | 40 | B.720(19) but annulet over R of SCOTOR. Bodleian. |
| 914/H | 38.8 | 2.51 | 220 | B.720(19). Hunter. |

III. (open mantle, single arched crown, rounded shield, trefoil stops)

915/H	42.9	2.78	180	B.706(1) but obv. stops reversed. P 1964 Q & LTR, Rigghead Hoard.
916/H	32.9	2.13	240	As 915/H. Neilson, Unknown Hoard.
	(broken			
	fragment)			
917/H	34.7	2.25	140	B.706(2). Neilson, Unknown Hoard.
	(edge			
	incomplete)			
918/H	40.1	2.60	30	B.706(3). Neilson, Unknown Hoard.

PLATE 47

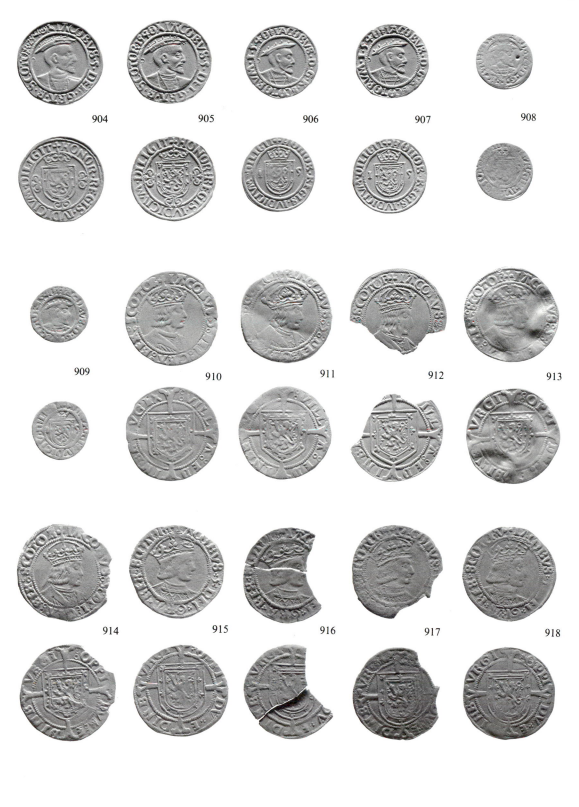

904   905   906   907   908

909   910   911   912   913

914   915   916   917   918

	Weight		*Die*	
	gr	gm	axis	
919/H	37.1	2.40	90	B.706(3). Neilson, Unknown Hoard.
	(edge			
	incomplete)			
920/H	16.2	1.05	0	B.706 variety uncertain. Neilson, Unknown Hoard.
	(fragment)			
921/H	27.8	1.80	0	B.706 variety uncertain. Neilson, Unknown Hoard.
	(fragment)			
922/A	41.8	2.71	350	B.707(4) but O**R**V. Hird.
923/H	31.1	2.53	180	B.707(4). Neilson, Unknown Hoard.
	(broken			
	fragment)			
924/H	39.4	2.55	130	B.707(5). Hunter.
925/H	40.9	2.65	315	B.707(5). Neilson, Unknown Hoard.
926/H	33.9	2.20	310	B.707 variety uncertain. Neilson, Unknown Hoard.
	(edge			
	incomplete,			
	broken)			
927/A	41.6	2.70	210	B.712(8) but : behind head. Hird.
928/H	41.8	2.71	60	B.712(8). P 1964 Q & LTR, Rigghead Hoard.
929/H	41.7	2.70	310	B.712(8). P 1964 Q & LTR, Rigghead Hoard.
930/H	42.8	2.77	150	B.712(9). P 1964 Q & LTR, Rigghead Hoard.
931/H	35.7	2.31	0	B.713(10). Neilson, Unknown Hoard.
	(fragment)			
932/A	40.1	2.60	0	B.714(12) Browne Willis.
933/A	41.5	2.69	70	B.716(14). Hird.

PLATE 48

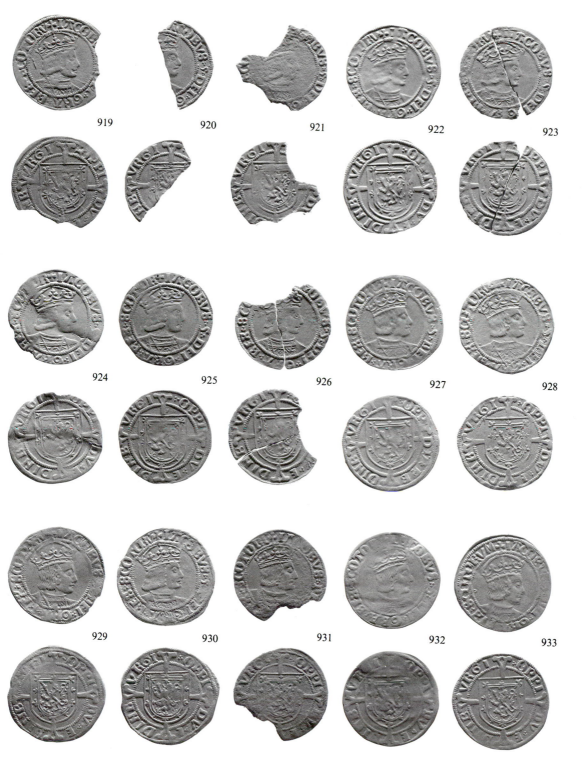

919   920   921   922   923

924   925   926   927   928

929   930   931   932   933

	Weight		Die	
	gr	*gm*	*axis*	
934/A	41.0	2.66	80	B.716(14) Bodleian.
935/H	41.5	2.69	130	B.717(15) but does not show chain. Hunter.
	(buckled)			
936/H	31.2	2.02	0	B.717(15). Neilson, Unknown Hoard.
	(edge			
	incomplete)			
937/A	41.2	2.67	150	B.718(16a) but nine pellets in crown. Bodleian.

IV. (as III but lis either side of the central cross in the crown and colon or trefoil stops)

938/A	39.2	2.54	80	B.709(7) but R**V**. D 1968 Stewart, Thorburn.

One Third Groat (Nos. 939–43)

IV. (as III but crown of five lis and colon stops)

939/A	13.5	0.88	270	B.710(1) but possibly I**A**COR**V**S. Bodleian.
940/H	12.8	0.83	90	B.710(1) but no pellet in **V** or **OPPIDV**. Neilson, Unknown Hoard.
941/A	12.8	0.83	330	B.711(3) but I**A**COBVS. Merton College.
942/A	11.2	0.73	10	B.711(4) but **A** in I**A**COBVS. Browne Willis.
	(chipped)			
943/H	14.1	0.91	220	B.711(4) but **SOTORV**. Hunter.

BILLON

First Coinage (1513–26)

Plack (Stops: star, trefoil, pellet. Nos. 944–50)

944/H	37.1	2.40	30	B.— /B.760(4), see Burns, ii, p. 255, Mules I—old English lettering on obv. as specimen from Creggan Hoard noted (James IV/James V mule). P 1964 Q & LTR, Linlithgow Hoard.
945/A	28.7	1.86	160	B.759(2a)—James IV/James V mule. D 1957, Executors of R. C. Lockett, Lockett 278 (part).
946/A	26.8	1.74	160	B.762(8) but stops uncertain. Hird.
947/H	24.6	1.59	300	B.767(12d) but single pellet after **REX**. Hunter.
948/A	32.4	2.10	190	B.768(13a). Browne Willis.

PLATE 49

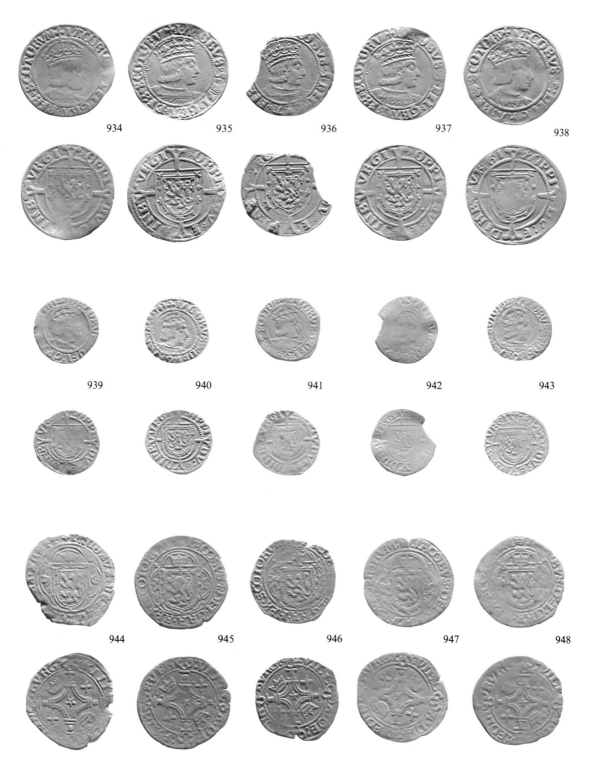

934   935   936   937   938

939   940   941   942   943

944   945   946   947   948

	Weight		*Die*	
	gr	*gm*	*axis*	
949/A	25.7	1.67	60	B.768(13). Christ Church.
950/A	31.6	2.05	200	B.760(4) but stops differ. Bodleian.

Third Coinage (1538–42)

Bawbee (Stops: pellet except trefoil as noted. Nos. 951–73)

I. without annulet, closed crown with pellets on points and trefoil after **OPPIDUM** (Stewart 2a)

| 951/H | 25.9 | 1.68 | 0 | B.775(4) but pellet after **OPPIDUM** as noted by Burns. P 1964 Q & LTR, Rigghead Hoard. |
| 952/H | 27.8 | 1.80 | 220 | As 951/H. P 1964 Q & LTR, Rigghead Hoard. |

II. without annulet, closed crown without pellets and trefoil after **OPPIDUM** (Stewart 2b)

953/H	25.5	1.65	270	B.776(5). P 1964 Q & LTR, Rigghead Hoard.
954/H	29.8	1.93	20	B.776(5). P 1964 Q & LTR, Rigghead Hoard.
955/H	18.4	1.19	310	B.776(5). P 1964 Q & LTR, Rigghead Hoard.
	(pierced)			
956/H	11.1	0.72	270	B.776(5). Neilson.
	(fragment)			
957/A	17.6	1.14	0	B.776(5). Bodleian, marked '?Willis d. at death'.
	(chipped)			
958/A	25.1	1.63	350	B.776(5). Bodleian.

III. with annulet over initial, closed crown with pellets (Stewart 1a)

959/A	27.1	1.76	300	B.772(1). Christ Church.
960/H	30.3	1.96	0	B.772(1). Hunter.
961/H	32.3	2.09	230	B.772(1). Hunter.
962/H	27.8	1.80	70	B.772(1) but no pellets on crown. P 1964 Q & LTR, Rigghead Hoard.
963/H	30.3	1.96	90	As 962/H. P 1964 Q & LTR, Rigghead Hoard.
964/H	27.8	1.80	40	B.772(1). P 1964 Q & LTR, Rigghead Hoard.
965/H	25.9	1.68	60	B.772(1). P 1964 Q & LTR, Rigghead Hoard.
966/H	30.6	1.98	300	B.772(1). P 1964 Q & LTR, Rigghead Hoard.
967/H	30.1	1.95	90	B.772(1) but annulet unclear. P 1964 Q & LTR, Rigghead Hoard.
968/H	28.7	1.86	130	B.772(1) with large annulet. P 1964 Q & LTR, Rigghead Hoard.

IV. with annulet to left of crown which is closed and without pellets (Stewart 1b)

| 969/A | 25.4 | 1.65 | 140 | B.774(3) with striated cross. Bodleian. |
| 970/H | 30.4 | 1.97 | 0 | B.774(3) but annulet unclear. P 1964 Q & LTR, Rigghead Hoard. |

PLATE 50

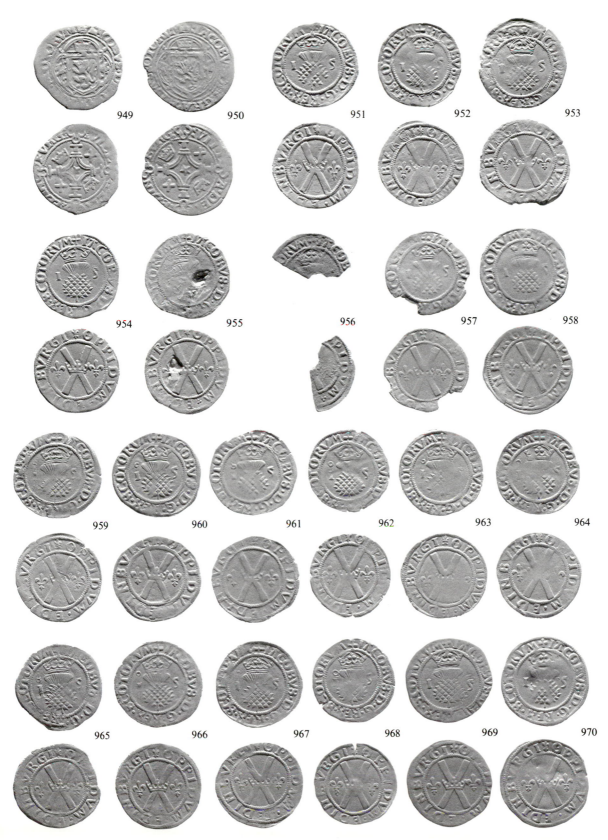

949 950 951 952 953

954 955 956 957 958

959 960 961 962 963 964

965 966 967 968 969 970

	Weight		Die	
	gr	gm	axis	
971/H	28.1	1.82	180	B.774(3). P 1964 Q & LTR, Rigghead Hoard.

V. with annulet to left of crown which is open and with pellets (Stewart 1c).

972/H	26.7	1.73	190	B.773(2). P 1964 Q & LTR, Rigghead Hoard.
973/A	23.3	1.51	70	B.772–6 but group uncertain; ?forgery; see 1031/A and 1072/A from same source. P 1940, 'said to have been found in Yorkshire'.

Half Bawbee (Stops: pellet. Nos. 974–5)

974/A	13.1	0.85	350	B.777(1) annulet over initial but double-struck and reads RR·SCO (Stewart 1a). Bodleian.
975/H	14.9	0.97	100	B.779(2a) annulet over numeral (Stewart 1b). P 1964 Q & LTR, Rigghead Hoard.

MARY (1542-67)

Stops: pellet unless otherwise noted.

Period 1. Pre-Marriage 1542–58 (title: **MARIA DEI GRATIA REGINA SCOTORUM**)

GOLD

Crown (Crucis arma sequamur. Nos. 976–7)

	Weight		Die	
	gm	gr	axis	
976/A	52.1	3.38	140	B.808(3) same dies. Hird, Cochran-Patrick 58, Wigan.
977/H	52.8	3.42	90	B.808(3). Hunter.

Twenty Shilling Piece 1543 (Ecce ancilla Domini. See Murray 1979. No. 978)

978/H	44.8	2.90	120	B.809(1); Murray no. 2 (this coin). Hunter.

Forty-Four Shilling Piece (Diligite justiciam 1553. Murray 1968. Nos. 979–84)

979/H	78.1	5.06	180	B. — but specimen noted Bii, p. 287; Murray Ib(C5) (this coin noted). Hunter.
980/A	79.9	5.18	210	B.813(4) same dies, same rev. die as 981/A; Murray IIa (E6) (this coin noted). Hird.
981/A	79.1	5.13	240	1555. B.813(5), same rev. die as 980/A; Murray IIa (F6). Hird, Thellusson 164.
982/H	79.3	5.14	60	B.813(6); Murray IIa(F7). Hunter.
983/H	78.3	5.07	90	B.812(3) but no stop after **SCOTORVM**; Murray IIb (G8) (this coin noted). Hunter.
984/H	78.9	5.11	220	B.813(4) but no stop before **DILIGITE**; Murray IIb (I8) (this coin noted). Hunter.

PLATE 51

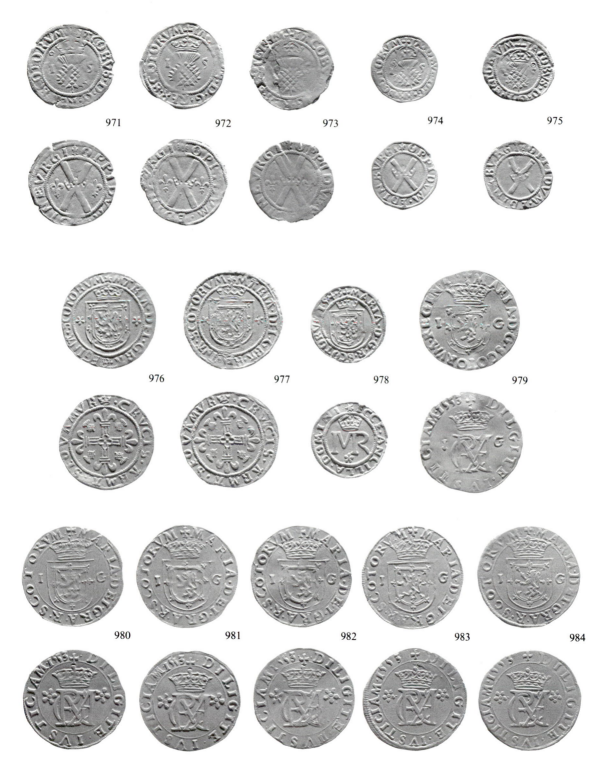

971   972   973   974   975

976   977   978   979

980   981   982   983   984

MARY (*cont.*)

Twenty-two Shilling Piece (Nos. 985-9)

	Weight		Die	
	gr	gm	axis	
985/A	39.2	2.54	80	B.817(4) but no inner circle on obv.; Murray A(3)2(1) (this coin noted). Hird, Brand.
986/H	39.5	2.56	330	B.817(4); Murray A(3)2(1) (this coin noted). Hunter.
987/A	37.6	2.44	320	B.814(1) but **MARIA** / B.814(2) same rev. die; Murray B(1c)3(2) (this coin noted). Hird, Newcomer, Pollexfen 342.
988/A	39.5	2.56	0	B.814(1) but **MARIA** and with stops on obv.; Murray B(2b)3(1) (this coin noted). Hird, Brand, Murdoch 208.
989/A	39.0	2.53	30	B.818(6) but **MARIADEIGRSCOTORV** and no stop before date; Cochran-Patrick 1875, 162, pl. III, 7 (this coin); Murray D(2)4(2). Hird, Cochran-Patrick 63, Wigan.

Three Pound Piece (Justus fide vivit 1555 [-57, -58]. See J. K. R. Murray 1979. Nos. 990-5)

990/A	117.9	7.64	30	1555. B.819(1) but *recte* obv. figured as 820; Murray 1A and pl. 24A (this coin). Knight, Barrett.
991/H	117.0	7.58	240	1555. B.819(1) but *recte* obv. figured as 820 but no wedges above crown and stop before and after rev. legend; Murray 5E and pl. 25, 7 (this coin). Hunter.
992/A	117.9	7.64	40	1555. B.819(3); Murray 7D and pl. 24, D (this coin). Hird, Cochran-Patrick 64, Wigan.
993/A	115.9	7.51	240	1555. B.819(1) but *recte* obv. figured as 820; Murray 13E and pl. 24, E (this coin). Hird, Browne 494.
994/A	117.6	7.62	200	1557. B.821(5) but *recte* without initial cross; Murray 14G. Hird, Huth 656, Murdoch 214.
995/H	114.9	7.45	110	1558. B.822(6); Murray 18I and pl. 24, I (this coin). Hunter.

Thirty Shilling Piece (See J. K. R. Murray 1979. Nos. 996-9)

996/A	58.0	3.76	60	1555. B.822-2(8); Murray 1A (this coin noted). Knight, Barrett.
997/H	58.8	3.81	90	1555. B.822-2(8); Murray 1A (this coin noted). Hunter.
998/A	54.0	3.50	340	1555. B.822-2(8); Murray 1B (this coin noted); ?forgery by Jons. Hird.
999/A	56.6	3.67	40	1557. B.—; Murray 4c and pl. 24,C and 4 (this coin). Hird, Bute 187.

PLATE 52

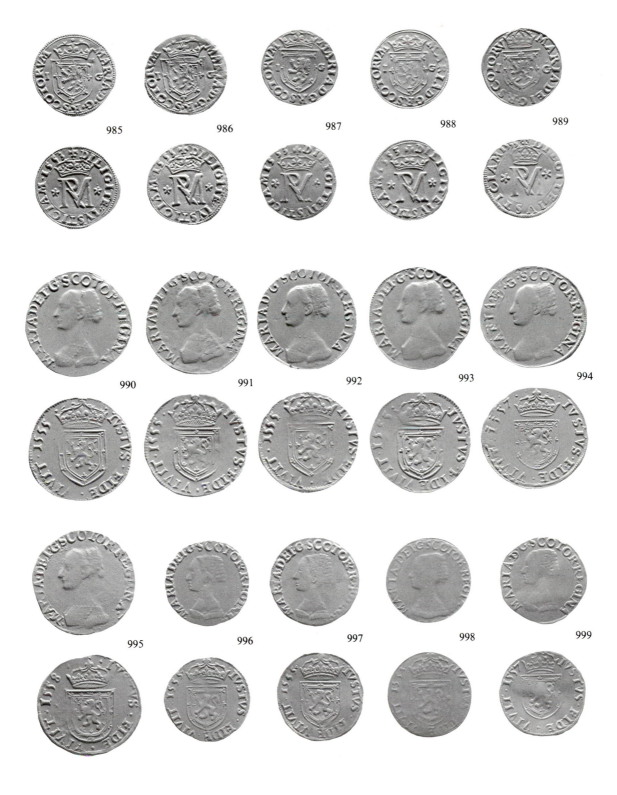

985   986   987   988   989

990   991   992   993   994

995   996   997   998   999

SILVER

Testoons (as Stewart 1967 groups below)

Group I. 1553 (Da pacem domine 1553. See Murray 1968 and especially 1981, 397 for a full list of known specimens. Nos 1000–2)

	Weight		Die	
	gr	gm	axis	
1000/H	77.5	5.02	230	B.780(1); Murray (1968) E4 (this coin noted) and (1981) no. 12 (this coin). Hunter.
1001/H	73.9	4.79	30	B.780(1); Murray (1968) E4 (this coin noted) and (1981) no. 13 (this coin). Hunter.
1002/A	72.3	4.69	190	B.780(1) but stop before **DA**; Murray (1968) E5 (this coin noted) and (1981) no. 20 (this coin). Browne Willis.

Group II. 1555 (Dilici domini cor humile. Nos. 1003–4)

1003/H	117.3	7.60	60	B.782(3) but no stop after date, reads **HVMILIE** and no trefoil before **COR**. Hunter.
1004/A	112.2	7.27	320	B.785(5) but with countermark. Somerville College.

Group III. 1556–8 (In virtute tua libera me. Nos. 1005–18)

1005/H	95.1	6.16	240	1556. B.786(7) but stops on obv. Hunter.
1006/A	93.2	6.04	260	1556. B.788(11) but no inner circles and with countermark. Ashmolean.
1007/H	94.2	6.10	310	1556. B.788(11) but no stop after dates. Hunter.
1008/H	95.1	6.16	40	1556. B.791(15) but **VIRTVTE**. Hunter.
1009/H	90.5	5.86	250	1556/7 mule. B.791(16) but 1556 and no stops on obv., also with countermark. Hunter.
1010/A	89.6	5.81	230	1557. B.791(16). Christ Church.
1011/H	92.9	6.02	280	1557. B.791(16) but stop at end of obv. legend and no stop after **LIBERA**. Hunter.
1012/H	87.8 (pierced)	5.69	160	1557. B.791(16). D 1942, W. F. Thomson.
1013/A	92.7	6.01	140	1557. B.793(18) but annulet below **M** and **R** and stops both sides. Browne Willis.

PLATE 53

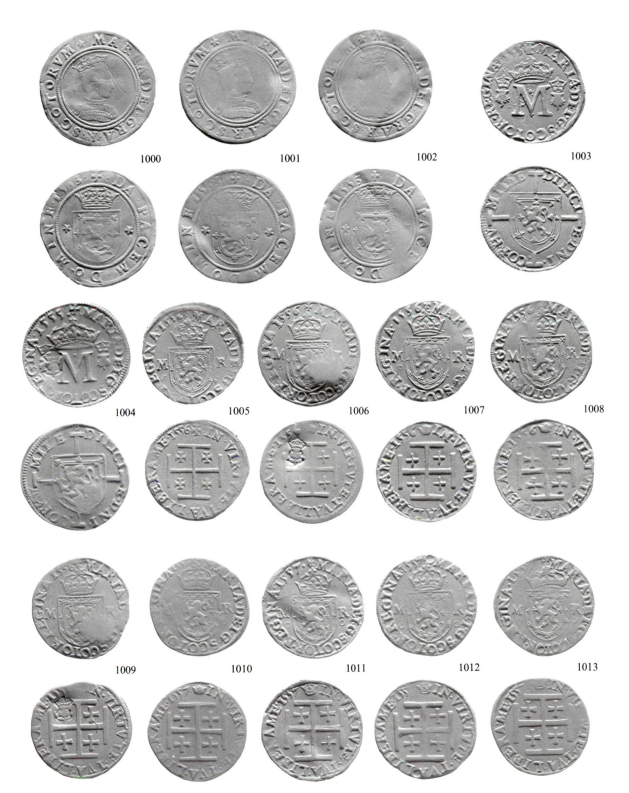

1000   1001   1002   1003

1004   1005   1006   1007   1008

1009   1010   1011   1012   1013

MARY (*cont.*)

	Weight		*Die*	
	gr	*gm*	*axis*	
1014/H	94.8	6.14	310	1557/8 mule. B.794(19) but no stop after **ME**. Hunter.
1015/H	84.4	5.47	250	1558. B.795(20) but *recte* stop after obv. date, but with countermark. Hunter.
1016/H	89.9	5.83	310	1558. B.797(22) but *recte* stop after obv. date, but **VIRTVTE**. Hunter.
1017/H	95.6	6.19	90	1558. B.798(24) but stops differ. Hunter.
1018/H	94.5	6.12	0	1558. B.798(25) but no stops after dates. Hunter.

Half Testoon (as testoons groups II and III. Nos. 1019–20)

1019/H	59.1	3.83	180	group II 1555. B.784(1) but no stops obv. and R not contracted, stop and trefoil after **DNI**. Hunter.
1020/H	48.0	3.11	330	group III 1558. B.—/B.806(15) but stop after date. Hunter.

BILLON

Bawbee (Edinburgh, Stirling. Nos. 1021–58)

Edinburgh

Class I

1021/H	24.4	1.58	330	B.823(1). P 1964 Q & LTR, Rigghead Hoard.
1022/H	30.9	2.00	160	B.823(1) but pellet in **V** of **SCOTORV**. P 1964 Q & LTR, Rigghead Hoard.
1023/H	28.6	1.85	220	B.823(1). P 1964 Q & LTR, Rigghead Hoard.
1024/H	30.7	1.99	120	As 1022/H. P 1964 Q & LTR, Rigghead Hoard.
1025/H	31.7	2.05	200	B.824(3) but **SCOTORVM**. P 1964 Q & LTR, Rigghead Hoard.
1026/H	30.1	1.95	100	B.825(4). P 1964 Q & LTR, Rigghead Hoard.
1027/H	28.6	1.85	30	B.825(4) but pellet in **V** of **SCOTORV**. P 1964 Q & LTR, Rigghead Hoard.
1028/A	27.4	1.78	60	B.825(7). Browne Willis.

PLATE 54

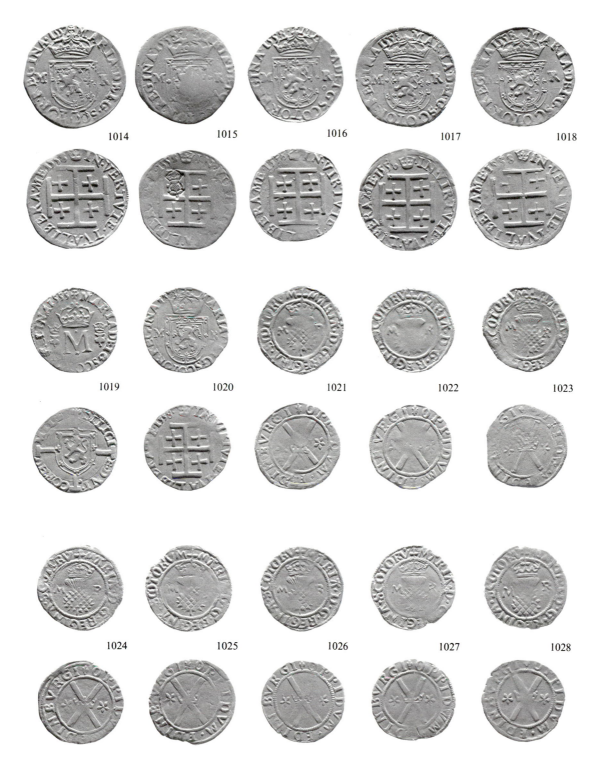

1014   1015   1016   1017   1018

1019   1020   1021   1022   1023

1024   1025   1026   1027   1028

	Weight		Die	
	gr	*gm*	*axis*	
1029/H	30.9	2.00	10	B.825(7) but pellet in **V** of **SCOTORV**. P 1964 Q & LTR, Rigghead Hoard.
1030/H	27.8	1.80	30	B.827(1). P 1964 Q & LTR, Rigghead Hoard.

Class II

1031/A	27.4	1.78	170	B.829(13) as text not plate, same obv. die as 1032/A. P 1940, 'said to have been found in Yorkshire' (cf. 973/A and 1072/A from same provenance).
1032/A	31.9	2.07	30	B.829(13) but fluted cross, same obv. die as 1031/A. Bodleian, marked '?Willis d. at death'.
1033/A	22.8	1.48	320	B.829(14) same obv. die. D 1923, found on Aberdeen golflinks.
	(pierced)			
1034/H	30.7	1.99	200	B.829(14). P 1964 Q & LTR, Rigghead Hoard.
1035/H	33.4	2.16	130	B.831(17). P 1964 Q & LTR, Rigghead Hoard.

Class III

1036/H	32.9	2.13	320	B.834(22). P 1964 Q & LTR, Rigghead Hoard.
1037/H	24.7	1.60	270	B.834(23) but no stop after **EDINBURGI**. P 1964 Q & LTR, Rigghead Hoard.
1038/H	34.6	2.24	350	B.835(26). Hunter.

Class IV

1039/H	31.4	2.03	110	B.837(29) but stops before **OPPIDVM**. Hunter.
1040/H	31.8	2.06	50	B.837(31). Hunter.
1041/H	30.4	1.97	130	B.837(31). P 1964 Q & LTR, Rigghead Hoard.

Class V

1042/H	26.6	1.72	150	B.839(34). P 1964 Q & LTR, Rigghead Hoard.
1043/H	29.7	1.92	60	B.839(34) but arch uncertain, a pellet above. P 1964 Q & LTR, Rigghead Hoard.

Class VI

1044/H	20.6	1.33	230	B.847(46) but fluting incomplete. Hunter.
1045/H	31.4	2.03	0	B.848(52) but stop before **MARIA** and after **EDINBURGI**. Hunter.
1046/A	28.1	1.82	270	B.850(55). P 1982.
1047/A	18.3	1.19	250	B.850(57). Browne Willis.
1048/H	25.3	1.64	200	B.851(58) but stop after **EDINBURGI**. P 1964 Q & LTR, Rigghead Hoard.
1049/H	18.2	1.18	220	B.851(58). D J. R. Lockie.
1050/H	24.3	1.57	0	B.852(61). Hunter.
1051/H	26.3	1.70	150	B. ? uncertain. D 1936, Miss Buchanan.

Class VII

1052/A	27.4	1.78	180	B.856(65). Keble College.

PLATE 55

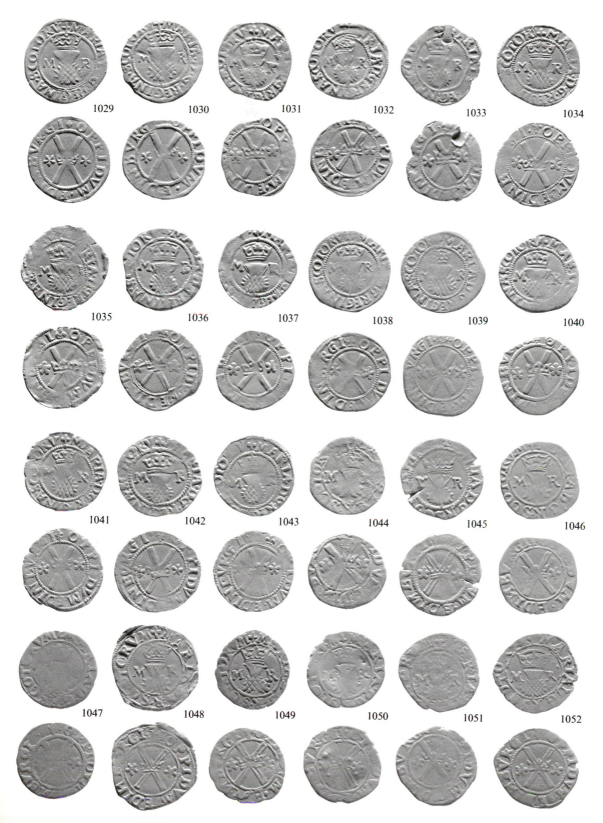

1029   1030   1031   1032   1033   1034

1035   1036   1037   1038   1039   1040

1041   1042   1043   1044   1045   1046

1047   1048   1049   1050   1051   1052

	Weight		Die	
	gr	*gm*	*axis*	
1053/A	29.4	1.91	160	B.856(66/68). Keble College.

Stirling

Class I

1054/A	27.9	1.81	0	B.860(76) but crown too near inner circle to show arch. Christ Church.
1055/H	27.2	1.76	210	B.860(76) but pellet in **V** of **SCOTORV**. P 1964 Q & LTR, Rigghead Hoard.
1056/A	27.3	1.77	280	B.861(77). Browne Willis.
1057/H	28.3	1.83	80	B.861(77) but pellet in **V** of **SCOTORV**. Hunter.
1058/H	24.1	1.56	180	B.861(77). P 1964 Q & LTR, Rigghead Hoard.

Half Bawbee (as bawbee—Edinburgh only. Nos. 1059–64)

Class I (plain cross)

1059/A	12.3	0.80	290	B.862(1). Somerville College.

Class II (fluted cross)

1060/A	18.0	1.17	0	B.863(3). Christ Church.
1061/A	14.9	0.97	330	B.863(3). Bodleian.
1062/H	13.9	0.90	310	B.863(3). Hunter.
1063/H	15.3	0.99	270	B.863(3). Hunter.
1064/H	14.4	0.93	40	B.863(3). Hunter.

Penny (Nos. 1065–7)

type 1a.

1065/A	12.5	0.81	200	B.864(1). Bodleian.
1066/H	9.3	0.60	320	B.864(2). Hunter.

type 3.

1067/A	12.2	0.79	40	B.866(7). P 1980.

Lion or Hardhead (Vicit veritas 1555. Nos. 1068–9)

1068/A	15.7	1.02	80	B.868(4). P 1982.
1069/A	9.8	0.64	330	B.867(3). P 1982.

Penny (Vicit veritas 1556. No. 1070)

1070/A	8.8	0.57	30	B.869(2); P. 1957, Lockett 327b.

Plack (Servio et usu teror 1557. Nos. 1071–80)

1071/A	27.0	1.75	270	B.870(1) but pellet above obv. crown and small cross pattée in centre of rev. Bodleian.
1072/A	19.6	1.27	0	B.870(1–2 uncertain) but no pellet above obv. crown and large cross pattée in centre of rev. and with countermark. P 1940, 'said to have been found in Yorkshire' (cf. 973/A and 1031/A from same provenance).
1073/H	27.5	1.78	90	B.870(1) but stop after obv. date. Hunter.
1074/H	27.0	1.75	210	B.870(1) but no stops. Hunter.
1075/H	22.1	1.43	120	B.870(1) but no stops and with countermark. Hunter.
1076/A	26.8	1.74	220	B.870(2). P 1982.

PLATE 56

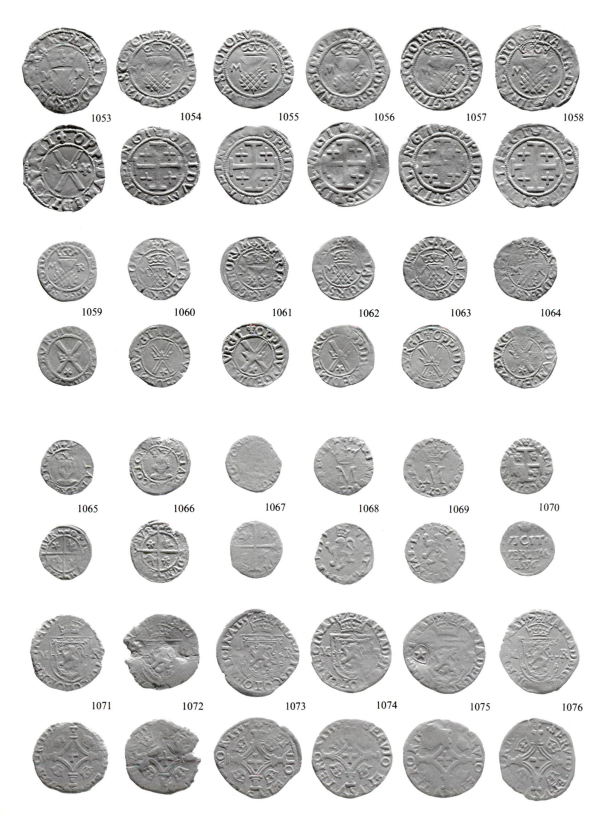

1053   1054   1055   1056   1057   1058

1059   1060   1061   1062   1063   1064

1065   1066   1067   1068   1069   1070

1071   1072   1073   1074   1075   1076

	Weight	*Die*	
	gr	*gm*	*axis*
1077/H	28.7	1.86	200	B.870(2) but with countermark. Unknown, Edzell Hoard.
1078/A	27.1	1.76	330	B.871(5). P 1982.
1079/H	32.2	2.09	210	B.871(5). Hunter.
1080/H	30.3	1.96	200	B.871(5). Hunter.

Lion or Hardhead (as before but 1558. Nos. 1081–3)

1081/H	13.7	0.89	150	B.875(7) with countermark. Neilson.
1082/A	11.1	0.72	270	As 1081/H. P 1980, Sheriff Mackenzie lot 311 (part).
1083/A	13.4	0.87	180	As 1081/H. Somerville College.

Period 2. Marriage to Francis 1558–60 (title: A—FRANCIS ET MARIA DEI GRATIA REX REGINA SCOTORUM DELPHINVS DELPHINA VIEN; B—FRANCIS ET MARIA DEI GRATIA REX REGINA FRANCORUM SCOTORUMQUE)

SILVER

Testoon

Group I. (Fecit utraque unum, 1558–9. Nos. 1084–7)

1084/H	94.3	6.11	180	B.877(1) but **DEI** and stop before **FECIT**. Hunter.
1085/H	91.4	5.92	180	B.878(2) but stop before **FECIT** and none after 1558. Hunter.
1086/H	87.2	5.65	270	B.879(6) but **DEI** and stop before and after rev. legend. Hunter.
1087/H	92.5	5.99	180	As 1087/H. Hunter.

Group II. (Vicit leo de tribu Juda 1560–1. See Murray 1967, 95. Nos. 1088–94)

1088/A	93.3	6.05	150	B.881(8) but no stop before rev. legend or after obv. legend; 1st type. Ashmolean.
1089/H	91.5	5.93	90	B.881(9) with countermark; 1st type. Hunter.
1090/H	95.1	6.16	340	B.882(11) but stop after date; 1st type. Hunter.
1091/H	92.5	5.99	50	B.883(12) but obv. i.m. plain cross, one stop before **FRAN** read **SCO·TO·R·Q·** and **LEO·DE·**; Murray intermediate variety 3, fig. 4 (this coin). Hunter.

PLATE 57

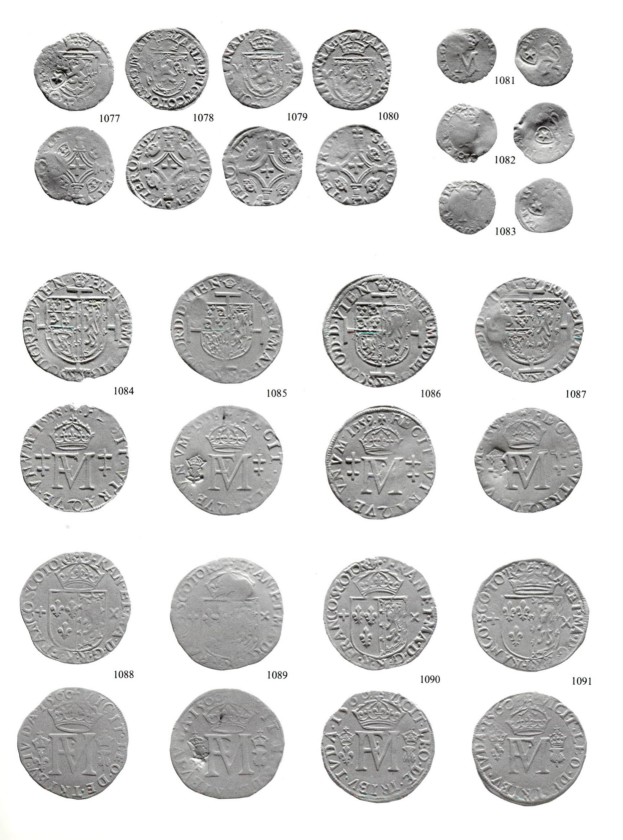

1077   1078   1079   1080

1081

1082

1083

1084   1085   1086   1087

1088   1089   1090   1091

	Weight		*Die*
	gr	gm	axis
1092/A	89.8	5.82	260	B.884(13) but stop after date and countermark; 2nd type. Browne Willis.
1093/A	90.7	5.88	90	B.884(14) but stop after Ω; 2nd type. Knight.
1094/H	92.8	6.01	270	B.884(14) but no stop before and after Ω; 2nd type. D 1936, Miss Buchanan.

Half Testoon (Nos. 1095–1100)

1095/A	45.3	2.94	240	B.880A(2a) but stops after **VIEN**. Browne Willis.
1096/H	46.0	2.98	130	B.880A(2a) but **SCOTO**; Group I. Hunter.
1097/H	45.1	2.92	120	B.886(3) but no stop start obv. legend, stop end of rev. legend and with countermark; group II, 1st type. Hunter.
1098/A	43.6	2.83	60	B.886(4); group II, 1st type. Browne Willis.
1099/A	41.2	2.67	130	As 1098/A. Christ Church.
1100/H	48.6	3.15	310	B.888(6); group II, 2nd type. Hunter.

BILLON

Nonsunt (Iam non sunt duo sed una caro, 1558–9. Nos. 1101–8)

1101/H	24.1	1.56	270	1558. B.889(1) but no stops end of obv. legend and after **NON, SED**, and **VNA**. Hunter.
1102/H	27.7	1.79	290	1559. B.890(4) but on rev. stops only: **·CARO·· 1559**. Hunter.
1103/H	23.3	1.51	40	1559. B.890(4). Hunter.
1104/A	21.3	1.38	100	1559. B.890(5). Christ Church.
1105/H	25.9	1.68	340	1559. B.890(5) but appear no stops obv. and before and after **CARO** and date on rev. Hunter.

PLATE 58

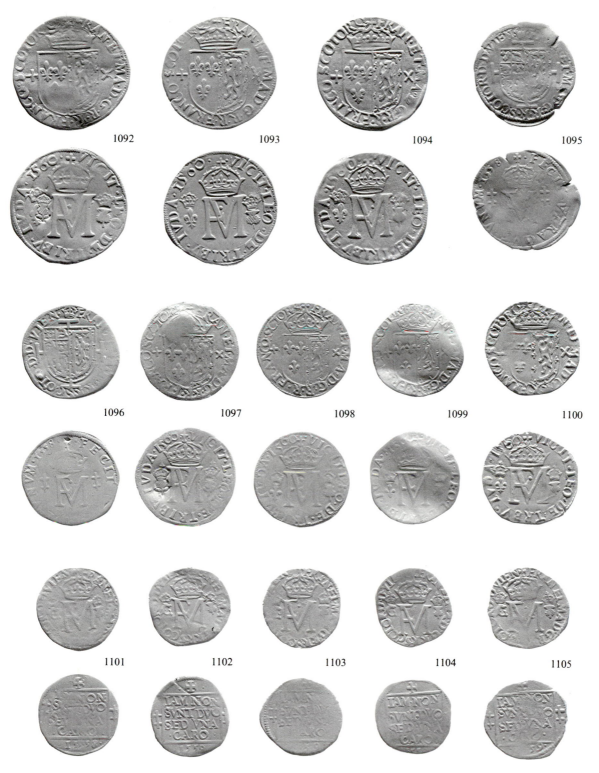

1092   1093   1094   1095

1096   1097   1098   1099   1100

1101   1102   1103   1104   1105

MARY (*cont.*)

	Weight		Die	
	gr	*gm*	*axis*	
1106/A	30.5	1.98	70	1559. B.891(8). Knight.
1107/A	23.6	1.53	280	1559. B.891(8). Bodleian.
1108/H	28.1	1.82	110	1559. B.891(8). Hunter.

Lion or Hardhead (1558–60. Nos. 1109–10)

1109/H	12.9	0.84	0	B.894–5 uncertain date, dolphins left. Hunter.
1110/H	11.1	0.72	270	As 1109/H. Unknown, Edzell Hoard.

Period 3. First Widowhood 1560–5 (title: **MARIA DEI GRATIA REGINA SCOTORUM**)

SILVER

Testoon (Salvum Fac populum tuum domine. Nos. 1111–16)

1111/H	93.7	6.07	300	1561. B.897(2) but seems five pellets on fillet. Hunter.
1112/H	90.2	5.84	300	1561. B.897(3) with countermark. Hunter.
1113/A	93.9	6.09	260	1562. B.899(4). Christ Church.
1114/A	87.3	5.66	80	1562. B.899(4) but with countermark. Bodleian.
1115/A	86.1	5.58	50	1562. B.900(5) with countermark. Bodleian.
1116/H	88.8	5.75	40	1562. B.900(5) with countermark. Hunter.
	(chipped)			

Half Testoon (Nos. 1117–18)

1117/H	40.6	2.63	210	1561. B.901(1) but stop after **DOMINE** and with countermark. Hunter.
1118/H	47.4	3.07	330	1561. B.902(2) but plain cross above crown. Hunter.

PLATE 59

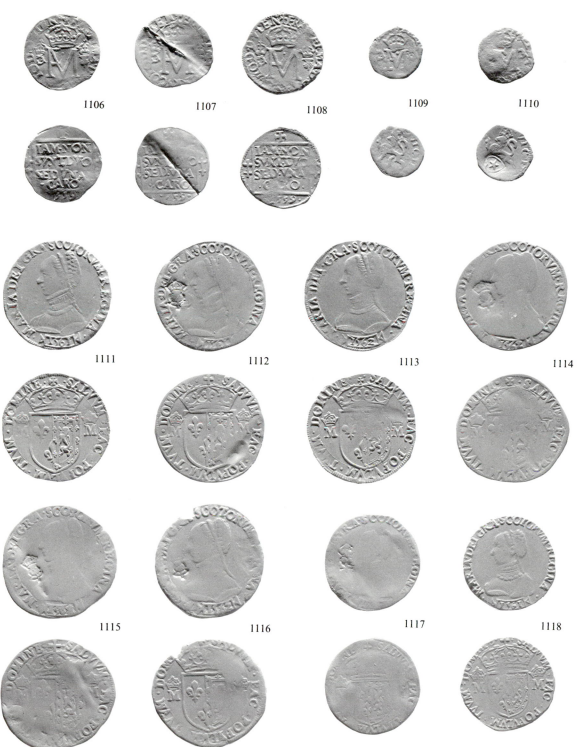

1106

1107

1108

1109

1110

1111

1112

1113

1114

1115

1116

1117

1118

MARY (*cont.*)

Period 4, Marriage to Lord Darnley 1565-7 (title: **MARIA ET HENRICUS REGINA ET REX SCOTORUM**)

SILVER

Ryal (Exurgat Deus et dissipentur inimici eius and Dat gloria vires, 1565-7. Nos. 1119-25)

	Weight		Die	
	gr	gm	axis	
1119/A	470.5	30.49	270	1565. B.904(1). Knight, Barrett.
1120/H	470.9	30.51	90	1565. B.904(1) but pellet in **V** of **SCOTORV** and under **R** of **DISSIPENTR**. Hunter.
1121/H	470.2	30.47	180	1565. B.904(2) with countermark. Hunter.
1122/H	470.6	30.49	90	1566. B.905(5) but no stop after **EXURGAT** and stops before and after FI9. Hunter.
1123/A	459.7	29.79	350	1566. B.905(6) with countermark but stop under 9 of EI9. Browne Willis.
1124/H	470.2	30.47	160	1566. B.905(6) with countermark but stop after EI9. Hunter.

PLATE 60

1119   1120   1121

1122   1123   1124

	Weight		*Die*
	gr	gm	axis

1125/H 464.8 30.12 0 1567. B.906(8) with countermark but stop before **MARIA**. Hunter.

Two Thirds Ryal (Nos. 1126–8)

1126/A 314.5 20.38 210 undated. B.—; Lockett lot 343 same rev. die; see Murray 1966, 94. P 1980.
1127/H 316.1 20.48 60 1565. B.907(9) but stop end of obv. legend. Hunter.
1128/A 304.1 19.71 80 1565. B.907(11) but with stop end of obv. legend and with countermark. Browne Willis.

One Third Ryal (Nos. 1129–30)

1129/A 150.9 9.78 70 1565. B.910(17). Knight.
1130/H 153.1 9.92 270 1565. B.910(17) but stop end of obv. legend. Hunter.

PLATE 61

1125

1126

1127

1128

1129

1130

MARY (*cont.*)

SILVER

Ryal (Nos. 1131–4)

	Weight		Die	
	gm	*gr*	*axis*	
1131/H	466.2	30.21	60	1567. B.912(1) but **MARIA** and **SCOTORUM**. Hunter.
1132/A	457.8	29.67	50	doublestruck 1567. B.912(2) with countermark. Christ Church.
1133/A	468.5	30.36	110	doublestruck 1567. B.912(2) but without countermark, same rev. die as 1134/A. D 1930, E. S. Bouchier.
1134/A	468.3	30.35	90	1567. As 1133/A. Browne Willis.

Two Thirds Ryal (Nos. 1135–6)

1135/H	315.2	20.42	120	1567. B.913(4). Hunter.
1136/H	304.0	19.70	90	1567. B.913(4) but with countermark. Hunter.

PLATE 62

1131 1132 1133

1134 1135 1136

MARY (*cont.*)

One Third Ryal (Nos. 1137–8)

	Weight		Die	
	gr	gm	axis	
1137/A	156.4	10.14	120	1567. B.915(7) but no stop at start of rev. legend, same obv. die. Browne Willis.
1138/H	151.3	9.80	0	1567. B.915(7) but without countermark. Hunter.

JAMES VI/I (1567–1625)

Before accession to English throne 1567–1603

GOLD

Twenty Pound Piece (In utrunque paratus 1575–6 and Parcere subiectis et debellare superbos. Nos. 1139–41)

1139/A	470.5	30.49	140	1575. B.947(–) but 1575. Hird, Gordon Cumming.
1140/H	470.4	30.48	150	1575. B.947(–) but 1575 and **GRA** and stop only before **&** on rev. Hunter.
1141/A	466.3	30.22	0	1576. B.947(1) but *recte* as plate, same dies. Hird, Earl of Haddington, Cochran-Patrick 66.

Ducat or Four Pound Piece (Exurgat Deus et dissipentur inimici eius 1580. Nos. 1142–43)

1142/H	93.7	6.07	240	1580. B.948(1) but **D·EI GRA**. Hunter.
1143/A	89.2	5.78	120	1580. B.948(2) but *recte* **DISSIIP**, same dies. Hird, Wormser, Sotheby May 1902 248.

Lion Noble (Post 5 & 100 proavos invicta manent haec and Deus judicium tuum regi da 1584–6, 1588. Nos. 1144–6)

1144/A	77.6	5.03	270	1584. B.949(1) but **HEC·**, same obv. die as 1145/A. Hird, Lingford 832.
1145/A	77.6	5.03	90	1585. B.949(–) but 1585 and **HEC·**, same obv. die as 1144/A. Hird, Bute 190.

PLATE 63

1137   1138

1139   1140   1141

1142   1143   1144   1145

	Weight		Die
	gr	gm	axis
1146/H	77.2	5.00	270	1585. B.949(–) but 1585 (this coin noted by Burns). Hunter.

Two Thirds Lion Noble (1584–5, 1587. No. 1147)

| 1147/H | 51.7 | 3.35 | 120 | 1585. B.950(1). Hunter. |

Thistle Nobles (Florent sceptra piis regna his Jova dat numeraque. Nos. 1148–52)

1148/A	117.4	7.61	110	B.951(1) same dies. Hird, Newcomer.
1149/A	118.0	7.65	340	B.951(1) but **NVMERATO·** and small cross-like quatrefoil initial marks. Hird, Thellusson 162 (part).
1150/A	116.2	7.53	100	B.951(2) but with bar on tail of Q composed of two dots, same obv. die as 1152/A. Hird.
1151/H	117.8	7.63	240	B.951(3). Hunter.
1152/A	117.8	7.63	100	B.951(4), same obv. die as 1150/A. Christ Church.

Hat Piece or Four Pound Piece (Te solum vereor 1591–3. All same obv. die. Nos. 1153–8)

| 1153/A | 67.9 | 4.40 | 220 | 1591. B.952(1) but stop after date. Hird, Cochran-Patrick 70, Wingate 314. |
| 1154/H | 69.0 | 4.47 | 160 | 1591. B.952(1). Hunter. |

PLATE 64

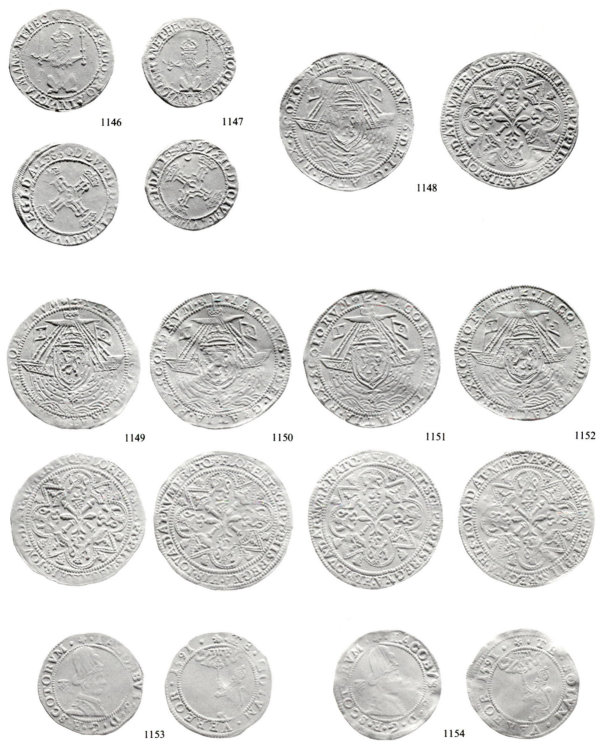

1146   1147

1148

1149   1150   1151   1152

1153   1154

	Weight		*Die*	
	gr	gm	axis	
1155/H	69.2	4.48	130	1592. B.952(2). Hunter.
1156/A	69.3	4.49	160	1592. B.952(3) same dies. Hird.
1157/A	68.0	4.41	110	1593. B.952(4). Christ Church.
1158/H	69.2	4.48	40	1593. B.952(4). Hunter.

Rider or Five Pound Piece (Spero meliora 1593–5, 1598–9, 1601. Nos. 1159–70)

1159/A	78.2	5.07	170	1593. B.953(1) same obv. die. Hird.
1160/A	78.2	5.07	60	1593. B.954(2) but stop before date. Hird, Duke of Atholl.
1161/A	77.1	5.00	130	1594. B.954(4) but stop before date. Hird.
1162/H	77.6	5.03	110	1594. As 1161/A. Hunter.
1163/A	78.1	5.06	50	1594. B.954(6), same obv. die as 1164/A. Hird.
1164/A	78.4	5.08	330	1594. As 1163/A. Christ Church.
1165/H	77.6	5.03	20	1595. B.954(7) but no stops by date. Hunter.
1166/A	77.6	5.03	280	1595. B.954(8) but without beading on cuisses and no stop by date. Hird, Dakers 463.
1167/A	78.5	5.09	250	1595. B.954(8) but no stops by date. Hird.
1168/A	77.0	4.99	250	1598. B.954(–) but 1598. Hird.
1169/A	76.0	4.93	250	1599. B.954(9). Hird, Bearman, Stobart.

PLATE 65

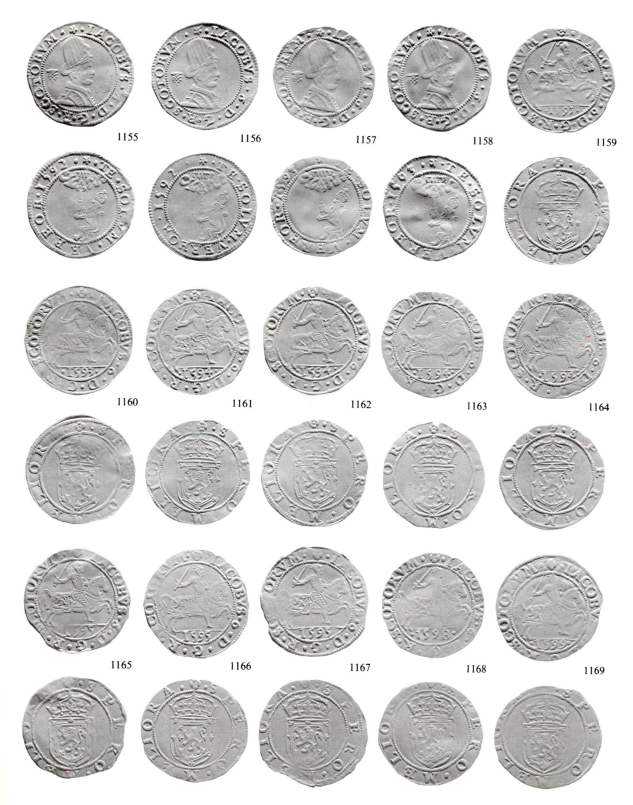

1155 1156 1157 1158 1159

1160 1161 1162 1163 1164

1165 1166 1167 1168 1169

	Weight		*Die*
	gr	gm	axis
1170/H	75.8	4.91	200	1599. B.954(9) but stop before date. Hunter.

Half Rider or Fifty Shilling Piece (Nos. 1171–80)

1171/A	38.4	2.49	200	1593. B.955(1) same dies as 1172/A. Hird, Lingford 848, Shand 254.
1172/A	38.2	2.48	40	1593. B.955(1) same dies as 1171/A. Hird, Drabble (1939) 226 (part).
	(pierced)			
1173/H	37.7	2.44	50	1593. B.955(1) but stop before date. Hunter.
1174/A	37.2	2.41	40	1594. B.955(2) same obv. die as 1175/A and 1176/A. Hird.
1175/A	38.4	2.49	30	1594. B.955(2) but no points on band of crown, same obv. die as 1174/A and 1176/A. Hird, Newcomer.
1176/A	38.6	2.50	60	1594. B.955(2) same obv. die as 1174/A and 1175/A. Christ Church.
1177/H	39.8	2.58	300	1594. B.955(2) but stop before date. Hunter.
1178/H	38.6	2.50	330	1595. B.955(–) but 1595 (this coin noted by Burns). Hunter.
1179/A	37.9	2.46	270	1599. B.955(4) but stop before date. Hird.
1180/H	38.6	2.50	190	1601. B.955(6). Hunter.

Sword and Sceptre or Six Pound Piece (1601–4. Nos. 1181–93)

1181/A	78.7	5.10	160	1601. B.956(1). Hird.
1182/H	77.3	5.01	300	1601. B.956(1). Hunter.
1183/A	76.0	4.93	270	1601. B.956(1) same rev. die, same rev. die as 1184/A. Corpus Christi College.
1184/A	75.4	4.89	10	1601. B.956(2)/(1) same rev. die, same rev. die as 1183/A. Christ Church.
1185/A	78.2	5.07	160	1602. B.956(4). Hird.

PLATE 66

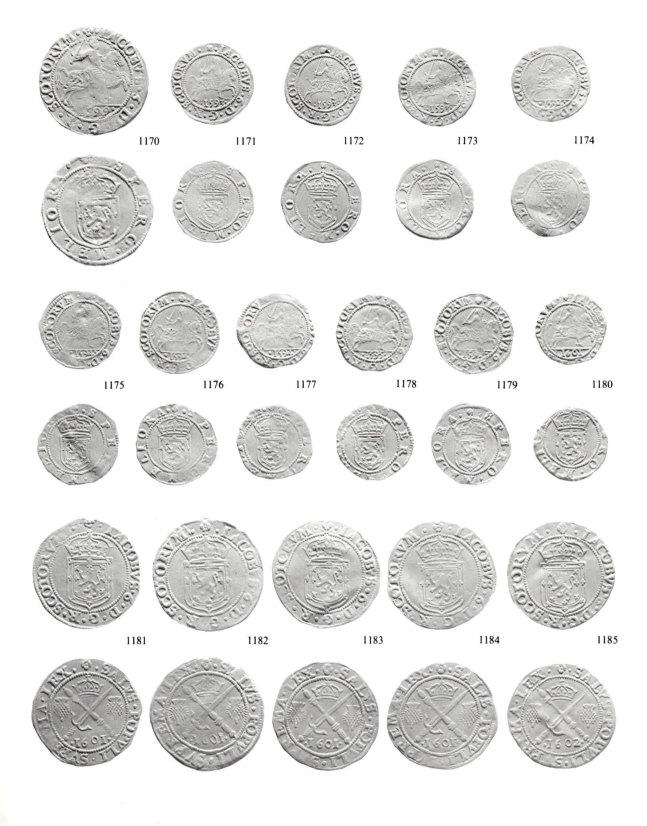

1170   1171   1172   1173   1174

1175   1176   1177   1178   1179   1180

1181   1182   1183   1184   1185

	Weight		*Die*	
	gr	gm	axis	
1186/A	77.9	5.05	150	1602. B.956(3) same rev. die as 1187/A. Hird.
1187/A	77.4	5.02	270	1602. B.956(3) same rev. die as 1186/A. Ashmolean, found on the site of Keble College 1868.
1188/A	74.2	4.81	310	1602. B.956(3). Knight.
1189/A	77.3	5.01	60	1602. B.956(4?). Christ Church.
1190/H	77.9	5.05	270	1602. B.956(4). Hunter.
1191/A	77.9	5.05	300	1603. B.956(5). Hird.
1192/H	76.1	4.93	300	1603. B.956(5). Hunter.
1193/A	78.1	5.06	120	1604. B.956(–) but 1604. Hird.

Half Sword and Sceptre or Three Pound Piece (Nos. 1194–1201)

1194/A	39.5	2.56	310	1601. B.957(1) same dies. Hird, Drabble (1939) 226 (part).
1195/H	37.8	2.45	0	1601. B.957(1). Hunter.
1196/A	37.6	2.44	320	1601. B.957(2) same rev. die as 1197/A. Hird.
1197/A	36.8	2.39	250	1601. As 1196/A. Christ Church.
1198/A	37.3	2.42	70	1602. B.957(3) same rev. die as 1199/A. Hird.
1199/A	39.2	2.54	200	1602. As 1198/A. Hird.
1200/H	39.1	2.53	120	1602. B.957(3). Hunter.
1201/A	38.1	2.47	230	1604. B.957(4) but no pellets on belt of crown. Hird.

PLATE 67

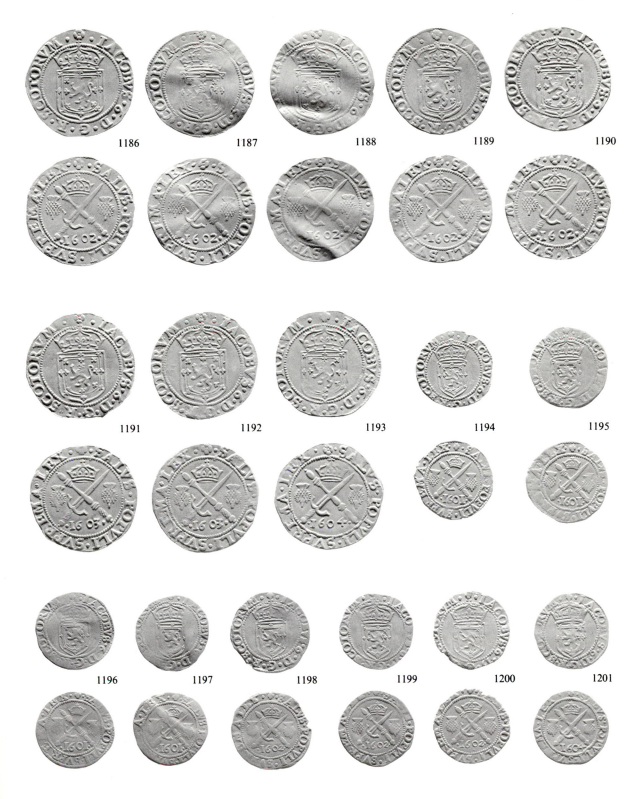

1186   1187   1188   1189   1190

1191   1192   1193   1194   1195

1196   1197   1198   1199   1200   1201

SILVER

Ryal (Pro me si mereor in me 1567–71. Nos. 1202–13)

	Weight		Die	
	gr	gm	axis	
1202/A	460.6	29.85	30	1567. B.921(2) but three pellets at end of both legends. Bodleian.
1203/H	468.7	30.37	10	1567. B.921(2) but three pellets at end of rev. legend. Hunter.
1204/H	461.4	29.90	310	1567. B.921(2) but three pellets at end of rev. legend and with countermark. Hunter.
1205/A	469.4	30.42	160	1567. B.921(1) but with countermark. Browne Willis.
1206/H	469.8	30.44	310	1568. B.921(3) but single pellet both ends obv. legend and end of rev. legend and without countermark. Hunter.
1207/H	469.3	30.41	270	1569. B.921(4) but with countermark. Hunter.

PLATE 68

1202

1203

1204

1205

1206

1207

| | Weight | | Die | |
	gr	*gm*	*axis*	
1208/A	468.7	30.38	200	1570. B.921(5) but three pellets at ends of both legends and without countermark (70 punched over 69?—see Stewart 1958, pl. 1). Bodleian.
1209/A	469.0	30.39	100	1570. B.921(5) but three pellets at ends of both legends and with countermark. Christ Church.
1210/H	463.1	30.01	150	1570. As 1209/A. Hunter.
1211/H	469.9	30.45	300	1570. B.921(5) but three pellets at ends of both legends and without countermark. Hunter.
1212/H	462.5	29.97	340	1571. B.921(6). Hunter.
1213/A	463.9	30.06	150	1571. B.921(7) with countermark but loops above outer arch of crown on rev. Keble College.

PLATE 69

1208

1209

1210

1211

1212

1213

Two Thirds Ryal (Nos. 1214–16)

	Weight		Die	
	gr	gm	axis	
1214/H	305.9	19.82	90	1569. B.922(4). Hunter.
1215/H	304.2	19.71	250	1570. B.922(5) with countermark. Hunter.
1216/H	315.3	20.43	320	1570. B.922(5) but no stop at end of obv. legend, pellets on obv. crown and without countermark. Hunter.

One Third Ryal (No. 1217)

1217/H	150.8	9.77	210	1568. B.923(3) but three pellets at both ends obv. and before rev. legend and with countermark. Hunter.

Half Merk (Salvum fac populum tuum domine 1572–7, 1580. Nos. 1218–27)

1218/A	102.7	6.66	340	1572. B.924(1). P 1982, Lingford 1146 (part).
1219/H	90.8	5.88	30	1572. B.924(1). Hunter.
1220/A	98.4	6.38	300	1573. B.924(4) but pellets on fillet of crown vary. Somerville College.
1221/H	103.7	6.72	200	1573. B.924(5). Neilson.
1222/H	101.7	6.59	290	1573. B.924(5) but no pellets on fillet of crown. Hunter.
1223/A	98.0	6.35	90	1574. B.925(6). Bodleian.

PLATE 70

1214   1215   1216   1217

1218   1219   1220   1221

1222   1223

	Weight		Die	
	gr	gm	axis	
1224/H	103.3	6.69	230	1574. B.925(6) but pellets on fillet of crown. Hunter.
1225/A	89.6	5.81	210	1577. B.925(10). Bodleian.
1226/H	102.5	6.64	10	1577. B.925(11). Hunter.
1227/H	100.9	6.54	40	1580. ·B.926(13). Hunter.

Quarter Merk or Forty Penny Piece (Nos. 1228–30)

1228/H	48.8	3.16	0	1572. B.927(1). Hunter.
1229/H	48.5	3.14	0	1573. B.928(2). Hunter.
1230/A	53.7	3.48	180	1580. B.929(8). P 1982, Lingford 1149 (part).

Two Merk (Nemo me impune lacesset 1578–80. Nos. 1231–3)

1231/H	334.1	21.65	320	1578. B.930(1a) but *recte* stop before and after obv. legend. Hunter.
1232/A	342.1	22.17	160	1579. B.930(1) same dies. Dakers 479.
1233/H	327.7	21.23	270	1579. B.930(1) but stop after obv. legend. Hunter.

Revaluation of 1578

Previous silver issues of Mary and James VI countermarked with a crowned thistle.

Mary	period 1	*testoons:*	1004/A, 1006/A, 1009/A, 1015/H
	period 2	*testoons:*	1085/H, 1087/H, 1089/H, 1092/H
		half-testoon:	1097/H
	period 3	*testoons:*	1112/H, 1114/A, 1115/A, 1116/A
		half-testoon:	1117/H
	period 4	*ryals:*	1121/H, 1123/A, 1124/H, 1125/H
		$\frac{2}{3}$ *ryal:*	1128/A
	period 5	*ryal:*	1132/A
		$\frac{2}{3}$ *ryal:*	1136/A
		$\frac{1}{3}$ *ryal:*	1137/A
James VI		*ryals:*	1204/H, 1205/A, 1207/H, 1209/A, 1210/H, 1213/A
		$\frac{2}{3}$ *ryal:*	1215/H
		$\frac{1}{3}$ *ryal:*	1217/H

PLATE 71

1224

1225

1226

1227

1228

1229

1230

1231

1232

1233

Sixteen Shilling Piece (Nemo me impune lacesset 1581. No. 1234)

	Weight		Die
	gr	gm	axis
1234/A	165.6	10.73	250	1581. B.930C(1a) same obv. die. P 1982, Lingford 1153, Dakers 482, Morrieson 968.

Eight Shilling Piece (No. 1235)

1235/H	85.1	5.51	180	1581. B.930C(1a). Hunter.

Thirty Shilling Piece (Honor regis iudicium diligit 1581–5. Nos. 1236–9)

1236/A	341.9	22.16	220	1581. B.933(2) but 1581 (see Anderson 1739, p. 103, note x; apparently only ten shilling pieces were authorized before 14 April 1582). Bodleian.
1237/A	346.6	22.46	250	1582. B.933(2). Knight.
1238/H	348.3	22.57	180	1582. B.933(2). Hunter.
1239/A	353.7	22.92	190	1583. B.933(3). Browne Willis.

PLATE 72

1234

1235

1236

1237

1238

1239

Twenty Shilling Piece (1582–5. Nos. 1240–2)

	Weight		Die	
	gr	*gm*	*axis*	
1240/A	232.5	15.07	210	1582. B.934(1) but with stop after **SCOTORVM**. Browne Willis.
1241/H	231.7	15.01	280	1582. B.934(2) but **DILIGT**. Hunter.
1242/H	222.6	14.42	110	1582. B.935(3) but two stops after **DEI**. Hunter.

Ten Shilling Piece (1582–4. Nos. 1243–6)

1243/A	108.9	7.06	180	1582. B.936(1). Browne Willis.
1244/A	108.9	7.06	0	1582. B.936(1). Bodleian.
1245/H	116.2	7.53	20	1582. B.936(1) but stop after obv. legend. Hunter.
1246/A	115.4	7.48	260	1582. B.936(2). Christ Church.

Balance Half Merk (His differt rege tyrannus 1591–3. Nos. 1247–51)

1247/A	67.9	4.40	250	1591. B.937(2). Bodleian.
1248/H	69.5	4.50	30	1591. B.937(2). Hunter.

PLATE 73

1240   1241   1242

1243   1244   1245   1246

1247   1248

	Weight		*Die*	
	gr	gm	axis	
1249/H	69.9	4.53	40	1592. B.937(4) but peculiar **6** and no stops after **D G R SCOTORVM**. Hunter.
1250/A	68.2	4.42	310	1593. B.937(5). Ashmolean.
1251/A	63.2	4.10	70	date uncertain. B.937(?). Browne Willis.

Balance Quarter Merk (1591 only. Nos. 1252–4)

1252/A	35.6	2.31	140	1591. B.938(1). Christ Church.
1253/A	29.7	1.93	180	1591. B.938(1). Browne Willis.
1254/H	33.2	2.15	350	1591. B.938(3) but no stop before **IACOBVS**. Hunter.

Ten Shilling Piece (Nemo me impune lacesset 1593–5, 1598–1601. Nos. 1255–68)

1255/H	93.7	6.07	0	1593. B.939(1). Hunter.
1256/A	93.3	6.05	180	1594. B.939(2). Bodleian.
1257/A	89.3	5.79	240	1594. B.939(2). Bodleian, marked '? Willis d. at death'.
1258/A	92.9	6.02	200	1594. B.939(2). Christ Church.
1259/H	90.5	5.86	40	1594. B.939(2). Hunter.
1260/A	92.7	6.01	310	1595. B.939(3). Oriel College.

PLATE 74

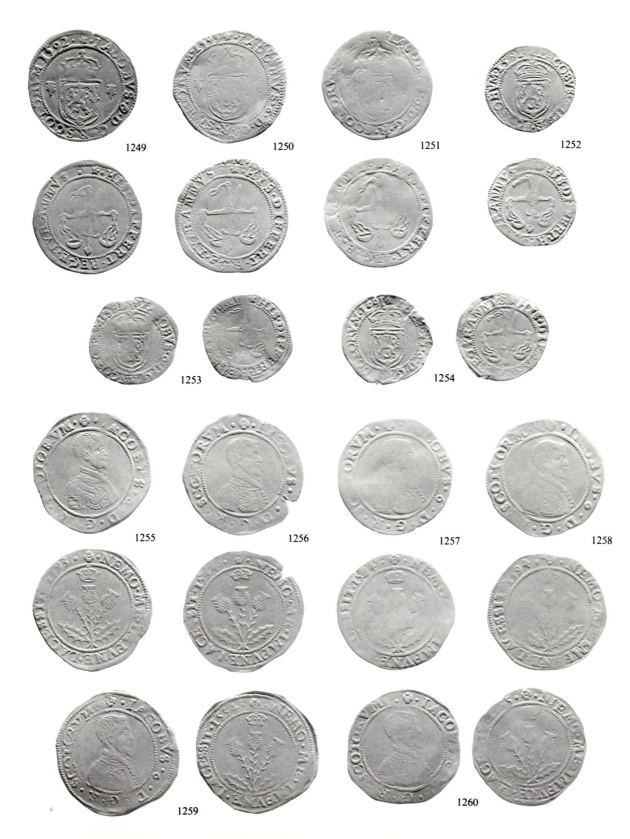

1249   1250   1251   1252

1253   1254

1255   1256   1257   1258

1259   1260

	Weight		*Die*	
	gr	gm	axis	
1261/A	94.1	6.10	330	1595(?). B.939(3) date uncertain. Ashmolean.
1262/H	90.6	5.87	270	1595. B.939(3). Hunter.
1263/A	92.4	5.99	210	double-struck 1598. B.939(4) same rev. die as 1264/A. Bodleian.
1264/A	90.9	5.89	340	1598. As 1263/A. Christ Church.
1265/H	92.8	6.01	330	1598. B.939(4). Hunter.
1266/A	90.6	5.87	270	1599. B.939(6). Bodleian.
1267/A	89.3	5.79	310	1599. B.939(6). Keble College.
1268/H	94.5	6.12	270	1599. B.939(6). Hunter.

Five Shilling Piece (Nos. 1269–75)

1269/H	45.2	2.93	100	1593. B.940(–) but 1593. Hunter.
1270/A	46.0	2.98	220	1594. B.940(1). Browne Willis.
1271/A	43.5	2.82	290	1594. B.940(1). Merton College.
1272/H	44.5	2.88	150	1594. B.940(1). Hunter.
1273/A	43.0	2.79	340	1595. B.940(2). Bodleian.

PLATE 75

1261   1262   1263   1264

1265   1266   1267   1268

1269   1270   1271   1272   1273

	Weight		Die	
	gr	gm	axis	
1274/H	45.2	2.93	220	1595. B.940(2). Hunter.
1275/H	46.5	3.01	0	1599. B.940(3). Hunter.

Thirty Pence Piece (1594–6, 1598–9, 1601. Nos. 1276–9)

1276/H	20.6	1.33	250	1594. B.941(1). Hunter.
1277/H	23.1	1.50	220	1594. B.941(1). Neilson.
1278/H	22.4	1.45	270	1595. B.941(2). Hunter.
1279/A	22.8	1.48	60	date uncertain. B.941(–) but **SCOTOVM**. Browne Willis.

Twelve Pence Piece (1594–6. Nos. 1280–1)

1280/H	9.7	0.63	70	1595. B.942(1). Hunter.
1281/A	9.2	0.60	290	159?. B.942(–) legends off flan. Bodleian.
	(clipped)			

Thistle Merk (Regem Jova protegit 1601–4. Nos. 1282–90)

1282/A	100.0	6.48	180	1601. B.943(1). Bodleian.
	(pierced)			
1283/H	102.9	6.67	180	1601. B.943(1). Hunter.
1284/A	104.3	6.76	350	1602. B.943(3) but without lis between lion's feet. Christ Church.
1285/A	100.9	6.54	230	1602. B.943(3). Bodleian.
1286/A	101.8	6.60	230	1602. B.943(3). D 1921, F. L. Griffith.
1287/A	104.4	6.77	60	1602. B.943(3). Browne Willis.

PLATE 76

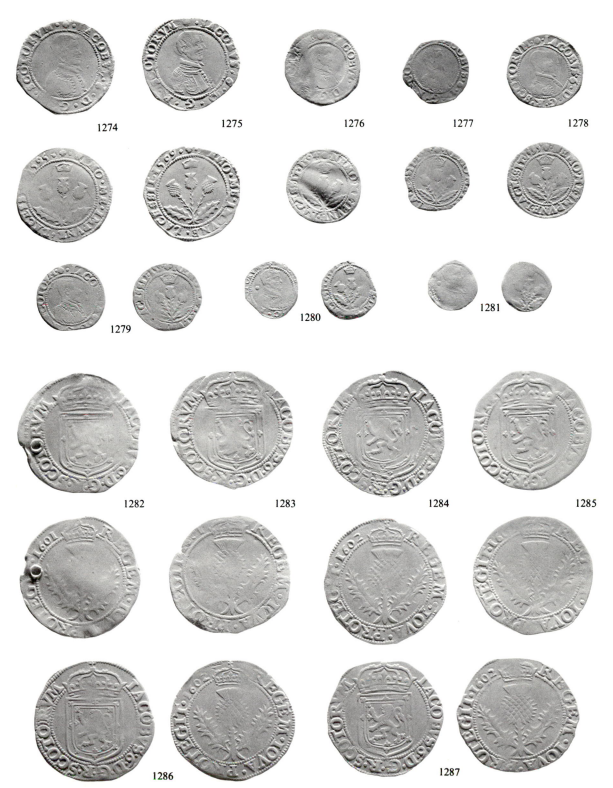

1274   1275   1276   1277   1278

1279   1280   1281

1282   1283   1284   1285

1286   1287

	Weight		Die	
	gr	gm	axis	
1288/H	103.3	6.69	20	1602. B.943(3). Hunter.
1289/A	98.4	6.38	180	1603. B.943(5) but stop after **SCOTORVM**. D 1921, F. L. Griffith.
1290/H	101.3	6.56	200	1603. B.943(5). Hunter.

Half Thistle Merk (Nos. 1291–9)

1291/A	50.7	3.29	110	1601. B.944(1). D 1921, F. L. Griffith.
1292/H	49.6	3.21	180	1601. B.944(1). Hunter.
1293/A	51.4	3.33	310	1602. B.944(2). Bodleian.
1294/A	50.7	3.29	210	1602. B.944(2). Christ Church.
1295/A	50.1	3.25	60	1602. B.944(2). Browne Willis.
1296/H	50.3	3.26	0	1602. B.944(2). Hunter.
1297/H	48.0	3.11	310	1603. B.944(3). Hunter.
1298/A	42.4	2.74	320	1604. B.944(4). Bodleian.
1299/H	47.6	3.08	0	1604. B.944(4) but stop after date. Hunter.

Quarter Thistle Merk or Forty Pence Piece (Nos. 1300–5)

1300/A	23.7	1.54	20	1602. B.945(2). Keble College.
1301/A	26.5	1.72	110	1602. B.945(2) same rev. die as 1302/A. Browne Willis.

PLATE 77

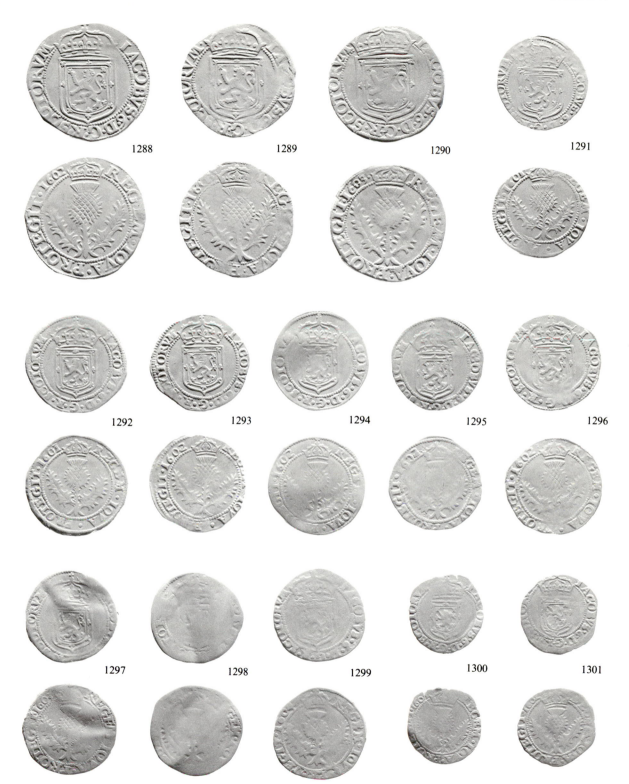

1288   1289   1290   1291

1292   1293   1294   1295   1296

1297   1298   1299   1300   1301

	Weight		Die	
	gr	gm	axis	
1302/A	25.9	1.68	310	1602. As 1301/A. Bodleian.
1303/H	24.4	1.58	270	1602. B.945(2). Hunter.
	(buckled)			
1304/H	25.2	1.63	130	1602. B.945(2). Hunter.
1305/A	25.1	1.63	10	1603. B.945(–) but 1603. D. 1915 W. Cozens.

Eighth Thistle Merk or Twenty Pence Piece (1601–3. Nos. 1306–11)

1306/A	10.0	0.65	0	1601. B.946(1). Bodleian.
1307/H	12.1	0.78	90	1601. B.946(1). Hunter.
1308/A	10.0	0.65	190	1602. B.946(2). Bodleian.
1309/A	12.8	0.83	210	1602. B.946(2). Ashmolean.
1310/A	10.9	0.71	40	1602. B.946(2). Browne Willis.
1311/H	13.6	0.88	90	1602. B.946(2). Hunter.

BILLON

Countermarking of 1575

Genuine billon placks and lions/hardheads of Mary countermarked with a heart and star

Mary   period 1   *placks:*   1072/A, 1075/H, 1077/H
        lion/hardhead (1558): 1081/H

Eightpenny Groat or Plack (Nos. 1312–19)

1312/A	43.0	2.79	0	B.959(1). P 1982, Lingford 1182 (part).
1313/A	22.8	1.48	300	B.959(1). P 1982, Lingford 1182 (part).
1314/H	28.4	1.84	270	B.959(1) but single stop after **D** and stop after **OPPIDVM**. Hunter.
1315/A	21.3	1.38	10	B.959–60 uncertain. Bodleian.
1316/A	29.0	1.88	320	B.961(5). P 1961.
1317/A	26.5	1.72	50	B.961(5). P 1980.
1318/H	21.8	1.41	30	B.961(5). Unknown, Edzell Hoard.
1319/A	28.7	1.86	90	B.962(6). P 1980.

Fourpenny Piece or Half Plack (No. 1320)

1320/A	10.1	0.66	250	B.963–4(3). P 1982, Lingford 1183 (part).

Twopenny Plack or Hardhead (Vincit veritas. 1321–35)

type I (crowned shield)

1321/A	21.9	1.42	20	B.965(1) but without obv. stops. P 1982, Lingford 1184 (part).

type II (lion rampant with two pellets behind)

1322/H	19.3	1.25	180	B.967(3). Hunter.
1323/H	19.3	1.25	320	B.967(2). Unknown, Edzell Hoard.
1324/H	19.0	1.23	30	B.967(3). Unknown, Edzell Hoard.
1325/H	20.7	1.34	210	B.967(3). Unknown, Edzell Hoard.
1326/H	22.9	1.48	220	B.967(3). Unknown, Edzell Hoard.
1327/H	24.1	1.56	220	B.967(3). Unknown, Edzell Hoard.
1328/H	21.3	1.38	0	B.967(3). Unknown, Edzell Hoard.
1329/H	26.1	1.69	270	B.967(3). Unknown, Edzell Hoard.

PLATE 78

1302   1303   1304   1305   1306   1307   1308

1309   1310   1311   1312   1313   1314   1315

1316   1317   1318   1319   1320   1321   1322

1323   1324   1325   1326   1327   1328   1329

	Weight		Die	
	gr	gm	axis	
1330/H	21.5	1.39	70	B.967(3). Unknown, Edzell Hoard.
1331/H	20.7	1.34	0	B.967(3). Unknown, Edzell Hoard.
1332/H	21.9	1.42	180	B.967(3). Unknown, Edzell Hoard.
1333/H	18.9	1.21	270	B.967(3). Unknown, Edzell Hoard.
1334/H	22.4	1.45	270	B.967(3) but no ' after **IACOB**. Hunter.
1335/A	24.2	1.57	160	B.967(5). Bodleian.

Penny or Half Hardhead (Nos. 1336–7)

1336/A	12.6	0.82	0	B.968(1). P 1982, Lingford 1184 (part).
1337/A	13.5	0.88	50	B.968(1). P 1982, Lingford 1184 (part).

Fourpenny or Saltire Plack (Nos. 1338–9)

1338/A	19.4	1.26	220	B.969(1). P 1982, Lingford 1184 (part).
1339/H	21.4	1.39	310	B.969(1). Hunter.

COPPER

Twopence or Turner (Nos. 1340–2)

1340/A	55.8	3.62	290	B.970(1). D 1969.
1341/H	57.3	3.71	330	B.970(1). Hunter.
1342/H	47.7	3.09	290	B.970(1). Unknown.

After accession to English Throne 1603–25 (title: **IACOBVS D G MAG BRIT FRAN & HIB REX**)

GOLD

Ninth Coinage 1604–9 (with English arms in first and fourth quarters of shield)

Unit (Faciam eos in gentem unam. Nos. 1343–4)

1343/A	154.4	10.01	0	B.987(1) but *recte* stop after **REX**, same obv. die, same obv. die as 1344/A. Hird, Wertheimer 195.
1344/A	154.1	9.99	90	As 1344/A. Christ Church.

Double Crown (Henricus rosas regna Iacobus. No. 1345)

1345/A	75.7	4.91	90	B.— (noted ii, pp. 430–1) same obv. die as 1355/A. Hird.

Britain Crown (No. 1346)

1346/A	39.6	2.57	270	B.— (noted ii, p. 431) same obv. die as 1357/A and 1358/A. Hird, Lingford 860, Cochran-Patrick 83.

Thistle Crown (Tueatur unita Deus. Nos. 1347–9)

1347/H	30.6	1.98	180	B.988(2) same dies. Hunter.
1348/H	31.5	2.04	330	B.988(2) but stop either side of rev. im. Hunter.
1349/A	30.4	1.97	170	As 1347/H. Hird.

Half Crown (Rosa sine spina and Tueatur unita Deus. No. 1350 stops: single pellets)

1350/A	18.8	1.22	0	B.— (noted ii, p. 433), same obv. die as 1359/A. Hird.

PLATE 79

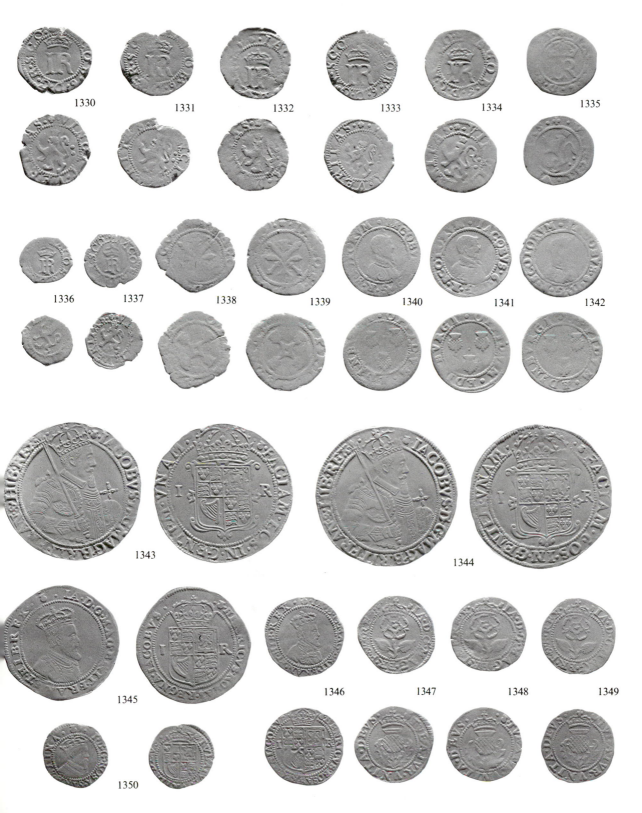

1330   1331   1332   1333   1334   1335

1336   1337   1338   1339   1340   1341   1342

1343   1344

1345   1346   1347   1348   1349

1350

Tenth Coinage 1609–25 (with Scottish arms in first and fourth quarters of shield)

Unit (Nos. 1351–3)

| | *Weight* | | *Die* | |
	gr	*gm*	*axis*	
1351/A	153.8	9.97	230	B.990(4). Hird.
1352/A	152.6	9.89	180	B.990(4) same obv. die. Bodleian.
1353/H	152.2	9.86	140	B.990(4). Hunter.
	(pierced)			

Double Crown (Nos. 1354–6)

1354/A	75.7	4.91	70	B.— (noted ii, p. 434). Hird, Bearman, Pollexfen 403.
1355/A	76.0	4.93	140	B.— (noted ii, p. 434) reading IA'., same obv. die as 1345/A. Hird.
1356/H	78.9	5.11	180	B.— (noted ii, p. 434). Hunter.

Britain Crown (Nos. 1357–8)

1357/A	37.2	2.41	250	B.991(5) but IACOB on rev., same obv. die as 1346/A and 1358/A. Hird, Browne 499a, Murdoch (1903) 311.
1358/A	37.3	2.42	220	B.991(5) same dies, same obv. die as 1346/A and 1357/A. Hird, Bute 203.

Half Crown (No. 1359)

1359/A	18.8	1.22	250	B.992(6) same dies, same obv. die as 1350/A. Hird, Browne 499b.

PLATE 80

1351   1352   1353

1354   1355   1356   1357

1358   1359

SILVER

Ninth Coinage 1604–9 (with English arms in first and fourth quarters)

Sixty Shilling Piece (Quae Deus coniunxit nemo separet. Nos. 1360–2)

	Weight		*Die*	
	gr	*gm*	*axis*	
1360/A	462.0	29.94	180	B.972(1) same rev. die, same dies as 1361/A, same obv. die as 1369/A. Christ Church.
1361/A	462.2	29.95	200	As 1360/A. Merton College.
1362/H	462.5	29.97	180	B.972(1). Hunter.

Thirty Shilling Piece (No. 1363)

1363/A	229.0	14.84	40	B.973 but stop after G varies. Bodleian.

Twelve Shilling Piece (No. 1364)

1364/H	85.9	5.57	310	B.974(2) but & for ET and countermark VII in front of King's face. Unknown.

Six Shilling Piece (No. 1365)

1365/H	41.7	2.70	130	1609. B.975(–) but 1609. Unknown.

Two Shilling Piece (Nos. 1366–8)

1366/A	13.5	0.88	0	B.976(4). P 1981.
1367/A	12.5	0.81	220	B.976(4) but without im on obv. P 1981.
1368/H	14.1	0.91	190	B.976(4) but stop before legends, stop after SPINA. P 1980.

PLATE 81

1360   1361   1362

1363   1364   1365

1366

1367

1368

Tenth Coinage 1609–25 (with Scottish arms in first and fourth quarters)

Sixty Shilling Piece (No. 1369)

	Weight		Die	
	gr	gm	axis	
1369/A	411.1	26.64	100	B.983(1) same dies, same obv. die as 1360/A and 1361/A. Bodleian.

Thirty Shilling Piece (Nos. 1370–4)

1370/A	229.1	14.85	40	B.984(14). Bodleian.
1371/A	230.2	14.92	0	B.984(14). Bodleian.
1372/A	229.4	14.87	320	B.984(14). Ashmolean.
1373/A	183.0	11.86	240	B.984(14). Bodleian.
1374/H	230.1	14.91	140	B.984(14). Hunter.

PLATE 82

1369   1370   1371

1372   1373   1374

Twelve Shilling Piece (Nos. 1375–6)

	Weight		Die	
	gr	*gm*	*axis*	
1375/A	86.5	5.61	310	B.985(15). Bodleian.
1376/H	91.2	5.91	340	B.985(15). Hunter.

Six Shilling Piece (Nos. 1377–9)

1377/A	42.6	2.76	350	1611. B.986(16) but 1611, **D'G'** and **R·EX**. Bodleian.
1378/A	43.5	2.82	330	1613. B.986(16) but 1613. Bodleian.
1379/A	42.6	2.76	310	1622. B.986(16). Bodleian.
	(chipped)			

COPPER

Twopence

Issue of 1614 (Title on obverse and reverse with Francie et Hibernie. Nos. 1380–3)

1380/A	36.4	2.36	90	B.993(1). Browne Willis.
1381/A	37.5	2.43	0	B.993(1). P 1980.
1382/H	38.2	2.48	320	B.993(1). Hunter.
1383/H	26.8	1.74	0	B.933(1). Unknown.

Issue of 1623 (as last but Fran & Hib. Nos. 1384–7)

1384/A	26.8	1.74	180	B.995(4). D 1937.
1385/A	33.1	2.15	0	B.995(4). Bodleian.
1386/A	32.8	2.13	270	B.995(4). P 1980.
1387/H	24.1	1.56	90	B.995(4). Hunter.

PLATE 83

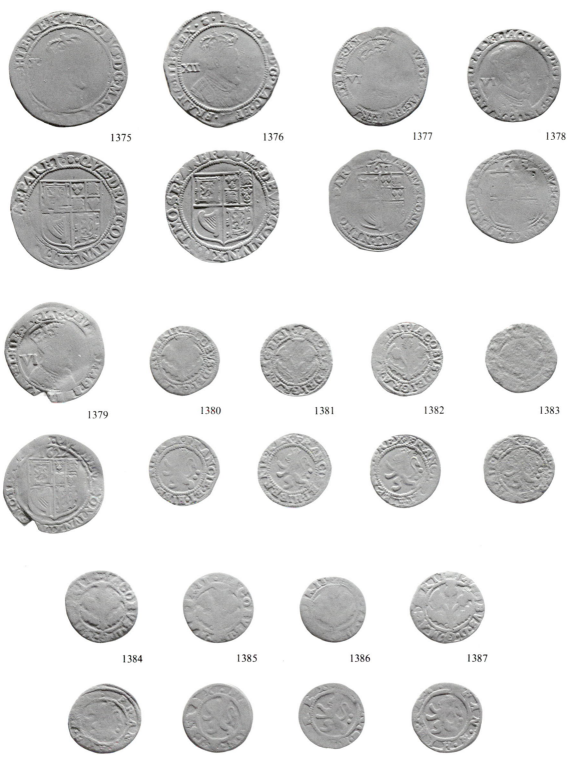

1375   1376   1377   1378

1379   1380   1381   1382   1383

1384   1385   1386   1387

CHARLES I 1625–49

(title: either **CAROLVS D G MAG BRIT FRAN & HIB REX** or **CAROLVS D G SCOT ANG FR & HIB R**)

GOLD (see Murray 1970)

First coinage 1625–34

Unit (Nos. 1388–90)

	Weight		*Die*	
	gr	*gm*	*axis*	
1388/A	152.0	9.85	0	B.1031(1) but recte stop after **VNAM**, same obv. die; Murray O1/R2 (this coin noted). Hird.
1389/A	148.4	9.62	0	B.1030(1) but *recte* stop after **VNAM**, Murray O2/R3 (this coin noted). Browne Willis.
1390/H	154.2	9.99	40	B.1030(1) but *recte* stop after **VNAM**, no stop after **CAROLVS**. Hunter.

Britain Crown (No. 1391)

1391/A	38.4	2.49	20	B.— (see ii, p. 481); Murray p. 131 (this coin noted). Hird, Duke of Atholl.
	(creased)			

Third Coinage 1637–42—Briot's Issue

Unit (His praesum ut prosim. Stops: lozenge. Nos. 1392–7)

1392/A	152.4	9.88	180	B.1032(3) but *recte* **VT** not **ET**, same dies, same dies as 1393/A, 1394/A, 1395/A, and 1396/H; Murray 1. Christ Church.
1393/A	152.7	9.90	180	As 1392/A. D 1925.
1394/A	152.6	9.89	180	As 1392/A. St John's College.

PLATE 84

1388   1389   1390

1391

1392   1393   1394

	Weight		*Die*	
	gr	gm	axis	
1395/A	153.2	9.93	180	As 1392/A. Browne Willis.
1396/H	154.2	9.99	180	As 1392/A. Hunter.
1397/A	152.4	9.88	180	B.1032(4) same dies. Knight.

Half Unit or Double Crown (Unita tuemur. Stops: lozenge. Nos. 1398–1402)

1398/A	76.8	4.98	0	B.1034(5) but *recte* no stop after **REX**, same dies; Murray 1(a/1). Knight.
1399/A	75.6	4.90	180	B.1035(6), same dies as 1400/A, same rev. die as 1401/A; Murray 3. Christ Church.
1400/A	76.2	4.94	180	As 1399/A. Hird.
1401/A	75.9	4.92	180	B.1035(6) but *recte* no stop after **REX**, same rev. die as 1399/A and 1400/A; Murray 2. Hird, Mallet.
1402/H	76.4	4.95	200	B.1035(6) but *recte* no stop after **REX**; Murray 2 but stop after **HIB**. Hunter.

Britain Crowns (Nos. 1403–5)

1403/A	37.0	2.40	200	B.— (see ii, p. 483); Cochran-Patrick 1875, pl. XIII, **6** with **B** at beginning of obv. legend; Murray 2(O1/R1). Browne Willis.
1404/H	38.1	2.47	200	B.— (see ii, p. 483); Murray 2. Hunter.
1405/A	38.1	2.47	200	B.1036(7) same dies; Murray 1. Hird, Cochran-Patrick 88, Wigan.

Half Crown (Nos. 1406–8)

1406/A	18.9	1.23	220	B.1037(8) same dies; Murray 1. Browne Willis.
1407/A	18.5	1.20	40	B.1038(9) same dies; Murray 2. Hird, Wills 194, Cochran-Patrick 89, Wingate 355.
1408/H	19.2	1.24	20	B.1038(9) same dies; Murray 2. Hunter.

Third Coinage 1637–42—Falconer's Issue

Half Unit or Double Crown (No. 1409)

| 1409/A | 74.7 | 4.84 | 180 | B.— (see ii, p. 483); Richardson 1901, p. 299, no. 104; Murray p. 137 (this coin noted). Hird. |

PLATE 85

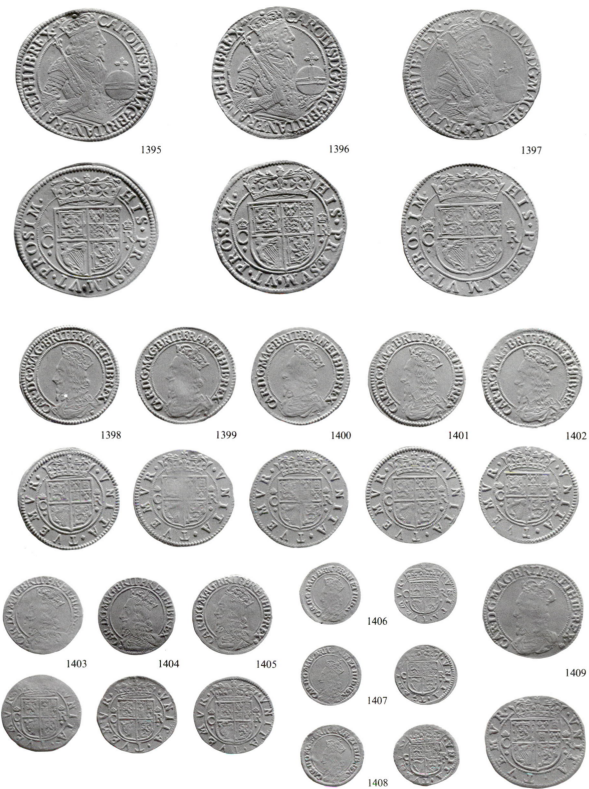

1395

1396

1397

1398

1399

1400

1401

1402

1403

1404

1405

1406

1407

1409

1408

SILVER (see Murray 1970)

First Coinage 1625–34

Sixty Shilling Piece (No. 1410)

	Weight		Die	
	gr	gm	axis	
1410/H	460.4	29.83	80	B.996(1); Murray pp. 121, 131 (this not die duplicate of B.996(1)). Hunter.

Thirty Shilling Piece (Nos. 1411–12)

1411/A	230.2	14.92	350	B.997(2) but with small thistle head im; Murray pp. 121, 131. Bodleian.
1412/H	229.2	14.85	160	B.997(2); Murray pp.121, 131. Hunter.

Twelve Shilling Piece (Nos. 1413–14)

1413/A	88.7	5.75	290	B.998(3) but small thistle head im rev., same obv. die; Murray pp. 121, 131. Knight.
1414/H	88.6	5.74	180	B.998(3) same obv. die; Murray pp. 121, 131. Hunter.

Six Shilling Piece (1625–34. Nos. 1415–18) (1625–34)

1415/A	40.9	2.65	310	1626. B.999(–) but 1626; Murray pp. 121, 132 (this coin noted). University College, Waddington.
1416/H	44.6	2.89	270	1626. B.999(–) but 1626; Murray pp. 121, 132 (this coin noted). Hunter.
1417/A	43.6	2.83	100	1631. B.999(–) but 1631; Murray pp. 121, 132 (this coin noted). Knight.
1418/H	45.4	2.94	320	1632. B.999(–) but 1632; Murray pp. 121, 132 (this coin noted). Hunter.

Two Shilling Piece (No. 1419)

1419/A	14.8	0.96	90	B.1000(6); Murray pp. 121, 123. P 1980.

PLATE 86

1410

1411

1412

1413

1414

1415

1416

1417

1418

1419

Second Coinage 1636

Half Merk Piece (Christo auspice regno. Nos. 1420–1)

	Weight		Die	
	gr	gm	axis	
1420/A	50.1	3.25	20	B.1001(1) but double pellets after HIB; Murray *c.* and same obv. die as pl. IV, 29. Knight.
1421/H	40.3	2.61	300	B.1001(1); Murray *a.* D 1936 Miss Buchanan.

Forty Pence Piece (Salus Reipublicae suprema lex. No. 1422)

1422/A	23.6	1.53	340	B.1002(2); Murray *a.* Bodleian.
	(pierced)			

Milled Patterns

Twenty Pence Piece (Justitia thronum firmat. Stops: lozenge. No. 1423)

1423/H	12.4	0.80	180	B.1004(4) same dies; Murray pp. 122, 133 (this coin noted). Hunter.

Third Coinage 1637–42

I. Briot's Issue (Stops: lozenge or pellet)

Sixty Shilling Piece (Nos. 1424–6)

1424/A	457.4	29.64	180	B.1005(5) same dies; Murray pp. 124, 133. Browne Willis.
1425/H	461.9	29.93	180	As 1424/A. Hunter.
1426/H	457.7	29.66	180	As 1424/A. Coats.
	(pierced)			

Thirty Shilling Piece (Nos. 1427–9)

1427/A	229.1	14.85	180	B.1006(6) same dies; Murray pp. 124, 133. Radcliffe.

PLATE 87

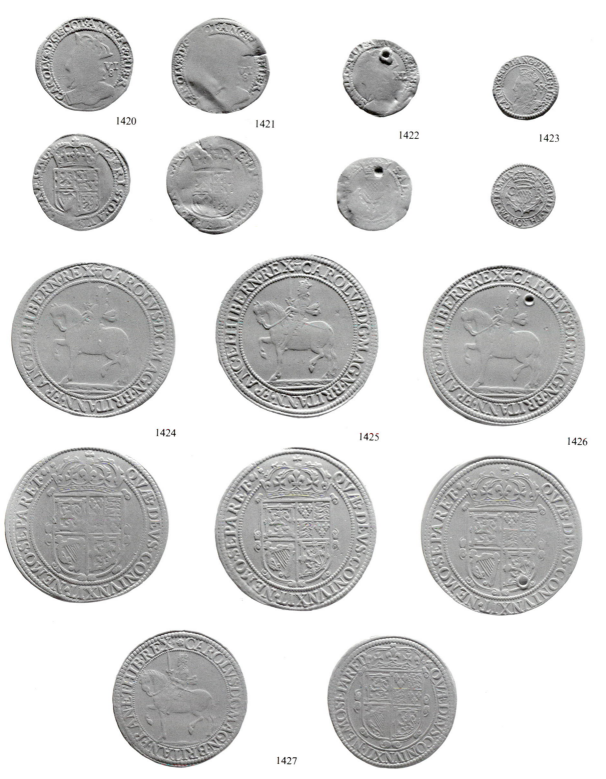

1420   1421   1422   1423

1424   1425   1426

1427

	Weight		*Die*	
	gr	*gm*	*axis*	
1428/H	228.3	14.79	180	As 1427/A. Hunter.
1429/H	221.8	14.37	180	As 1427/A. Unknown.

Twelve Shilling Piece (Nos. 1430–2)

1430/A	85.9	5.57	180	B.1007(7) same dies, same dies as 1431/A and 1432/H; Murray pp. 124, 133. Bodleian.
1431/A	89.3	5.79	180	As 1430/A. Bodleian.
1432/H	90.6	5.87	120	As 1430/A. Hunter.

Six Shilling Piece (Nos. 1433–7)

1433/A	44.4	2.88	180	B.1008(8); Murray 6. Bodleian.
1434/H	45.1	2.92	200	B.1008(8); Murray 6. Hunter.
1435/H	45.1	2.92	180	B.1008(9); Murray 1 (this coin noted). Hunter.
1436/H	45.2	2.93	180	B.—; Murray 3 (this coin noted). Hunter.
1437/H	45.1	2.92	180	B.—; Murray 5 (this coin noted). Hunter.

Half Merk Piece (Nos. 1438–44)

1438/A	49.0	3.18	180	B.1010(11) same dies, same rev. die as 1439/A and 1440/A; Murray O4/R1 (this coin noted). Knight.
1439/A	46.4	3.01	210	B.1010(11) same rev. die, same rev. die as 1438/A and 1440/A; Murray O1/R1, same dies as pl. IV, 31 (this coin noted). Browne Willis.
1440/A	50.3	3.26	200	B.1010(11) same rev. die, same rev. die as 1438/A and 1439/A; Murray O2/R1 (this coin noted). Bodleian.

PLATE 88

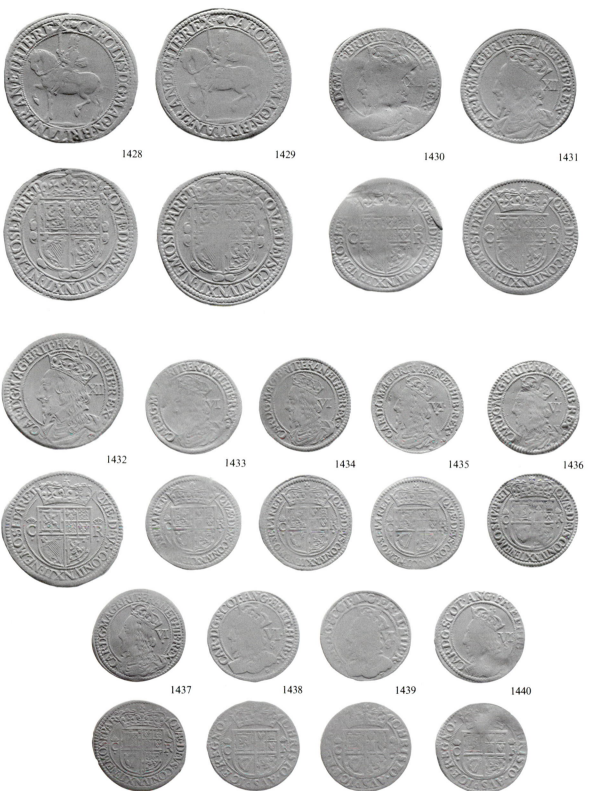

1428   1429   1430   1431

1432   1433   1434   1435   1436

1437   1438   1439   1440

	Weight		Die
	gr	gm	axis
1441/A	50.9 (pierced)	3.30	180	B.1010(11–12), same rev. die as 1442/A; Murray O5/R3 (this coin noted). University College, Waddington.
1442/A	58.1	3.77	0	B.1010(11–12), same rev. die as 1441/A; Murray O7/R3. Christ Church.
1443/A	46.0	2.98	180	B.1010(11–12); Murray O6/R4. Christ Church.
1444/H	50.3	3.26	200	B.1010(11); Murray O1/R1. Hunter.

Forty Pence Piece (Nos. 1445–7) (Stops: double lozenges or pellets)

1445/H	24.9	1.61	90	B.1012(13) but stop after R and before **SALVS**; Murray *d*/?*c*. Hunter.
1446/A	29.0	1.88	180	B.1013(14); Murray *h*/*g*. Browne Willis.
1447/H	29.8	1.93	90	B.1012(13) but *recte* stop after R and B under bust/B.1013(14); Murray *h*/*g*. Hunter.

Twenty Pence Piece (Nos. 1448–56)

1448/A	11.8	0.77	180	B.1014(15) but without B on obv. or lozenges; Murray *l*/*c*. Knight.
1449/A	16.6	1.08	180	B.1014(16), same dies as 1450/A; Murray *a*/*i*. Bodleian.
1450/A	11.4	0.74	200	As 1449/A. Christ Church.
1451/A	15.9	1.03	220	B.1014(–) but B below thistle on rev; Murray *a*/*e*. Bodleian.
1452/H	11.4	0.74	180	B.1014(–); Murray *a*/*c*. Hunter.
1453/H	15.3	0.99	180	B.1014(17) but most stops missing on obv; Murray *c*/?*l*. Hunter.
1454/A	12.0	0.78	190	B.1014(19) but without B on obv., same dies as 1455/A; Murray *l* but R·/*m*. Bodleian.
1455/A	12.3	0.80	180	As 1454/A. Bodleian.
1456/A	10.0	0.65	120	B.1014 (uncertain); Murray *g*/?*c*. Ashmolean.

II. Intermediate Issue

Thirty Shilling Piece (as Briot's issue. No. 1457)

1457/H	229.4	14.86	180	B.1015(20) but *recte* B.1015 not B(21), same dies; Murray pp. 125, 137. Hunter.

PLATE 89

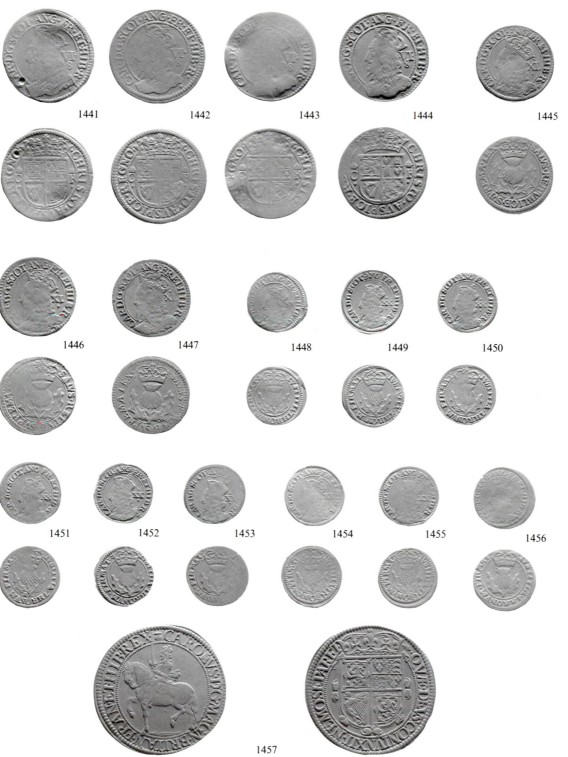

1441   1442   1443   1444   1445

1446   1447   1448   1449   1450

1451   1452   1453   1454   1455   1456

1457

CHARLES I (*cont.*)

Twelve Shilling Piece (as Briot's issue. Nos. 1458–9)

	Weight		Die	
	gr	gm	axis	
1458/A	89.8	5.82	270	B.—(21) same dies; Murray pp. 125, 137, pl. III, 20. Christ Church.
1459/H	91.8	5.95	270	As 1458/A. Hunter.

III. Falconer's First Issue

Twelve Shilling Piece (Nos. 1460–5)

1460/A	86.5	5.61	270	B.1017(24) same dies, same dies as 1461/A–1465/H; Murray pp. 126, 138. Christ Church.
1461/A	90.4	5.86	270	As 1460/A. Knight.
1462/A	88.5	5.74	270	As 1460/A. Bodleian, marked '?Willis d. at death'.
	(pierced)			
1463/A	90.2	5.85	270	As 1460/A. Ashmolean.
1464/A	89.9	5.83	270	As 1460/A. D F. P. Barnard, 'The first coin I ever bought. Gt. Yarmouth'.
1465/H	90.3	5.85	270	As 1460/A. Hunter.

Six Shilling Piece (Nos. 1466–8)

1466/A	45.5	2.95	180	B.—(26); Murray O4/R1. Knight.
1467/H	44.2	2.86	270	B.—(26); Murray O4/R3. Hunter.
1468/A	46.0	2.98	270	B.— variety without initial mark on obv. as noted B.ii p. 466; Murray O7/R4. Knight.

PLATE 90

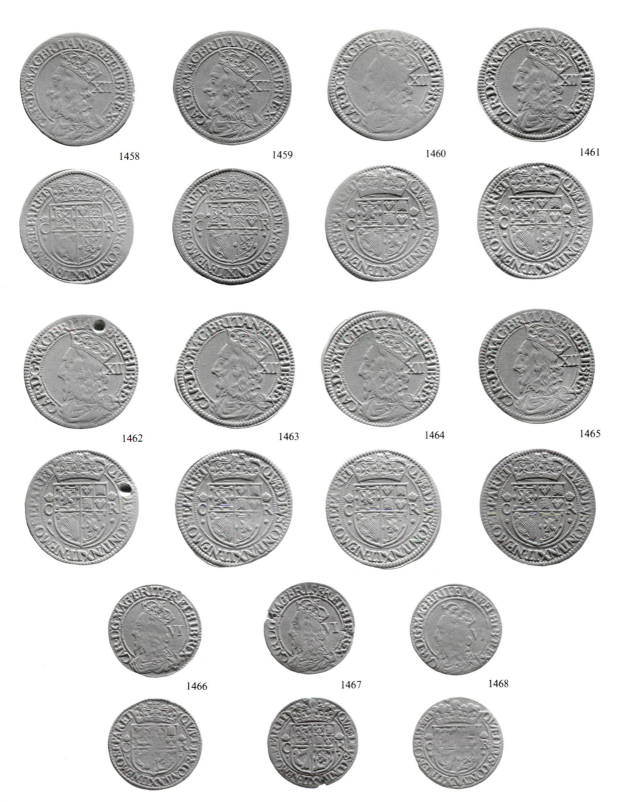

1458   1459   1460   1461

1462   1463   1464   1465

1466   1467   1468

Forty Pence Piece (Nos. 1469–83)

	Weight		Die	
	gr	gm	axis	
1469/A	21.0	1.36	210	B.—(28), same rev. die as 1476/A; Murray *f/g*. Bodleian.
1470/H	22.7	1.47	180	B.—(28); Murray *f/f*. Hunter.
1471/A	21.6	1.40	200	B.—(29) but stop after R and before **SALVS**; Murray *c/f*? Bodleian.
1472/H	29.9	1.55	180	B.—(29) but no stop before **CAR**; Murray *d/f*. Hunter.
1473/H	26.3	1.70	200	B.—(29); Murray *e/f*. D 1943 W. McLelland, found Trongate, Glasgow.
1474/H	24.6	1.59	180	B.—(29); Murray *e?/f*. D 1943 W. McLelland, found Trongate, Glasgow.
1475/H	20.2	1.31	180	B.—(29) but no stop before **CAR**; Murray *e/f*. Neilson.
1476/A	29.1	1.89	200	B.—(30) but *recte* illustrated as Fig. 1016 and with F over crown but nothing by mound, same obv. die as 1482/A, same rev. die as 1469/A; Murray *c/g*. Knight.
1477/H	25.6	1.66	280	B.—(30) but *recte* illustrated as Fig. 1016; Murray *c/c*. Hunter.
1478/H	21.5	1.39	270	B.—(30) but *recte* illustrated as Fig. 1016 and with F facing out and small **X** in **LEX**; Murray *c/e*. D 1936 Miss Buchanan.
1479/A	31.1	2.02	270	B.—(32); Murray *j/i*. Radcliffe.
1480/A	22.6	1.47	190	B.—(30) but *recte* illustrated as Fig. 1016, same dies; Murray *c/c*. Bodleian.
1481/A	25.9	1.68	200	B.—(27) but without lozenges by value and F and point above crown on rev.; Murray *d/g*. Christ Church.
1482/A	25.0	1.62	200	B.—(30)? same obv. die as 1476/A; Murray *c/*?. Bodleian.
1483/A	20.0	1.30	290	B.1016(22); Murray *c/e*. University College, Waddington.

Twenty Pence Piece (Nos. 1484–91)

1484/A	14.0	0.91	20	B.1018(35) (fig. *recte*), same dies; Murray *b/a*. Ashmolean.
1485/H	7.4	0.48	0	B.1019(35) (fig. *recte*); Murray *b/a*. Hunter.
1486/H	14.1	0.91	210	B.1019(35) (fig. *recte*) but F upright; Murray *b/g*. Hunter.
1487/H	9.1	0.59	20	B.1019(35) (fig. *recte*) but F over crown; Murray *b/i*. Hunter.
1488/A	13.4	0.87	290	B.1019(36) but **BRIT** and **R.**; Murray *f/*?. Bodleian.
1489/H	12.1	0.78	0	B.— without F; Murray *m/s*. Hunter.
1490/H	12.8	0.83	180	B.— without F; Murray *l/s*. D 1937 L. A. Lawrence.
1491/A	8.9	0.58	200	B. ? details uncertain; Murray ? Christ Church.

PLATE 91

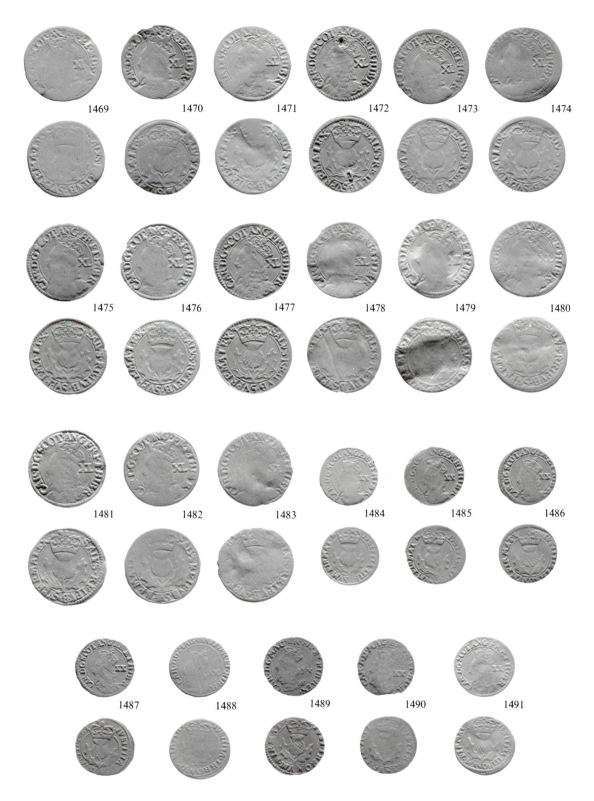

1469　　1470　　1471　　1472　　1473　　1474

1475　　1476　　1477　　1478　　1479　　1480

1481　　1482　　1483　　1484　　1485　　1486

1487　　1488　　1489　　1490　　1491

IV. Falconer's Second Issue

Thirty Shilling Piece (Nos. 1492–1501)

	Weight		Die	
	gr	gm	axis	
1492/H	227.9	14.77	180	B.—(38); Murray 5. Hunter.
1493/A	228.2	14.79	180	B.—(38), same dies as 1494/A, same obv. die as 1495/A and 1496/A; Murray 5. Christ Church.
1494/A	223.0	14.45	180	As 1493/A. Keble College.
1495/A	227.7	14.76	180	B.—(38) but rev. im thistle head and stop at end of rev. legend, same dies as 1496/A, same obv. die as 1493/A and 1494/A; Murray 7. Bodleian.
1496/A	211.7	13.72	180	As 1495/A. Christ Church.
1497/A	226.7	14.69	190	B.—(39); Murray 4. Bodleian.
1498/H	227.2	14.72	180	B.—(39); Murray 4. Hunter.
1499/H	231.9	15.03	180	B.—(41); Murray 3. Hunter.
1500/A	220.5	14.29	190	B.—; Murray 2. University College, Waddington.
1501/H	225.3	14.60	180	B.—; Murray 2. Hunter.

PLATE 92

1492   1493   1494   1495

1496   1497   1498   1499

1500   1501

CHARLES I (*cont.*)

	Weight		Die	
	gr	gm	axis	
1502/A	88.9	5.76	180	B.1020(42) same dies, same dies as 1503/A–1507/H; Murray 1. Bodleian.
	(pierced)			
1503/A	91.3	5.92	180	As 1502/A. Bodleian.
1504/A	84.4	5.47	180	As 1502/A. Bodleian.
1505/A	91.0	5.90	180	As 1502/A. University College, Waddington.
1506/H	87.9	5.70	180	As 1502/A. Hunter.
1507/H	90.5	5.86	180	As 1502/A. Hunter.
1508/H	92.3	5.98	180	B.1020(42) but plain inner circles; Murray 7. Hunter.
1509/A	91.2	5.90	180	B.1020(43), same dies as 1510/A; Murray 6. Bodleian.
1510/A	90.1	5.84	180	As 1509/A. Ashmolean.
1511/H	92.5	5.99	180	B.1020(43); Murray 6. Hunter.
1512/A	88.5	5.74	180	B.1020(44) but rev. stops differ and triple pellets after **SEPARET**; Murray 8. Christ Church.

PLATE 93

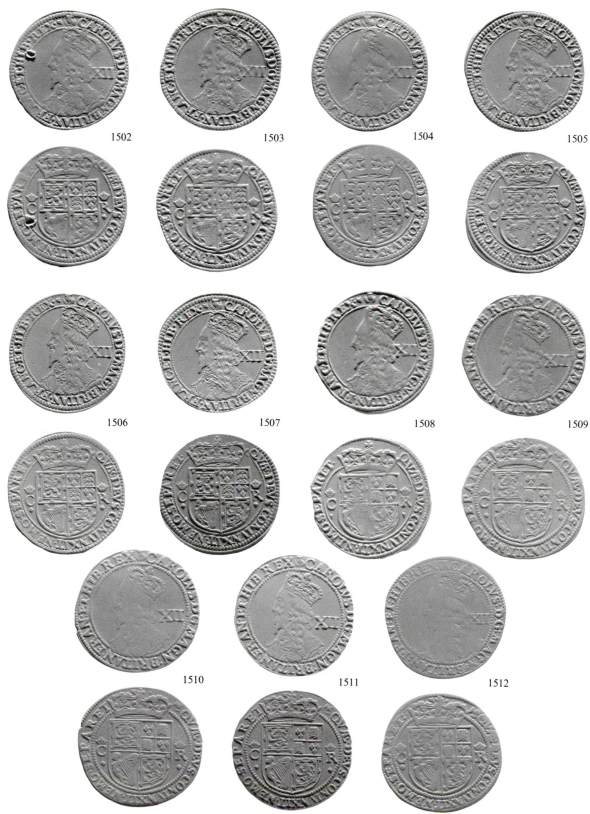

1502   1503   1504   1505

1506   1507   1508   1509

1510   1511   1512

Six Shilling Piece (No. 1513)

	Weight		Die	
	gr	gm	axis	
1513/H	43.4	2.81	180	B.—(45) but **SEP** with two pellets above P and one to right above crown; Murray 1. Hunter.

Twenty Pence Piece (Nos. 1514–18)

1514/H	11.4	0.74	180	B.1021(46) but without im; Murray *f/b*. Hunter.
1515/H	14.5	0.94	210	B.1021(47); Murray *c/b*. D 1937. L. A. Lawrence.
1516/A	15.7	1.02	180	B.1022(49) but without im and with F and pellet over crown and stop after **CAR**; Murray *e/b*. Bodleian.
1517/H	12.4	0.80	180	B.1022(49); Murray *b/b*. Hunter.
1518/A	11.7	0.76	270	B.1021(46) but F not visible; Murray *a/*? D 1932 J. G. Milne, found in Port Meadow allotments, Oxford.

V. Falconer's Anonymous Issue

Thirty Shilling Piece (No. 1519)

1519/H	229.5	14.87	180	B.1023(51); Murray 4. Hunter.

Twelve Shilling Piece (Nos. 1520–3)

1520/A	87.6	5.68	180	B.—(54), same dies as 1521/A; Murray 3. D 1921 F. L. Griffith.
1521/A	90.1	5.84	180	As 1520/A. D 1921 F. L. Griffith.
1522/A	93.2	6.04	180	B.—(54); Murray 2. Bodleian.
1523/H	91.2	5.91	180	B.—(54); Murray 2. Hunter.

Six Shilling Piece (Nos. 1524–5)

1524/A	42.9	2.78	180	B.—(55) but *recte* **QVAE**, same dies; Murray pp. 128, 143, pl. IV, 28. Knight.
1525/H	46.0	2.98	180	As 1524/A. Hunter.
	(pierced)			

Twenty Pence Piece (Nos. 1526–33)

1526/A	10.9	0.71	40	B.—; Murray *b/b*. University College, Waddington.
1527/A	11.5	0.75	0	B.—; Murray *b/a*. Ashmolean.

PLATE 94

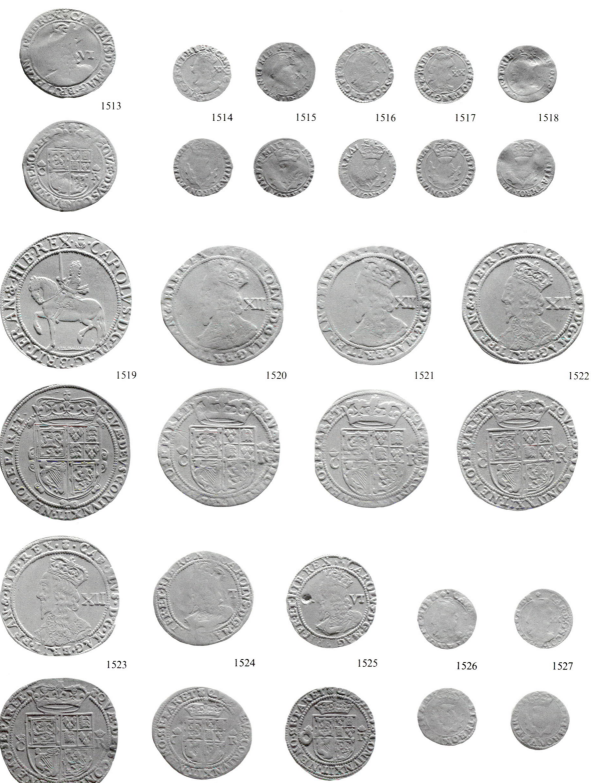

1513

1514 1515 1516 1517 1518

1519 1520 1521 1522

1523 1524 1525 1526 1527

	Weight		*Die*	
	gr	*gm*	*axis*	
1528/A	15.4	1.00	0	B.—; Murray *a/a*. Bodleian.
1529/A	10.5	0.68	110	B.—; Murray *a/b*. D 1921 F. L. Griffith.
1530/A	12.8	0.83	180	B.—: Murray *h/b*. D 1921 F. L. Griffith.
1531/A	10.3	0.67	0	B.—; Murray *b/b*. Oriel College.
1532/H	12.4	0.80	90	B.—(58) but stop after **R** and **FIRMAT**; Murray *j/a*. Hunter.
1533/A	12.0	0.78	180	B. and Murray uncertain. Rawlinson.
	(bent)			

Fourth Coinage 1642

Three Shilling Piece (Salus reipublicae suprema lex. Nos. 1534–5)

1534/A	19.9	1.29	80	B.1029(68) same dies; Murray *a/b*. Bodleian.
1535/H	23.0	1.49	180	B.1029(68) but *recte* stop before **CAROLVS**, same obv. die; Murray *a/b*. Hunter.

Two Shilling Piece (Justitia thronum firmat. Nos. 1536–43)

1536/A	20.6	1.39	200	B.1026(63) same dies, same dies as 1537/A; Murray 1 noting this coin. Rawlinson.
1537/A	14.0	0.91	200	As 1536/A. Bodleian.
1538/H	23.3	1.51	180	B.1026(63) but *recte* **D:G** and stop after **FIRMAT**; Murray 1. Hunter.
1539/A	12.9	0.84	0	B.1027(64); Murray 2(i)a. Rawlinson.
1540/A	18.2	1.18	270	As 1539/A. Bodleian.
1541/H	17.5	1.13	270	As 1539/A. Hunter.
1542/H	9.6	0.62	180	As 1539/A. Hunter.
1543/A	18.9	1.23	0	B.1028(66) but with **ANG** and **· & HIB**; Murray 2(ii)c. Bodleian.

COPPER

Issue of 1629

Twopence or Turner (Nos. 1544–7)

1544/A	22.8	1.48	80	B.1039(1). D 1975 H. de S. Shortt, J. Birkett (Salisbury).
1545/A	18.8	1.22	0	B.1039(1). Bodleian.
1546/A	25.0	1.62	300	B.1039(1). Bodleian.
1547/H	26.4	1.71	220	B.1039(1). Hunter.

Issue of 1632–9 (The Earl of Stirling Coinage—see Stevenson 1959)

Twopence or Turner (Nemo me impune lacesset. Nos. 1548–55)

1548/A	11.7	0.76	180	B.1043(7); Stevenson 3. Bodleian.
1549/A	16.9	1.10	180	B.1043(7); Stevenson 3. Bodleian.
1550/H	15.7	1.02	180	B.1043(7); Stevenson 3. Hunter.
1551/H	10.6	0.69	170	B.1043(8); Stevenson 11. Neilson.

PLATE 95

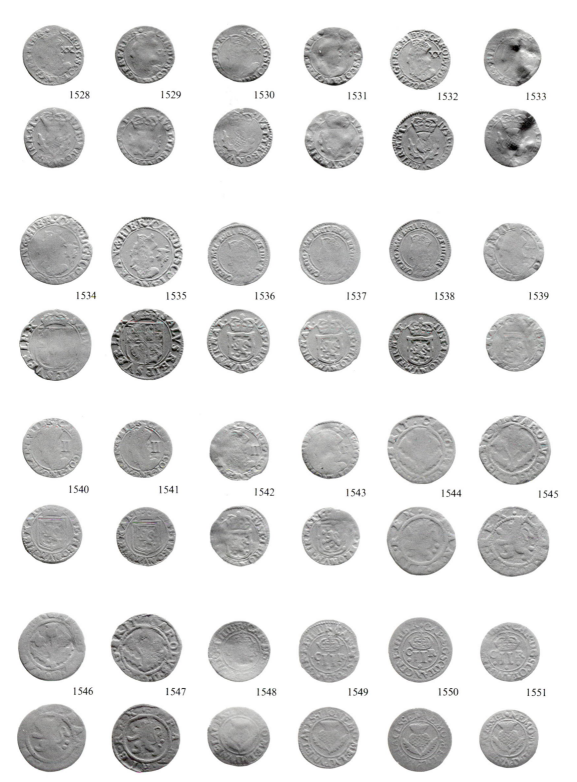

1528   1529   1530   1531   1532   1533

1534   1535   1536   1537   1538   1539

1540   1541   1542   1543   1544   1545

1546   1547   1548   1549   1550   1551

CHARLES I (*cont.*)

	Weight		Die	
	gr	gm	axis	
1552/H	9.10	0.59	180	B.1043(10); Stevenson 19. Hunter.
1553/A	11.7	0.76	190	B.1043(1) but anemone im both sides; Stevenson 19–24. Bodleian.
1554/A	13.1	0.85	100	B.1043(11); Stevenson 39. Bodleian.
1555/H	11.9	0.77	90	B.1043(12); Stevenson 40. Neilson.

Issue of 1642–50 (See Murray and Stewart 1972)

Twopence or Turner (*no* mark of value. Nos. 1556–65)

1556/A	41.5	2.69	270	B.—; M & S Ia. Bodleian.
1557/A	39.8	2.58	340	B.—; M & S Ia with broken C punch. Bodleian.
1558/A	42.2	2.74	280	B.—; M & S IIa. Bodleian.
1559/A	40.1	2.60	60	B.—; M & S IIc. Bodleian.
1560/H	45.3	2.94	80	B.1046(8); M & S IIIa. Hunter.
1561/H	17.7	2.15	0	B.1046(8); M & S IIIa. Unknown.
1562/A	38.7	2.51	170	B.—; M & S IVb. Bodleian.
1563/A	43.5	2.82	100	B.—; M & S IVb. Bodleian.
1564/A	47.2	3.06	270	B.—; M & S IVb. Bodleian.
1565/A	41.9	2.72	180	B.—; M & S IVb. Bodleian.

CHARLES II (1649–85)

SILVER (see Murray 1969)

First Coinage 1664–75

Four Merk (1664–5, 1670, 1673–5. Nos. 1566–8)

1566/H	410.5	26.60	0	1664. B.1048(1) but two-leaved thistle under bust; Murray 1a. Hunter.
1567/H	403.9	26.17	90	1673. B.1048(3) but stop after GRA and not after HIB; Murray 4. Hunter.
1568/A	408.9	26.50	0	1674. B.1048(4); Murray 5b. Browne Willis.

PLATE 96

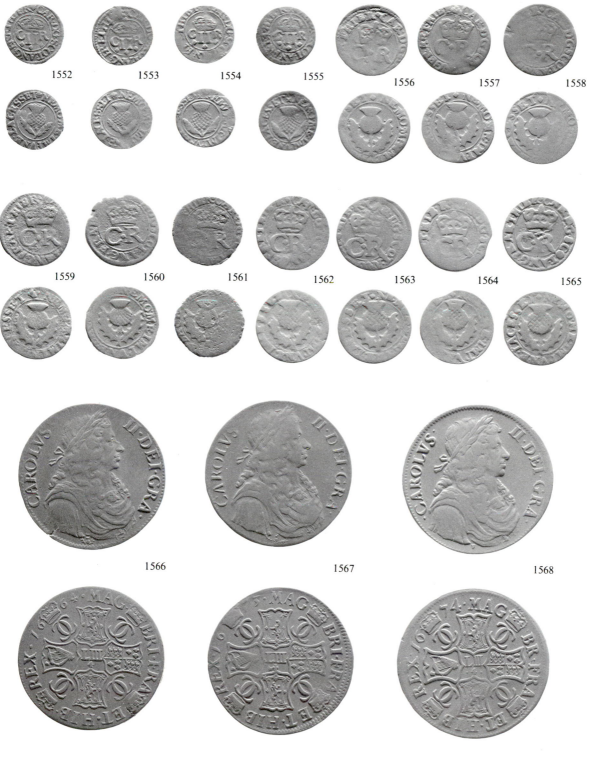

1552 1553 1554 1555 1556 1557 1558

1559 1560 1561 1562 1563 1564 1565

1566 1567 1568

Two Merk (1664, 1670, 1673–5. Nos. 1569–74)

	Weight		Die	
	gr	gm	axis	
1569/H	206.5	13.38	180	1664. B.1049(1) but no stops after **CAROLVS** and **GRA**; Murray 7. Hunter.
1570/A	198.4	12.86	90	1673. B.1049(2) same dies; Murray 9. Bodleian.
1571/H	198.5	12.86	270	1673. B.1049(2) but stops differ; Murray 9. Hunter.
1572/A	199.7	12.94	180	1675. B.1050(4) but small **F** and no colon after **DEI**, same obv. die as 1573/A; Murray 11. Knight.
1573/A	201.5	13.06	0	1675. B.1050(4) but small **F** and colon after **DEI**, no stop after **BR**, Murray 11a same obv. die as 1572/A. Browne Willis.
1574/H	200.6	13.00	0	1675. B.1050(4) but rev. stops differ, same obv. die; Murray 11b. Hunter.

Merk (1664–6, 1668–75. Nos. 1575–95)

1575/A	97.5	6.32	90	1664. B.1051(1); Murray 12. Knight.
1576/A	96.9	6.28	180	1664. B.1051(1) but stops differ; Murray 12. Christ Church.
1577/H	41.7	6.55	270	1664. B.1051(1); Murray 12. Hunter.
1578/A	95.3	6.18	270	1669. B.1051(5); Murray 16. Bodleian.

PLATE 97

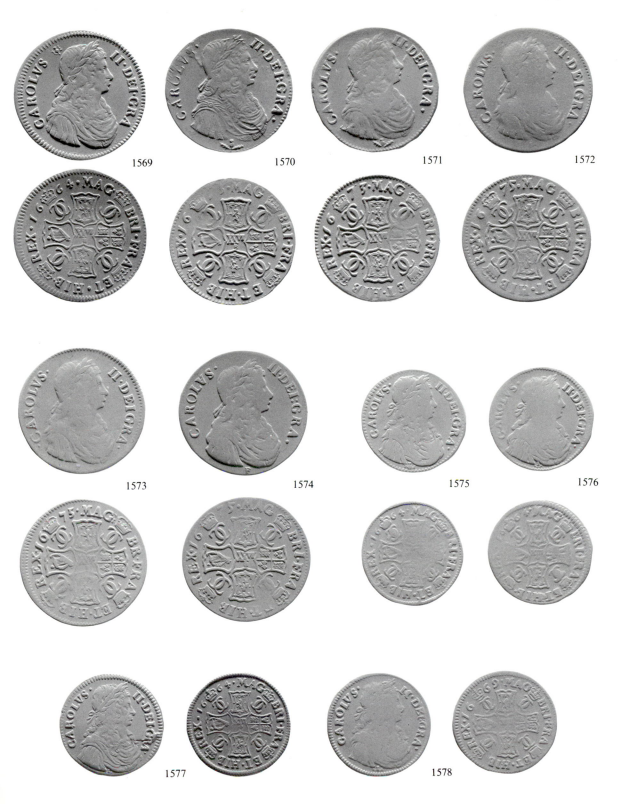

1569   1570   1571   1572

1573   1574   1575   1576

1577   1578

	Weight		*Die*	
	gr	gm	axis	
1579/A	96.4	6.25	0	1669. B.1051(5) but colon after date; Murray 16. Lincoln College.
1580/H	95.1	6.17	0	1669. B.1051(5) but colon after date; Murray 16. Hunter.
1581/A	87.6	5.68	90	1670. B.1051(6) but stops on obv.; Murray 17. Ashmolean.
1582/H	93.1	6.03	40	1670. B.1051(7) but single pellet after DEI; Murray 17. P 1980.
1583/H	87.2	5.65	90	1671. B.1051(8); Murray 18. D 1814, P. Millet.
1584/A	85.2	5.52	90	1671. B.1051(9); Murray 18. P 1980.
1585/H	91.2	5.91	90	1671. B.1051(9); Murray 18. Hunter.
1586/H	90.6	5.89	90	1671. B.1051(9); Murray 18. Unknown.
1587/A	89.6	5.81	90	1672. B.1052(10) but *recte* stop after date; Murray 19. D 1834, R. Finch.
1588/H	98.0	6.35	180	1672. B.1052(10) but single stop after DEI; Murray 19. Hunter.
1589/H	88.0 (pierced)	5.70	0	rev. ghosting on obv. 1672. B.1052(10) but single pellet after DEI; Murray 19. D 1936 Miss Buchanan.
1590/A	85.6	5.55	90	1673. B.1052(11), same dies as 1591/A; Murray 20. Bodleian.
1591/A	86.4	5.60	90	1673. As 1590/A. D 1921 F. L. Griffith.
1592/A	87.9	5.70	90	1673. B.1052(11); Murray 20. Browne Willis.
1593/H	94.6	6.13	90	1673. B.1052(11); Murray 20. Hunter.

PLATE 98

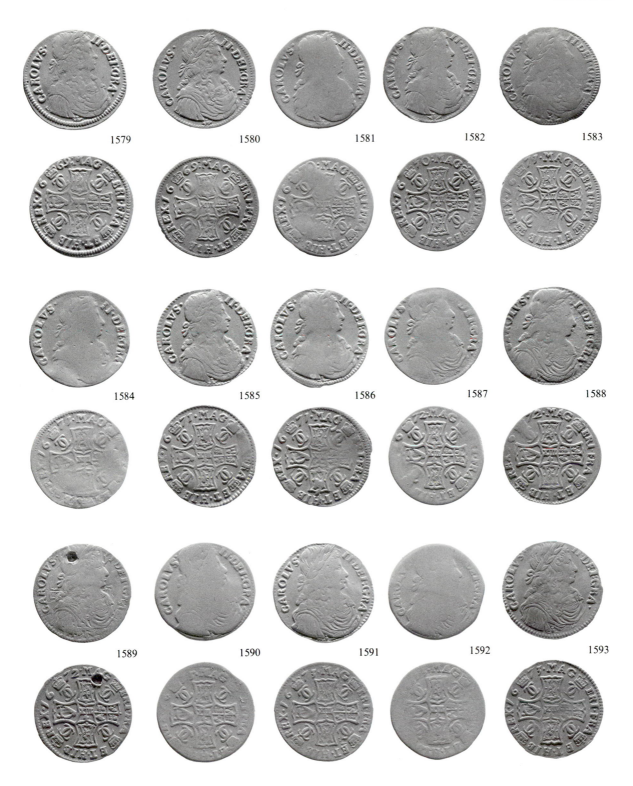

1579   1580   1581   1582   1583

1584   1585   1586   1587   1588

1589   1590   1591   1592   1593

	Weight		Die	
	gr	*gm*	*axis*	
1594/A	98.4	6.38	0	1675. B.1052(14), same dies as 1595/A; Murray 22. Bodleian.
1595/A	97.2	6.30	0	1675. As 1594/A. Lincoln College.

Half Merk (1664–73, 1675. Nos. 1596–1607)

1596/H	48.8	3.16	90	1665. B.1053(–) but 1665; Murray 24. Hunter.
1597/A	48.0	3.11	270	1666. B.1053(–) but 1666 and Irish arms in second quarter; Murray 25. Browne Willis.
1598/A	47.7	3.09	90	1669. B.1053(3) but no point after date; Murray 28. Bodleian.
1599/H	47.7	3.09	180	1669. B.1053(3); Murray 28. Hunter.
	(pierced)			
1600/H	45.7	2.96	270	1669. B.1053(3); Murray 28. D 1936 Miss Buchanan.
1601/A	39.8	2.58	90	1670. B.1053(5) but with stops on obv. and nothing after date; Murray 29. Bodleian.
1602/A	42.6	2.76	270	1672. B.1053(7) but colon after **DEI**, same dies as 1603/A; Murray 31. Ashmolean.
1603/A	48.4	3.14	90	1672. As 1602/A. Bodleian.
1604/H	48.9	3.17	90	1672. B.1053(7); Murray 31. Hunter.
1605/H	46.2	2.99	90	1673. B.1053(8) but colon after **DEI** and stops on rev.; Murray 32. P 1982 Q & LTR, Inverary Hoard.
1606/A	47.0	3.05	0	1675. B.1053(9); Murray 33. Bodleian.
1607/H	48.3	3.13	0	1675. B.1053(9) but stops on rev.; Murray 33. Hunter.

PLATE 99

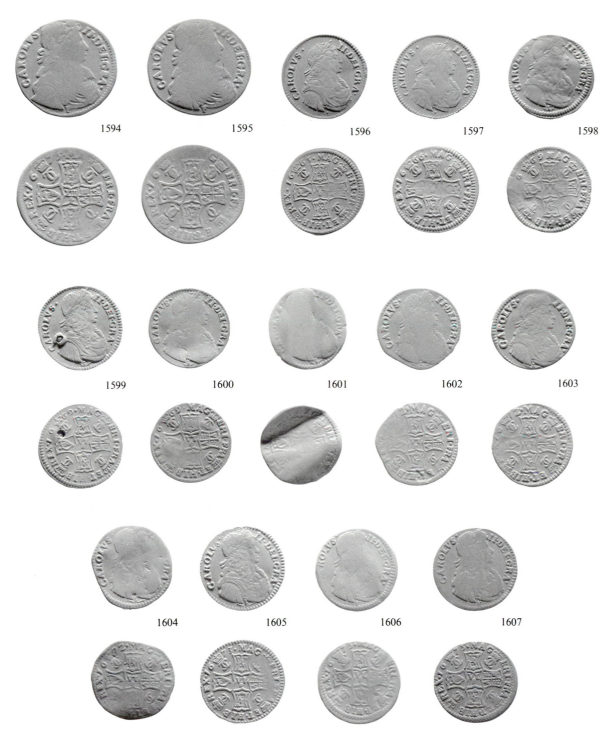

1594   1595   1596   1597   1598

1599   1600   1601   1602   1603

1604   1605   1606   1607

Second Coinage 1675–82

Dollar (1676, 1679–82. Nos. 1608–17)

	Weight		Die	
	gr	*gm*	*axis*	
1608/A	407.7	26.42	180	1676. B.1054(1) but no stops after **FR ET HIB**; Murray 34a. Bodleian.
1609/A	404.8	26.23	180	1679. B.1054(–) but 1679, same dies as 1610/A; Murray 35. Knight.
1610/A	411.1	26.64	180	1679. As 1609/A. Browne Willis.
1611/H	408.0	26.44	180	1680. B.1054(–) but 1680; Murray 36. Hunter.
1612/A	407.5	26.41	180	1681. B.1054(2); Murray 37. Bodleian.
1613/H	404.3	26.20	180	1681. As 1612/A. Hunter.

PLATE 100

1608　　　　　　　　　　　1609　　　　　　　　　　　1610

1611　　　　　　　　　　　1612　　　　　　　　　　　1613

	Weight		*Die*	
	gr	gm	axis	
1614/A	404.8	26.23	180	1682. B.1054(3), same dies as 1615/A and 1616/A; Murray 38. D 1921 F. L. Griffith.
1615/A	407.7	26.42	180	1682. As 1614/A. Bodleian.
1616/A	405.8	26.30	180	1682. B.1054(3)—obv. engraved Edward Kerby born 2 October 1790, same dies as 1614/A and 1615/A; Murray 38. D 1979 Mrs L. Sims.
1617/H	410.5	26.50	180	1682. B.1054(3); Murray 38. Hunter.

Half Dollar (1675–6, 1681. Nos. 1618–24)

1618/A	199.5	12.93	180	1675. B.1055(1); Murray 39. Christ Church.
1619/A	199.9	12.95	180	1675. As 1618/A. Browne Willis.
1620/A	200.7	13.01	180	1675. As 1618/A. Bodleian.

PLATE 101

1614

1615

1616

1617

1618

1619

1620

	Weight		*Die*	
	gr	*gm*	*axis*	
1621/H	199.0	12.90	180	1675. As 1618/A. Hunter.
1622/A	199.0	12.90	180	1676. B.1055(–) but 1676; Murray 40. Knight.
1623/H	201.6	13.06	180	1676. As 1622/A. Hunter.
1624/H	198.9	12.89	180	1681. B.1055(2); Murray 41. Hunter.

Quarter Dollar (1675–82. Nos. 1625–34)

1625/A	99.0	6.42	180	1676. B.1056(2); Murray 43. Christ Church.
1626/H	102.0	6.61	180	1676. As 1625/A. Hunter.
1627/H	101.9	6.60	180	1677. B.1056(4); Murray 44. Hunter.
1628/H	100.7	6.53	180	1677. B.1056(4); Murray 44. D 1936 Miss Buchanan.
1629/A	99.7	6.46	180	1679. B.1056(5); Murray 46. Knight.
1630/H	100.0	6.48	180	1679. As 1629/A. Hunter.
1631/H	102.2	6.62	180	1680. B.1056(6); Murray 47. Hunter.
1632/A	101.4	6.57	180	1681. B.1056(7); Murray 48. Bodleian.
1633/H	104.1	6.57	180	1681. B.1056(7); Murray 48. Hunter.
1634/A	100.3	6.50	180	1682. B.1056(8); Murray 49. Browne Willis.

PLATE 102

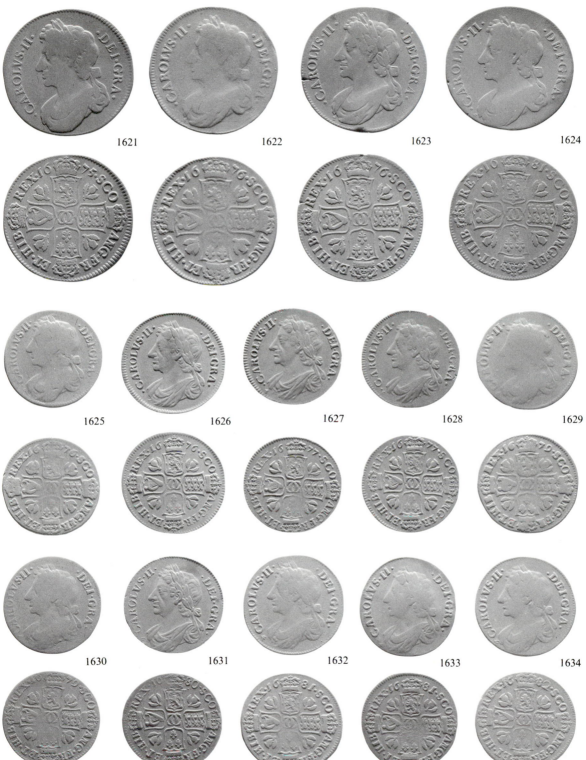

1621   1622   1623   1624

1625   1626   1627   1628   1629

1630   1631   1632   1633   1634

Eighth of Dollar (1676–80, 1682. Nos. 1635–40)

	Weight		Die	
	gr	gm	axis	
1635/A	49.7	3.22	90	1676. B.1057(1) but rev. stops differ, same rev. die as 1636/A; Murray 50. Bodleian.
1636/A	49.8	3.23	180	1676. As 1635/A. Browne Willis.
1637/H	50.3	3.26	180	1676. B.1057(1) with small **F**; Murray 50. Hunter.
1638/A	49.8	3.23	180	1677. B.1057(2); Murray 51. Ashmolean.
1639/A	49.5	3.21	180	1677. B.1057(2) but stop before **CAROLVS**; Murray 51. Christ Church.
1640/H	50.0	3.24	180	1680. B.1057(3); Murray 54. D 1936 Miss Buchanan.

Sixteenth Dollar (1677–81. Nos. 1641–8)

1641/A	25.3	1.64	180	1677. B.1058(1) but no stop before **CAROLVS**; Murray 56. Knight.
1642/H	24.1	1.56	180	1677. As 1641/A. Hunter.
1643/A	24.8	1.61	180	1678. B.1058(2); Murray 57. Christ Church.
1644/A	23.7 (pierced)	1.54	180	1679. B.1058(–) but **1679** with **9** over **7**; Murray 58. Bodleian.
1645/A	25.9	1.68	180	1681. B.1058(4); Murray 60. Ashmolean.
1646/A	25.1	1.63	180	1681. As 1645/A. Browne Willis.
1647/A	24.8	1.61	180	1681. As 1645/A. Bodleian.
1648/H	26.7	1.73	180	1681. B.1058(4); Murray 60. Hunter.

COPPER (see Murray and Stewart 1972)

Issue of 1663–8

Turner (Nemo me impune lacesset. Nos. 1649–57)

See B.1044, 1045, 1047

1649/A	35.3	2.29	0	M & S im uncertain/rosette 33. Bodleian.
1650/A	32.8	2.13	200	M & S im cross 21/uncertain. Bodleian.
1651/A	41.3	2.68	290	M & S im cross 21/rosette 32. Bodleian.
1652/A	28.2	1.83	70	M & S im cross 22–3/pellet cross. D 1981 I. C. G. Campbell.
1653/A	35.1	2.28	180	M & S im cross 21–3/uncertain with **LACESSNT**. Bodleian.
1654/A	29.1	1.89	90	M & S im cross 22/rosette 32–3. Bodleian.
1655/A	41.9	2.72	180	M & S im uncertain/pellet cross 30. Bodleian.
1656/H	31.8	2.05	180	B.1044(2); M & S im rosette 19/pellet cross 30. Hunter.
1657/H	37.6	2.44	0	B.1045 (?) uncertain; M & S uncertain. Neilson.

PLATE 103

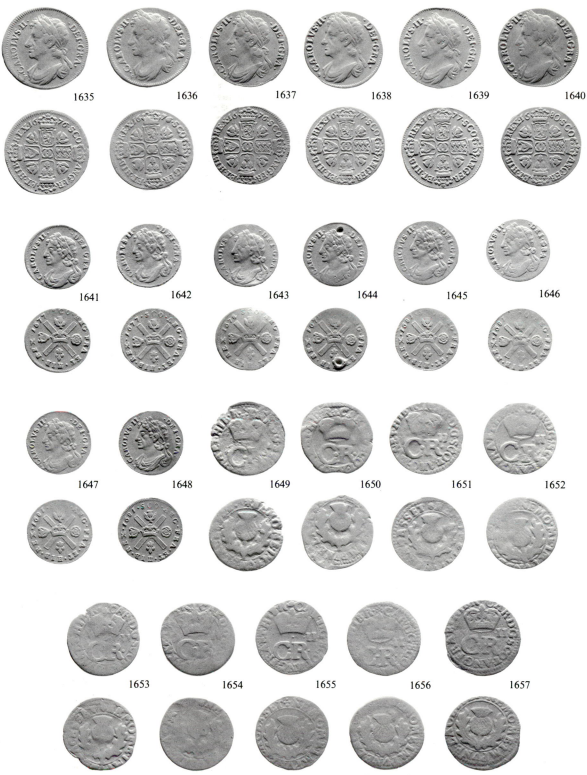

1635   1636   1637   1638   1639   1640

1641   1642   1643   1644   1645   1646

1647   1648   1649   1650   1651   1652

1653   1654   1655   1656   1657

Issue of 1677–9

Bawbee (Nemo me impune lacesset. 1677–9. Nos. 1658–71)

	Weight		Die	
	gr	gm	axis	
1658/A	140.4	9.10	180	1677. B.1059(1); M & S 1. Christ Church.
1659/A	124.3	8.06	180	1677. B.1059(2); M & S 4. Bodleian.
1660/A	125.1	8.11	180	1677. M & S 4. Bodleian.
1661/A	135.9	8.81	180	1677. M & S 4. Bodleian.
1662/H	132.9	8.61	180	1677. B.1059(2); M & S 4. Hunter.
1663/A	123.3	7.99	180	1678. B.1059(3); M & S 5. Bodleian.
1664/A	121.7	7.89	180	1678. M & S 5. Bodleian.
1665/A	118.5	7.68	180	1678. M & S 5. Bodleian.
1666/H	123.9	8.03	180	1678. B.1059(3) same dies; M & S 5. Hunter.
1667/A	123.6	8.01	180	1679. B.1059(4); M & S 6. Bodleian.
1668/H	125.6	8.14	180	1679. B.1059(4); M & S 6. Hunter.
1669/H	128.9	8.35	180	1679. B.1059(4); M & S 6. Hunter.
1670/A	124.7	8.08	180	1679. M & S 6. Bodleian.
1671/A	124.7	8.08	180	1677. B.1059(–); M & S 2. Bodleian.

Turner (1677–9. No. 1672–4)

1672/H	41.8	2.71	180	1677. B.1060(1); M & S 1. Hunter.
1673/A	40.7	2.64	180	1677. B.1060(–); M & S 2. Bodleian.
1674/H	43.5	2.82	180	1678. B.1061(2); M & S 7. Hunter.

PLATE 104

1658   1659   1660   1661   1662

1663   1664   1665   1666   1667

1668   1669   1670   1671

1672   1673   1674

JAMES VII (1685-9)

SILVER

Forty Shilling Piece (1687-8. Nos. 1675-8)

| | Weight | | Die | |
	gr	gm	axis	
1675/A	284.4	18.43	0	1687. B.1062(1). Browne Willis.
1676/H	284.5	18.42	0	1687. B.1062(1). Hunter.
1677/A	283.3	18.36	0	1688. B.1062(4) but **IACOBUS**. Browne Willis.
1678/H	283.0	18.34	0	1688. B.1062(4) but **IACOBUS**. Hunter.

Ten Shilling Piece (1687-8. Nos. 1679-87)

1679/A	68.3	4.43	0	1687. B.1063(1). D 1930 E. S. Bouchier.
1680/A	70.8	4.59	0	1687. B.1063(2). Bodleian.
1681/A	71.1	4.61	0	1687. B.1063(2). Merton College.
1682/H	71.0	4.60	0	1687. B.1063(2). Hunter.
1683/A	70.5	4.57	0	1687. B.1063(-) but stop before 10. Browne Willis.
1684/A	70.2	4.55	0	1687. B.1063(3). Ashmolean.
1685/A	69.1	4.48	0	1688. B.1063(4) but rev. stops differ. Browne Willis.
1686/A	67.6	4.38	0	1688. B.1063(4) but rev. stops differ. Christ Church.
1687/H	70.2	4.55	0	1688. B.1063(4). Hunter.

PLATE 105

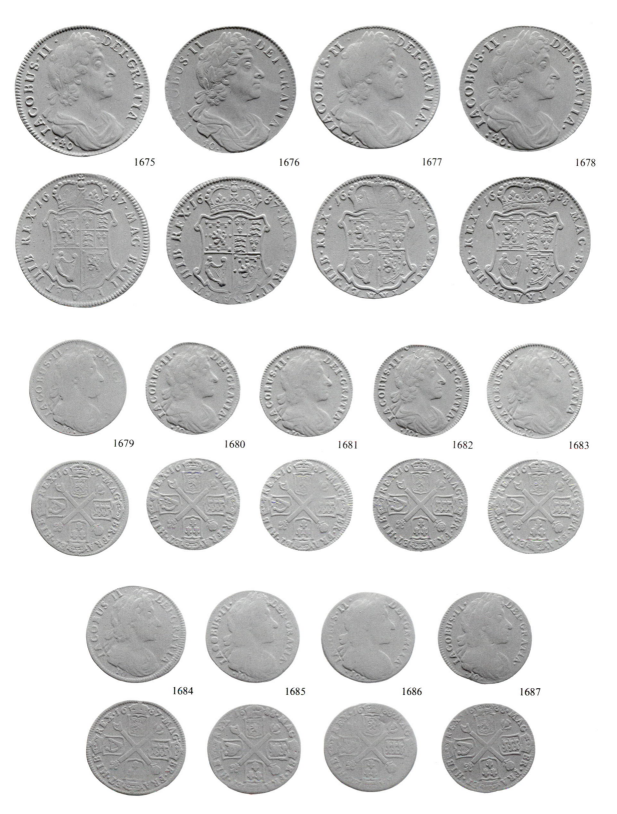

1675   1676   1677   1678

1679   1680   1681   1682   1683

1684   1685   1686   1687

WILLIAM AND MARY (1689–94)

(title: GVLIELMVS ET MARIA DEI GRATIA / MAG BR FR ET HIB REX ET REGINA)

SILVER

Sixty Shilling Piece (1691–2. Nos. 1688–91)

	Weight		Die	
	gr	gm	axis	
1688/A	428.4	27.76	0	1691. B.1065(1) same dies. Browne Willis.
1689/H	427.0	27.67	0	1691. As 1688/A. Hunter.
1690/A	424.5	27.51	0	1692. B.1065(2). D 1834 R. Finch.
1691/H	419.6	27.19	0	1692. B.1065(2). Hunter.

Forty Shilling Piece (1689–94. Nos. 1692–1701)

1692/A	284.4	18.43	180	1689. B.1066(1) but no stop after **GRATIA**. Browne Willis.
1693/H	284.3	18.42	180	1689. B.1066(1) but no stop after date. Hunter.

PLATE 106

1688   1689   1690

1691   1692   1693

WILLIAM and MARY (*cont.*)

	Weight		Die	
	gr	*gm*	*axis*	
1694/A	282.4	18.30	0	1691. B.1066(3). Merton College, Kilner (1767).
1695/H	283.2	18.35	0	1691. B.1066(3). Hunter.
1696/A	283.9	18.40	0	1692. B.1066(5). D 1921 F. L. Griffith.
1697/A	283.1	18.35	0	1692. B.1066(6). Bodleian.
1698/A	283.5	18.37	0	1692. B.1066(6). Christ Church.
1699/H	284.6	18.44	0	1692. B.1066(6). Hunter.
1700/A	284.5	18.44	30	1693. B.1066(7) but without lozenges on Dutch shield. Bodleian.
1701/H	284.9	18.46	10	1693. B.1066(7) but QVARTO. Hunter.

Twenty Shilling Piece (1693–4. Nos. 1702–3)

1702/A	140.7	9.12	0	1693. B.1067(1) but *recte* no stop after GRATIA. Bodleian.
1703/H	142.5	9.23	0	1693. B.1067(1) but *recte* no stop after GRATIA. Hunter.

PLATE 107

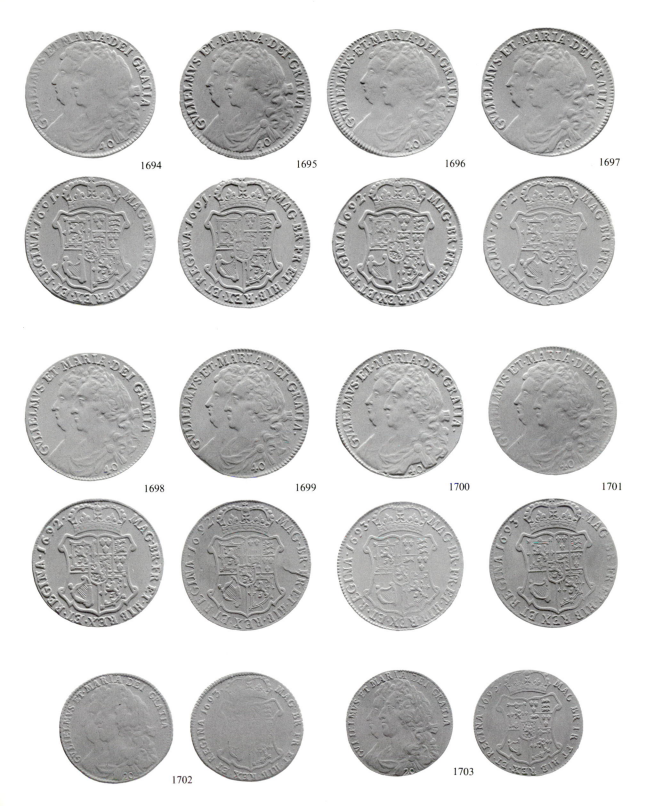

1694

1695

1696

1697

1698

1699

1700

1701

1702

1703

WILLIAM and MARY (*cont.*)

Ten Shilling Piece (1689–92, 1694. Nos. 1704–11)

	Weight		Die	
	gr	gm	axis	
1704/A	69.6	4.51	0	1690. B.1068(1) but *recte* stop after **GRATIA**. Bodleian.
1705/A	70.0	4.54	0	1690. As 1704/A. Browne Willis.
1706/A	70.5	4.57	0	1691. B.1069(2) but no stop after **GRATIA**. Merton College, Kilner (1767).
1707/H	71.0	4.60	10	1691. B.1069(2). Hunter.
1708/A	71.0	4.60	0	1691. B.1069(2). Christ Church.
1709/A	70.5	4.57	0	1691. B.1069(2). Ashmolean.
1710/A	70.5	4.57	0	1691. B.1069(3). Bodleian.
1711/A	71.0	4.60	180	1691. B.1069(4). Browne Willis.

Five Shilling Piece (1691, 1694. Nos. 1712–15)

1712/H	35.5	2.30	0	1691. B.1070(1) same dies. Hunter.
1713/A	34.8	2.26	0	1694. B.1071(2). Browne Willis.
1714/A	34.8	2.26	0	1694. B.1071(2). Bodleian.
1715/H	35.8	2.32	0	1694. B.1071(2) same dies. Hunter.

COPPER (see Murray and Stewart 1972)

Bawbee (1691–4. Nos. 1716–21)

1716/H	125.0	8.16	0	1691. B.1072(–) but 1691; M & S 3. Hunter.
1717/A	128.5	8.33	0	1692. B.1072(2) but *recte* im thistle; M & S 9. Bodleian.
1718/A	125.4	8.13	0	1692. B.1072(–); M & S 11. Knight.

PLATE 108

1704   1705   1706   1707   1708

1709   1710   1711   1712   1713

1714   1715   1716   1717   1718

WILLIAM and MARY (*cont.*)

	Weight		Die	
	gr	gm	axis	
1719/H	139.8	9.06	180	1692. B.1072(–) im uncertain; M & S uncertain. Hunter.
1720/H	201.7	13.07	0	1693. B.1072(4) with im star; M & S 15. Hunter.
1721/H	126.4	8.19	180	1694. B.1072(–) but 1794; M & S 18. Hunter.

Turner (1691–4. Nos. 1722–30)

1722/A	39.0	2.53	0	1691. M & S 2. Bodleian.
1723/A	43.6	2.83	0	1692. M & S 27/15. P 1980.
1724/A	41.6	2.70	0	1692. B.1073(–); M & S 10. Bodleian.
1725/A	39.5	2.56	0	1694. B.1073(–); M & S 31. Knight.
1726/A	37.5	2.43	0	1692. B.1073(2); M & S 5. Bodleian.
1727/H	42.4	2.75	0	1692. B.1073(2). Hunter.
1728/A	41.0	2.66	180	1694. B.1073(4); M & S 29. University College, Waddington.
1729/A	38.5	2.50	180	1694. B.1073(4); M & S 29. Bodleian.
1730/H	37.2	2.41	180	1694. B.1073(4) but **REGIN** and stop on rev. only after date. Hunter.

WILLIAM II (1694–1702)

(title: **GVLIELMVS DEI GRATIA / MAG BRIT FRA ET HIB REX**)

GOLD

Pistole or Twelve Pound Piece (1701. Nos. 1731–2)

1731/A	105.8	6.86	0	1701. B.1078(1) but *recte* no stop after **GVLIELMVS** and **MAG** same dies. Browne Willis.
1732/H	105.3	6.82	0	1701. As 1731/A. Hunter.

Half Pistole or Six Pound Piece (1701. Nos. 1733–4)

1733/A	52.7	3.42	0	1701. B.1079(2) same dies. Hird, Newcomer.
1734/H	52.8	3.42	0	1701. As 1733/A. Hunter.

PLATE 109

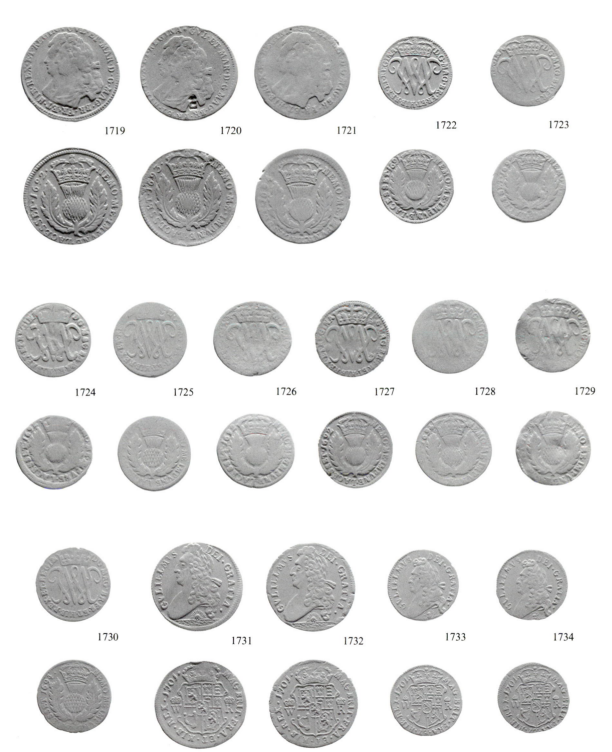

1719 1720 1721 1722 1723

1724 1725 1726 1727 1728 1729

1730 1731 1732 1733 1734

SILVER

Forty Shilling Piece (1695–1700. Nos. 1735–44)

	Weight		Die	
	gr	gm	axis	
1735/A	282.8	18.33	0	1695. B.1074(1) but **OCTAVO** and no stops after **DEI** and **GRATIA**. Merton College.
1736/A	280.7	18.19	0	1695. B.1074(3), same dies as 1737/A. Bodleian, '?Willis d. at death'.
1737/A	279.9	18.14	0	1695. As 1736/A. Bodleian.
1738/H	284.3	18.42	0	1695. B.1074(3) but stop after date. Hunter.
1739/H	283.7	18.38	0	1695. B.1074(4). D 1936, Miss Buchanan.
1740/A	283.9	18.40	0	1696. B.1074(5) same dies. Browne Willis.
1741/H	284.6	18.44	0	1696. As 1740/A. Hunter.
1742/A	275.6	17.86	0	1697. B.1074(6). Merton College, Kilner.
1743/H	298.0	18.31	0	1697. B.1074(6). Hunter.
1744/H	284.6	18.44	0	1698. B.1074(7). Hunter.
	(flan flawed)			

PLATE 110

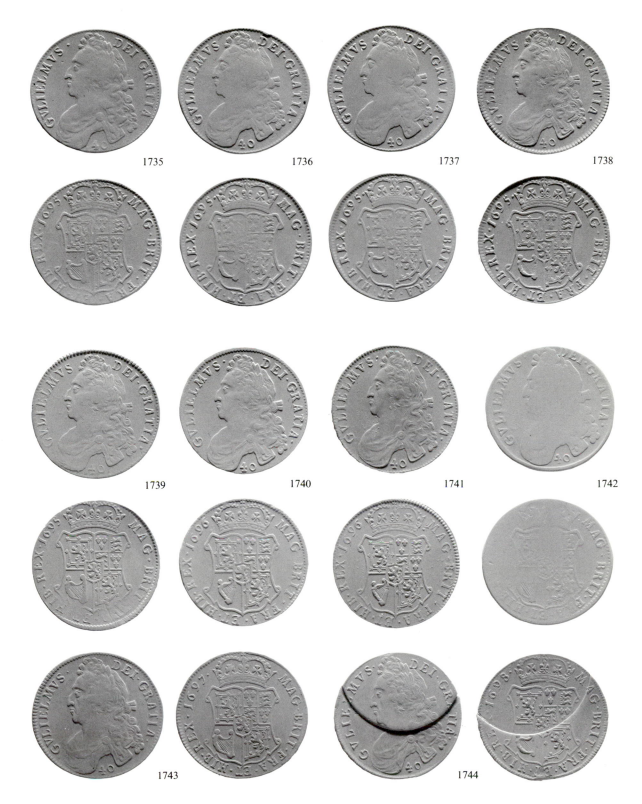

1735   1736   1737   1738

1739   1740   1741   1742

1743   1744

Twenty Shilling Piece (1695–9. Nos. 1745–51)

	Weight		Die	
	gr	gm	axis	
1745/A	141.8	9.19	0	1695. B.1075(1). Browne Willis.
1746/H	142.0	9.20	0	1695. B.1075(1). Hunter.
1747/A	143.0	9.27	0	1696. B.1075(2). Knight.
1748/H	140.5	9.10	0	1696. B.1075(2). Hunter.
1749/H	140.9	9.13	0	1698. B.1075(4) but stop after 20 and date. Hunter.
1750/A	142.4	9.23	0	1699. B.1075(5). Christ Church.
1751/H	142.6	9.24	0	1699. B.1075(5) but stop after date. Hunter.

Ten Shilling Piece (1695–9. Nos. 1752–9)

1752/H	71.0	4.60	0	1695. B.1076(1). Hunter.
1753/A	70.2	4.55	0	1696. B.1076(2). Bodleian.
1754/A	67.2	4.36	0	1696. B.1076(2). Knight.
1755/H	71.4	4.63	0	1696. B.1076(2). Hunter.
1756/H	71.6	4.64	180	1697. B.1076(3) but stop after date. Hunter.
1757/A	71.0	4.60	0	1698 (8 over 7). B.1076(–) but 1698. Bodleian.
1758/H	71.2	4.61	0	1698 (8 over 7). B.1076(–) but 1698. Hunter.
1759/H	68.3	4.43	0	1699. B.1076(–) but 1699. Neilson.

PLATE 111

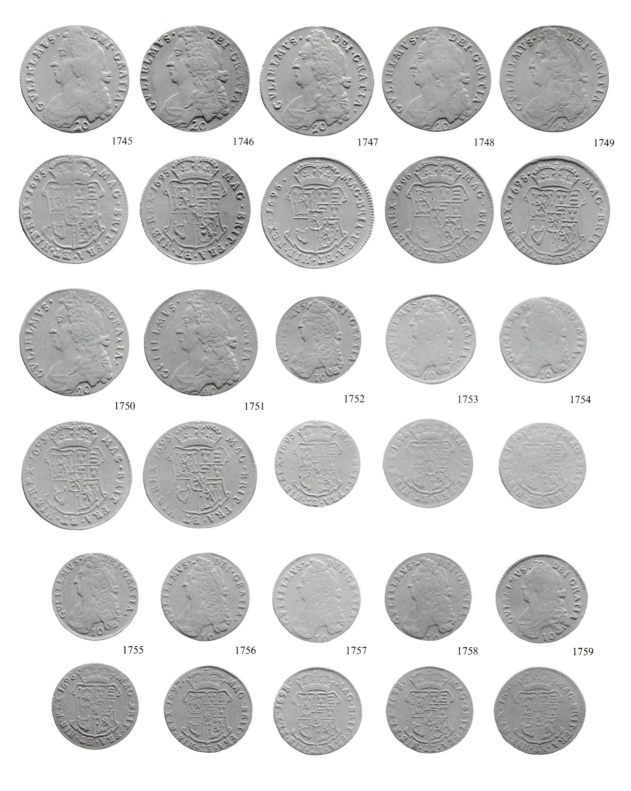

1745   1746   1747   1748   1749

1750   1751   1752   1753   1754

1755   1756   1757   1758   1759

Five Shilling Piece (1695–1702. Nos. 1760–71)

	Weight		Die	
	gr	*gm*	*axis*	
1760/H	33.0	2.14	0	1695. B.1077(1). D J. R. Lockie.
1761/H	35.7	2.31	0	1695. B.1077(1) but stop after **GVL**. Hunter.
1762/A	34.4	2.23	0	1696. B.1077(2) but stop before date. Bodleian.
1763/A	35.3	2.29	0	1696. As 1762/A. Christ Church.
1764/H	34.7	2.25	0	1696. B.1077(2). Hunter.
1765/A	31.8	2.06	180	1697. B.1077(3). Ashmolean.
	(pierced)			
1766/A	35.0	2.27	180	1697. B.1077(3). Knight.
1767/A	34.1	2.21	0	1697. B.1077(3). Christ Church.
1768/H	32.1	2.08	0	1697. B.1077(3) but with stops on rev. Hunter.
1769/H	37.1	2.40	0	1699. B.1077(4) but **GVL D G MAG BR**. Hunter.
1770/A	34.1	2.21	0	1700. B.1077(5). Bodleian.
1771/A	35.5	2.30	0	1702. B.1077(6). Browne Willis.

COPPER (see Murray and Stewart, 1972)

Bawbee (1695–7. Nos. 1772–3)

1772/H	115.9	7.51	0	1695. B.1080(1); M & S 3. Hunter.
1773/A	126.2	8.18	180	1697. B.1080(3); M & S 9. Knight.

Turner (1695–7. Nos. 1774–80)

1774/A	36.4	2.36	0	1695. B.1081(1); M & S 4. Bodleian.
1775/A	41.8	2.71	0	1695. B.1081(1) but dies = M & S 3. Bodleian.
1776/H	43.3	2.81	0	1695. B.1081(1) but *recte* stop after **REX**, not after date. Hunter.
1777/H	41.3	2.68	0	1695. B.1082(2). Hunter.
1778/A	44.7	2.90	0	1696. B.1082(3) but dies = M & S 20. Bodleian.
1779/A	42.6	2.76	180	1697. B.1082(4); M & S 28. Bodleian.
1780/H	42.1	2.73	0	1697. B.1082(4). Hunter.

PLATE 112

1760   1761   1762   1763   1764   1765

1766   1767   1768   1769   1770   1771

1772   1773

1774   1775   1776   1777   1778

1779   1780

ANNE (1702-14)

SILVER

Before Union

Ten Shilling Piece (1705-6. Nos. 1781-3)

	Weight		Die	
	gr	gm	axis	
1781/A	70.5	4.57	0	1705. B.1083(1). Knight.
1782/A	70.8	4.59	0	1705. B.1083(1). Bodleian.
1783/H	70.6	4.57	0	1705. B.1083(1) same dies. Hunter.

Five Shilling Piece (Nemo me impune lacesset. 1705-6. Nos. 1784-91)

1784/A	39.0	2.53	0	1705. B.1084(1) but stops after **GRATIA**. Knight.
1785/A	35.6	2.31	0	1705. As 1784/A. Merton College, Kilner.
1786/A	33.5	2.17	0	1705 (5 over 4). B.1084(2) but no stop after **&**, same dies as 1787/A and 1788/A, same rev. die as 1790/H. Bodleian.
1787/A	33.5	2.17	0	1705 (5 over 4). As 1786/A. Bodleian.
1788/A	32.4	2.10	0	1705 (5 over 4). As 1786/A. Christ Church.
1789/A	32.3	2.09	0	1705. B.1084(3) but no stops after **FR** and **&** nor on rev. Bodleian.
1790/H	36.1	2.34	0	1705 (5 over 4). B.1084(3) but no stops after **D, G, BR, FR, &**, and 5. Same rev. die as 1786-8/A Hunter.
1791/A	37.2	2.41	0	1706. B.1084(4) but no stops after **&** and R. Bodleian.

Post Union

Crown (1707-8. Nos. 1792-7)

1792/A	464.0	30.07	180	1707. B.1085(1). Knight.
1793/A	457.1	29.62	180	1707. B.1085(1) same rev. die. D 1930 E. S. Bouchier.
1794/H	460.4	29.83	180	1707. B.1085(1) but single stop after **REG**. Hunter.

PLATE 113

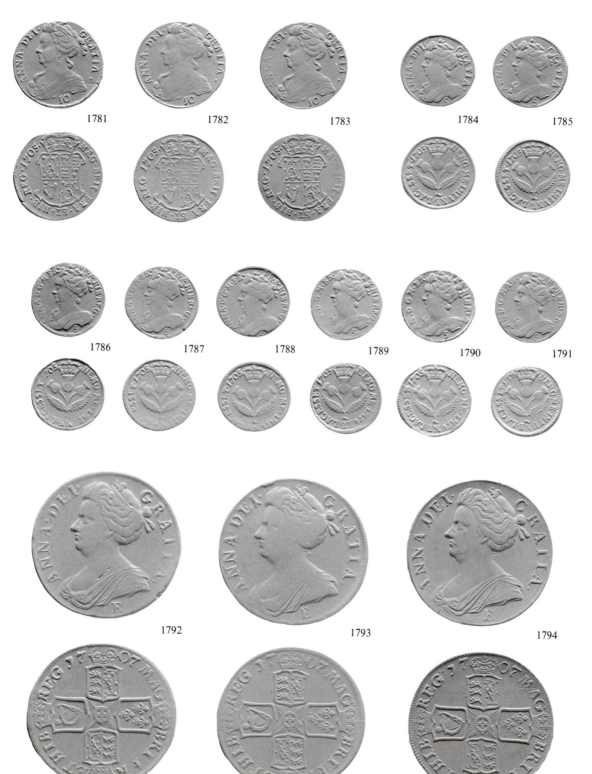

1781   1782   1783   1784   1785

1786   1787   1788   1789   1790   1791

1792   1793   1794

	Weight		Die	
	gr	gm	axis	
1795/A	459.8	29.80	180	1708. B.1085(2). D 1893 E. L. Hussey.
1796/A	463.1	30.01	180	1708. B.1085(2). D 1921 F. L. Griffith.
1797/H	462.7	29.98	180	1708. B.1085(2) but colon after **FR**. Hunter.

Half Crown (1707–9. Nos. 1798–1804)

1798/A	226.7	14.69	180	1707. B.1086(1). Bodleian.
1799/A	232.4	15.06	180	1707. B.1086(1). Ashmolean.
1800/A	232.2	15.05	180	1707. B.1086(1). Knight.
1801/H	232.1	15.04	180	1707. B.1086(1). Hunter.
1802/A	223.6	14.49	180	1708. B.1086(2). D 1924 Mary and Susan Field.
1803/A	221.7	14.37	180	1708. B.1086(2). Bodleian.
1804/H	229.0	14.84	180	1708. B.1086(2). Hunter.

PLATE 114

1795   1796   1797   1798

1799   1800   1801   1802

1803   1804

Shilling (1707–9. Nos. 1805–14)

	Weight		Die	
	gr	gm	axis	
1805/H	93.2	6.04	180	1707. B.1087(1) but stops on obv. and after **MAG** and **BRI**. Hunter.
1806/A	92.7	6.01	180	1707. B.1087(2) but with stops after **MAG**, **FR**, and **HIB**. Knight.
1807/A	90.9	5.89	180	1707. B.1088(4). D 1921 F. L. Griffith.
1808/H	92.2	5.97	180	1707. B.1088(4) but no stops on obv. Hunter.
1809/H	91.4	5.92	180	1708. B.1088(5). Hunter.
1810/H	91.7	5.94	180	1707. B.1089(7). Hunter.
1811/A	91.9	5.96	180	1707. B.1089(7). Ashmolean.
1812/H	89.9	5.83	180	1708. B.1089(8). Hunter.
1813/A	91.6	5.94	180	1708. B.1090(9). Bodleian.
1814/A	89.0	5.77	0	1709. B.1090(10) but no stops after **ANNA** and **GRATIA**. D 1935 T. R. Gambier-Parry.

Sixpence (1707–8. Nos. 1815–22)

1815/A	45.8	2.97	180	1707. B.1091(1) but rev. reads **MAG.BRI.FR.ET HIB REG.** 1707. D 1921 F. L. Griffith.
1816/A	46.9	3.04	180	1707. B.1091(1) but no stops on rev. Bodleian.
1817/H	46.7	3.03	180	1707. B.1091(1). Hunter.
1818/A	46.3	3.00	180	1707. B.1091(2/1). Knight.
1819/A	44.4	2.88	180	1707. B.1091(2) but rev. stops vary. P 1909.
1820/H	46.6	3.02	180	1708. B.1092(3) but no stops obv. Hunter.
1821/A	45.2	2.93	180	1708. B.1093(4). D 1921 F. L. Griffith.
1822/H	46.0	2.98	180	1708. B.1093(4) but no stops after **MAG**, **FRA**, and **HIB**. Hunter.

PLATE 115

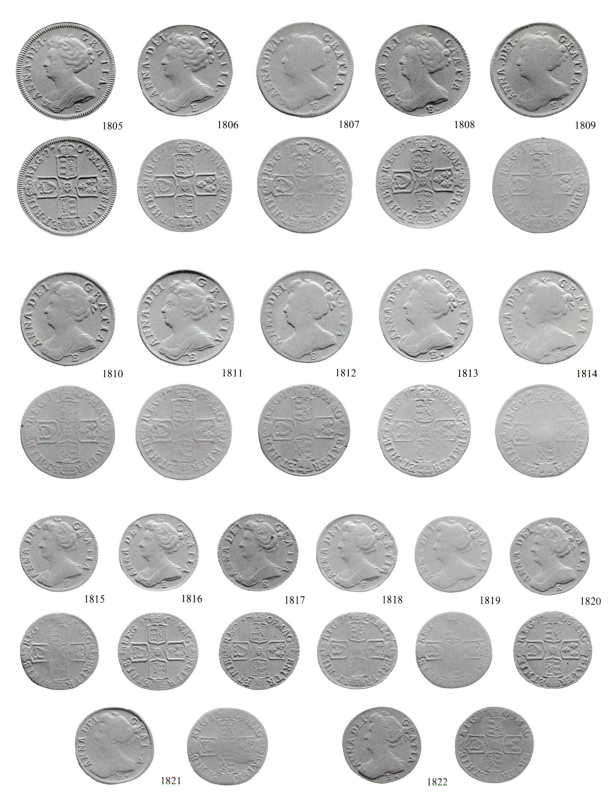

1805 1806 1807 1808 1809

1810 1811 1812 1813 1814

1815 1816 1817 1818 1819 1820

1821 1822

FORGERIES

Robert I *penny* (modern)
1823/H 25.5 1.65 180 B.225(1) but stop end of rev. Coats.

James I second variety fleur-de-lis *groat* Edinburgh (modern)
1824/H 52.6 3.41 50 B.477(39) but rev. legends, stops, and ornaments differ. Coats.

James IV billon *penny* Edinburgh (contemporary)
1825/H 11.4 0.74 180 B.—; Stewart III; legends end ORΛ and BOΘI. Hunter.

Mary period I gold *twenty shilling piece* 1543 (? 19th-century by Jons of Dunfermline, see—Murray, 1979, 85–6, no. 10, this coin)
1826/A 41.6 2.70 230 B.810(2). Hird, Dick Institute (Kilmarnock), Selkirk-Hunter.

Mary period I gold *three pound piece* 1555 (contemporary)
1827/H 70.2 4.55 260 copper. B.819(1) but crown and stops differ. Hunter.

Mary period I billon *bawbee* Edinburgh (contemporary)
1828/H 19.5 1.26 150 B.842(38) but SCOTOR.VM. and end of rev. uncertain. Hunter.

Mary period II F & M billon *nonsunt* 1559 (contemporary)
1829/A 32.1 2.08 80 B.891(–). Browne Willis.

Mary period II F & M billon *lion or hardhead* 1558 (contemporary)
1830/A 12.2 0.79 290 date rendered as 58. B.892(1–2) as fig. with inverted A for V in VIEN and VERITAS. P 1980.

As last
1831/A 10.1 0.66 240 D 1938 found 'in Bodleian trench in Broad Street' Oxford.

As last
1832/H 15.6 1.01 90 B.892(1) but *recte* VERITAS. P 1980.

James VI gold *sword and sceptre piece* 1602 (? contemporary)
1833/H 72.9 4.72 250 ? copper gilt. B.956(4). Hunter.

James VI silver *half merk* 1572 (contemporary)
1834/A 91.3 5.92 80 base. B.924(1). Browne Willis.

James VI billon *eightpenny groat or plack* (contemporary)
1835/A 34.2 2.22 0 B.960(–) with OPPIDVM EDINBVRG. P 1982, Lingford 1182 (part).

As last
1836/A 25.0 1.62 240 B.962(6). P 1982, Lingford 1183/4 (part).

As last
1837/A 26.8 1.74 20 B.959–62(–). P 1982, Lingford 1183/4 (part).

Charles I silver *twenty pence piece* (contemporary)
1838/A 6.1 0.49 250 B.1024–5(59–62). D Prof. M. A. Lawson (found in Botanic Gardens, Oxford 1883).
(pierced)

PLATE 116

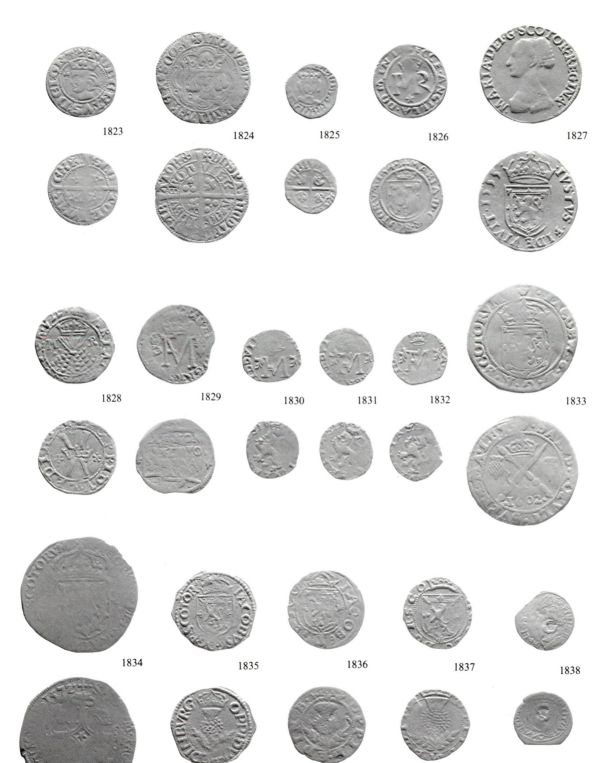

1823   1824   1825   1826   1827

1828   1829   1830   1831   1832   1833

1834   1835   1836   1837   1838

APPENDIX

THE SHORT-CROSS ALEXANDER III STERLING OF GLASGOW

by IAN STEWART

THE short-cross penny of Glasgow (no. 90) is one of the most significant and unexpected additions to the Scottish series that has appeared for many years. The collection from which it comes was largely formed by J. W. Spurway of Leicester in the period when he was a member of the British Numismatic Society, up to 1930. Traces of coloured wax on both sides suggest that a plaster cast was taken at some stage, but the existence of the coin did not apparently become known to the numismatic world in general until the collection was sent for sale in 1984. Since it is clearly legible, is undoubtedly authentic, and was palpably unpublished, it is odd that it was not sooner brought to light. It does not have the light brown patina or clean surface associated with coins from the Brussels hoard, but its rather blacker colouring, with slight encrustation visible under magnification, suggests a hoard origin rather than a single find. The surface of the coin is scratched, which might be the result of crude cleaning, since the scratches are prominent on areas in relief, but could perhaps represent the condition of the flan before striking. There are signs of double striking, more evident on reverse than obverse. Probably due to variation in the thickness of the blank, rather than to uneven striking, there is corresponding weakness in the impression at the top and back of the head, and in the adjacent inscription, and towards the bottom and right of the reverse.

Prior to discovery of this coin the only known mints for Alexander short-cross sterlings were Berwick and Roxburgh, and the only known (long-cross) moneyer for Glasgow was Walter.[1] The new coin, which may well be the earliest surviving product of the Glasgow mint, indicates that a decision to coin there was taken before the main decision to open a number of new mints for the purpose of converting the existing currency into coins of the new long-cross type, as had happened in England from 1247. According to Fordun's *Scotichronicon* the change took place in Scotland in 1250, the year following Alexander II's death, and this date gains support from the existence of a small number of short-cross Alexander sterlings with a beardless portrait, which presumably represents the young Alexander III. Glasgow was already known to be (with Aberdeen, Ayr, Lanark and Perth) one of the earliest new mints of Alexander III's long-cross recoinage, by virtue of its coins of type II, which predate the bulk of the recoinage (type III). But the Robert coin suggests that a mint

---

[1] For a full discussion of the Alexander voided-cross sterlings see chapter IV of 'Scottish Mints'.

at Glasgow may have been authorized before any of the others, and so perhaps lends credence to the idea that minting rights had been granted to the bishop.

One of the notable features of the Alexander III long-cross coinage is the recurrence of a few moneyers' names at several mints, indicating in all probability that individuals with these names had responsibilities in more than one burgh. Some mints—Ayr (Simon), Inverness (Gefrai), St Andrews (Thomas) and Stirling (Henri)—had a single moneyer whose name does not appear elsewhere. There are also some moneyers (e.g. Wales at Berwick, Ion Cokin at Perth and Michel at Roxburgh) who coined at the larger mints alongside other moneyers, and whose names are not found on the coins of more than one mint. Robert of Berwick had apparently been one of these. But it must be quite likely that he was the same man as the Robert who produced the new Glasgow coin, since he is known to have been an active moneyer at this period, and there is another case of an early unique coin of a moneyer for the mint, namely Wilam at Roxburgh in type II, unknown before the Colchester find of 1969,[2] but a name found at several other mints during the course of the long-cross coinage (including Lanark in the same type). Perhaps Robert at Glasgow and Wilam at Roxburgh each played a part in the new developments at these two mints before returning or moving to other mint-towns. At Glasgow all the known coins, apart from this one of Robert, have the name Walter. There are obverse die-links between Walter of Glasgow and Walter of other mints (*Dun*, *Fres* and *Mun*), which confirm that the same moneyer was involved in several different towns.[3] Walter is also the name of one of the Berwick moneyers and of the only moneyer at Renfrew.

Robert's Glasgow penny is from the same obverse die as most of the surviving type II Glasgow coins of Walter. It has a large head, uncrowned but with a small cap(?), facing right. The lettering is of the plain form described by Burns as class I.[4] The ER of *Alexander* are joined, there is a large stop before *Rex*, and the letters A, R (without curved tail) and X are notable for their simple form. On later strikings from this die there are flaws at the top of the second E and in the lower half of the third E. No such flaws are visible on the Robert coin, confirming that it was an early striking from the die. This would be consistent with the reasonable assumption that its use with a short-cross reverse was quickly discontinued, and most of its productive life was in combination with long-cross reverse dies of Walter. The only other known case of an obverse die being used with both short-cross and long-cross reverses is at Berwick[5] and again only a single specimen of the short-cross type is known, suggesting that short-cross reverse dies were withdrawn, even if only partially used, when the long-cross type was introduced in 1250. In England, when the type was changed in 1247, a distinctive new obverse design was introduced for the long-cross series and there was a clear administrative break between the

---

[2] Stewart 1974, pl. VI, no. 56 (printing error for S6).

[4] B. i, 121 and 143; and figs. 92C, D and E.

[3] 'Scottish Mints', chapter VIII.

[5] Burns, i, figs. 76B and 77.

short-cross and long-cross coinages. The use of the same obverse dies with both reverse types at two Scottish mints indicates the possibility that the change of reverse was in the first instance merely an act of conformity with the new English type, to assist the currency of new Scottish coins in England as had been the case during the short-cross coinage. Most of the new Scottish mints were not opened until type III, so the decision to carry out a full recoinage may not have been taken at the outset or, if it was, without the prior planning and preparation which was needed to implement it quickly.

Of the seven mints which produced long-cross coins earlier than type III, only Berwick and Glasgow had dies with the plain lettering of Burns class I. This confirms the evidence of the Glasgow short-cross coin that Glasgow was the first mint to be opened during the reign of Alexander III, joining Berwick which had continued its activity from the previous reign and possibly Roxburgh (although there may have been an interval between Roxburgh's short-cross issues under Alexander II and its earliest long-cross coins, of type II with 'florid'[6] lettering).

The obverse die used by Robert was evidently much more prolific than the other two dies known for Glasgow in type II, one of which has a left-facing bust and plain lettering, the other a small right-facing bust with the normal florid lettering of type II. According to A. H. Baldwin's manuscript catalogue of the Scottish coins in the Brussels hoard, there were 20 examples from the obverse die used by Robert in the hoard, three from the die with bust left,[7] and two from the third die.[8] Only Robert's die was represented in the Colchester hoard (six examples), and indeed I have no record of any specimens from the other two Glasgow type II obverse dies from any source other than Brussels. The obverse die with bust left is of remarkable quality: the profile is clearly defined, the face and neck full and the bust carefully modelled, with drapery on the shoulders; four neat locks of hair fall below the cap, finishing in three neat rows of pellets. There is no comparable die in the long-cross series; since the lettering is similar to that on Robert's die, it is certainly one of the first two (known) dies to have been supplied to the new mint at Glasgow. Indeed, except that the short-cross reverse die was actually used with the other early obverse die, the die with bust left might be thought, because of its unusual features and very high standard of craftsmanship, to have been the pair to the short-cross reverse, and indeed that is not impossible, since obverse and reverse dies were very indiscriminately paired in this coinage. Unlike any of the long-cross reverses, the Robert short-cross die has lettering of the same form as that on these two early Glasgow obverse dies. It reads ROBERT·ON·GLA· in clear, plain lettering, the nearest comparable reverse dies being those of Roxburgh by Pieres for Alexander II.[9]

---

[6] Burns class III lettering.
[7] For illustrations of two of these coins see Lockett, lot 48(B) and Stewart 1983, pl. 19, no. 5 (p. 323).
[8] Photographs of R. C. Lockett collection, plate II, nos. 72–3.
[9] B. figs. 70–2.

INDEX OF MINTS

Gold coins are not indexed and may be assumed to be Edinburgh, but see Stewart 1971, 232, 236, 239.

INDEX OF MONEYERS' NAMES

This is a list of moneyers' names occuring on coins in this volume. The same name does not always indicate the same moneyer.

INDEX OF FINDS